THE COTTAGE HOTEL

The History & Untold Tales of Mendon Hamlet's Legendary Stagecoach Inn & Tavern

Karen Mireau

Azalea Art Press
Sonoma | California

© Karen Mireau, 2023.
All Rights Reserved.

ISBN: 978-1-943471-71-3

Front Cover Art:
The *Cottage Hotel*, circa 1954
"The Friendly Inn" by Martin de Wolfe
Painting from the archive of
Rosemary (Heckman) Lewis

Dedication Page Art:
Hannah Whitney

Cover Designs:
Jim Edmon | jimedmon.com

for "Burdock"
John Urquhart Ross
(1943-1981)

and for all those who love
the Cottage Hotel
of Mendon, New York

In Memoriam
John Urquhart ("Burdock") Ross

This history of the Cottage Hotel is inspired by the special soul we came to know as Burdock.

When I was young, Burdock encouraged me to follow my fledgling dream of becoming a writer. Without him, my life would be vastly different.

I will always be profoundly grateful to him for that, and for the love and care he gave so freely to so many others trying to find their way.

CONTENTS

Preface by Karen Mireau   i

Chapter I   1

Ridin' in Style:
Stagecoach Days in Mendon Hamlet

The *Cottage Hotel* opened in 1822 in Mendon hamlet as a humble tavern and stagecoach inn. Traveling by stage to get there was a rollicking rumble of a ride, not without its share of danger and discomfort. But just like today, when you arrived at the front door, you were sure to be treated like royalty at *The Cottage* — no matter where you came from or what your station in life might be.

Chapter II   16

How to Construct a Lasting Legend:
The Building of The Cottage Hotel

The *Cottage Hotel* rests on a foundation of common field stones and perhaps a few 'cobbles,' or stones formed by the glaciers' retreat some 13,000 years ago. The construction of the cellar walls of the *Cottage Hotel* and the structure itself is a story that transcends space and time.

Chapter III 32

Burnt-Over, but Never Burnt Out: Give Me That Old Time Religion

Some say it was something in the air, or the water, or the very ground beneath our feet that drew a surprising number of people with spiritual aspirations to Mendon hamlet. With the opening of the Erie Canal, this part of Upstate New York soon became known as *The Psychic Highway*. Those ablaze with evangelical enthusiasm spawned religions, utopian communities, and spiritual societies that exist to this day, giving it the moniker *The Burned* or *Burnt-Over District*. We may never be entirely sure of what fanned those flames, but it added a fascinating note to our local history.

Chapter IV 53

All Aboard! Tales of Rails & Trails in the Hamlet

When the Lehigh Valley Railroad established a depot here in 1892, the clickety-clack of freight and passenger trains would rattle the streets in the hamlet nonstop for the next 84 years. When the last freight rumbled through in 1976, the hamlet returned to relative quiet, but many still miss the comforting calliope of the trains' steam whistles, signaling that there were many other exciting places in the world to see and experience.

Chapter V — 74

Last Call for Alcohol!
Prohibition Comes to Mendon Hamlet

When the nation goes "dry" in 1920 thanks to the passage of *The Volstead Act*, a loophole in that law allows the two stagecoach inns in the hamlet—the *Cottage Hotel* and the *Mendon Hotel*—to continue to serve alcohol. A few years later, in 1933, citizens in bars and saloons across the country will shout their hallelujahs—celebrating the end of a doomed experiment in legislating human behavior.

Chapter VI — 85

Yo Ocarinas!
The Lost Ocarina Factory of Mendon Hamlet

Mendon has many claims to fame, but none so astonishing and inventive as the ocarina factory that once existed on Parrish Road. It took many years to rediscover the amazing story of Rudolph Teschner, who produced his "sweet potato" flutes and sold them throughout the United States. Hearsay from one hamlet farmer and a little digging into local resources finally unearthed the clue to the exact location of the kiln where America's first ocarinas were forged.

Chapter VII 100

Let's Go Honky-Tonkin':
Our Local Watering Hole Finds its Mojo

It's fashionable now to be a "dive" bar and the *Cottage Hotel* is sometimes referred to as such, but you and I know that this is intended only as a term of endearment. *The Cottage* is and has always been, the real deal. No matter who you are, or why you're sitting at *The Cottage* bar, since the 1800s it has always been a place to relax, toss back a few, kick up your heels, and enjoy the show.

Chapter VIII 109

The Big Chill:
The Cottage's Beloved Bevador Gets a Facelift

You couldn't miss it. If there's one thing most remember about the *Cottage Hotel*, it's the iconic *Bevador*. Shaped like an almost 8-foot-tall beer bottle, it has stood in the right-hand corner of the bar since the 1950s and painted to resemble different beer labels over the years. *Genesee Lager*? *Labatt Blue*? *Heinekens*? *The Caged Alpha Monkey*? Which do you remember? Whatever the *Bevador* looked like while you were having such a good time at *The Cottage* says a lot about when you spent time there!

Chapter IX 119

Fearless Leaders:
Owners, Managers, & Lessees
Through the Years

There's no debating that those who made it their mission to tend to the business of the *Cottage Hotel* had enterprising natures. Most were men, others were women who took the helm, and many were married couples. No matter who was minding the store, the traditions of *The Cottage* as a 'home away from home' continued on thanks to the dedication and imagination of these special personalities.

Chapter X 158

Behind the Bar:
The Other Side of the Story

There's no more beloved and sacred a place to rest your bones than at the *Cottage Hotel* bar. What defines that experience, in great measure, are those who tend it. They're the ones who listen to our confessions, our tall tales, our rants and random ramblings . . . and are always there to lend an ear, pour us another shot, or one last beer. It's not an easy job, with dangers of its own. Here, now, for the first time, are their un-watered-down observations.

Chapter XI 177

Of Men, Women, & Mason Jars:
The Tradition of "The Mug Club"

A legendary (and some say genius) marketing idea developed by John Urquhart ("Burdock") Ross, the *Mug Club* on Tuesday nights at the *Cottage Hotel* and later, at the *Mason Jar* in Henrietta, found great success through the years. That tradition continues to this day, in revised but no less whistle-wetting form at *The Cottage Hotel of Mendon*, on *Mason Jar Wednesdays*.

Chapter XII 190

Our Haunted Hamlet:
Ghosts of the Cottage Hotel

It's haunted — there's no doubt about it! The *Cottage Hotel* has always had a reputation as being presided over by apparitions and departed spirits. From spectral presences to ghostly footsteps, to murmuring voices from long ago — many have had experiences at *The Cottage* that defy explanation.

Chapter XIII 202

What a Long, Strange Trip it's Been:
Sex, Drugs, & Rock 'n Roll at the Cottage Hotel

Shenanigans, horseplay, hijinks, hanky-panky, and misbehaviors of all kinds . . . some of the highlights what went on at *The Cottage* through the years are chronicled here. If you want to know the real inside story of the *Cottage Hotel*, this is the chapter for you. Kudos to those who honestly and unflinchingly shared their candid tales of the monkey business that went on at the *Cottage Hotel*!

Part One:
Dangerous Liaisons — 202

Part Two:
One Tequila, Two Tequila,
Three Tequila . . . Floor! — 205

Part Three
Musical Magic (& Mayhem) — 209

Part Four
Wild Things — 255

Chapter XIV — 267

And the Beat Goes On:
Cottage Hotel Kids Take the Stage!

No matter when they first arrive, the moment they cross the *Cottage Hotel* doorstep "*Cottage Kids*" play a special role in *Cottage* history. Their perspective is without question unique. Here are their fascinating tales of what it was and is like to be a child growing up at the *Cottage Hotel*.

Chapter XV — 288

Moonlight in Mendon
Tales of Love & Romance at the Cottage Hotel

Love has always been in the air at the *Cottage Hotel*. From one-night trysts to lifelong partnerships, here are the inspiring recollections of patrons about their experiences catching *The Cottage* "love bug."

Appendix I: — 303
Cottage Hotel
Owners & Lessees from 1818-2023

Appendix II: — 307
An Annotated History
of the Stagecoach Inns & Taverns
of Mendon Hamlet

Appendix III: — 318
A Compendium of Important Dates,
People & World Events
Affecting the Hamlet of Mendon, New York

Resources — 342

Acknowledgments — 351

Index — 364

About the Author — 373

Closing Time — 375

Contact & Book Orders — 376

Preface

Dear Reader:

In Hollywood, where I once worked with creators of cartoons, animators often encouraged one another to "get aboard a moving train."

This meant . . . get to the heart of things as directly and as genuinely as possible. Good advice in many life circumstances, wouldn't you say?

This collection is a literary train of sorts, coupling tales of the past to those in the present and, with any luck, to future stories of the *Cottage Hotel*.

It is also somewhat of an old-fashioned, rough-and-tumble stagecoach ride, intent on delivering you posthaste to the *Cottage Hotel*.

The Cottage — that magical portal in Mendon hamlet where good friends, both old and new, await your arrival — and all things are possible.

It is my hope that you will enjoy the trip and perhaps be inspired by the landscape along the way.

Happy Trails,

K.

Karen Mireau

Chapter I

Ridin' in Style: Stagecoach Days in Mendon Hamlet

Stagecoach passing through Canandaigua
(*Canandaigua Daily Messenger, December 9, 1847.*)

*The forests went down, the swamps were cleared
and the howl of the wolves was stilled.*

No longer was this "The Great Western Wilderness."

*The canals came and the steamboats and then the Iron Horse
and the horn of the stagecoach was forever inured.*

*The pioneers are gone. They are part of the earth
they cleared and conquered long ago.*

*But they left a rich heritage, the pioneering spirit
that has never been quenched in the Stage Coach Towns.*[1]

---

[1] Arch Merrill, *Stagecoach Towns*, (Louis Heindl & Sons, Rochester, NY, 1947).

A quick sharp crack of a braided whip and the sounding of the driver's brass bugle horn announce the arrival of the stage in Mendon hamlet. The number of blasts tells *Cottage Hotel's* innkeeper, Thomas "Yankee Tom" Finucane, how many guests to expect at the common table for supper.

In a flurry of dust and pungent horse sweat, the stage pulls to a halt and livery men, known as *hostlers*, skillfully unhook and take hold of the four exhausted horses, leading them to the stable for replacement with a fresh team. The grizzled driver and weary travelers disembark and head directly to either of the hamlet's two inns.

Those who have chosen the humble *Cottage Hotel* over its fancier neighbor the *Mendon Hotel* (earlier known as the *East Mendon Hotel*), are just as ready to fortify themselves with strong drink and a hot meal. They may decide to pay for a crowded sleeping room (often with up to eight others) before it's time to leave for their final destination.

Meanwhile, canvas sacks of mail are retrieved from the leather-covered "boot" at the back of the stage where luggage trunks are also kept, and exchanged for mail ready to continue to the next post office.

> *In 1847 mailers could buy stamps or let the recipient of the letter pay at the other end. Many people refused the letters because they*

did not have the money to pay, so prepaid mail became mandatory in 1855.[2]

Mail is a very valuable commodity and government contracts are quite lucrative. As you might imagine, competition among stage lines is keen. The sacks are unlocked from an iron ring with a key held only by the postmaster, for it is not uncommon for stages to be robbed.

Though sometimes less efficient than a rider on horseback, by 1800 the Post Office Department already owns coaches for mail transport, with stage lines subsidized by The Continental Congress.[3] There are added benefits. Paving of Mendon roads will not begin until 1920, and even a decade later most are still made of battened earth. "Post roads" are better maintained because of stagecoach traffic.

Let's not forget that the term *stagecoach* comes from the way coaches are run in segments for 10-20 miles, sometimes more, before being replaced with a new driver and fresh horses.

On smooth clear roads, with a seasoned driver, good time can be made even on the most challenging routes. A stage can travel from five to

---

[2] Rickie Longfellow, "Transportation in America's Postal System," *Back in Time* (June, 27, 2017), fhwa.dot.gov.
[3] Stage lines will be subsidized by the Continental Congress until 1845.

eight miles per hour, sometimes 60-70 miles per day — whereas a covered wagon might cover a tenth of that distance.

Village stagecoach inns like *The Cottage* and the *Mendon Hotel* play an important role in this kind of travel. In more rural areas, at farms known as *home stations*, passengers can also expect lodging and a hot meal. These stagecoach stops are sometimes 50 miles apart or more.

Most stage drivers are subcontractors, with stage proprietors like that in *The Old Mail Line*[4] in alliance to satisfy the growing demands of passengers. Mendon hamlet customers purchase their route ticket at the post office and the *waybill* is given to the driver saving him from having to collect fares.

But the driver is not a subservient character by any means. In fact, he is a respected individual, a celebrity known by name and welcomed at every village and inn. He holds a well-earned prestige — faithfully performing his duties in navigating his coach across the landscape with great skill and daring to deliver both passengers and mail — and with pride in keeping a tight and timely schedule.

---

[4] "The *Old Mail Line* and others were part of a well-organized conglomerate that employed hundreds of agents, drivers, station-keepers, runners, clerks, mechanics, blacksmiths, and tavern keepers. It is essentially a monopoly until 1828." Richard F. Palmer, "Getting There By Stages," *Stagecoach Days*, (September 2011), stagecoachdays.blogspot.com.

Attired in his well-weathered great coat, bearskin cap in winter, and thick buckskin gloves, he undoubtedly cuts a powerful, romantic figure.

Travel by stage is surely an adventure, including the close (perhaps too close for comfort) proximity of fellow riders. A typical coach measures 115 inches high by 78 inches wide, with a total length of 152 inches.

Interior of an Abbott Downing Concord Coach
(Courtesy: The Henry Ford.org.)

Nine people could squeeze inside a stagecoach; additional passengers sometimes traveled on the roof. Inside, three lucky passengers had the back seat. Three passengers sat in the middle seat, which had only a leather strap for a backrest, and three sat in the front seat, facing backwards. Middle and front seat passengers faced each other and had to interlock their legs.[5]

1891 Abbott Downing Concord Coach
(Courtesy: The Henry Ford.org.)

On steadier, well-maintained roads, the thick leather thorough-braces that buffer and hold the coach to its wheels bounce and sway back and forth, lulling passengers with a motion that some liken to being rocked in a cradle. On roads that receive less grooming, the ride can be "bone jolting," like being tossed about in a sack of potatoes. Heat or air conditioning, of course, is unheard of—blankets,

---

[5] "The United States Postal Service: An American History," https://about.usps.com/ publications/pub100.pdf, p. 16.

hand fans, and often smelling salts must do to maintain comfort.

Mile posts mark the stage's progress, but roads can be treacherous, especially in winter when wheels are sometimes replaced with a set of "bobs" or runners, or with a "bob sleigh" consisting of a long rectangular box. In spring, ruts, bogs, or mud can quickly conspire to quagmire a coach, as can an unexpected snowstorm—always a possibility in western Upstate New York, even in April or May.

Although the driver gives exceptional attention to the comfort of his nine to eleven passengers, it is part of the etiquette of travel (which includes no spitting, smoking, swearing, or drinking without sharing) that riders disembark and assist with getting the coach back on the road. This is sometimes done by prying out a nearby fence rail and levering the 2,200 to 2,400-pound coach out of its rut. No easy task!

The year of 1812 is a busy one for the hamlet. In May of that year, The Town of Mendon is officially annexed to Monroe County, Victor-Mendon Road is surveyed, and the first post office in the hamlet is established.[6] A log cabin tavern, the *Mendon Hotel* (also sometimes known as the *East Mendon Hotel*), is

---

[6] Timothy Barnard is the first postmaster at his residence a mile northwest of the hamlet.

7

built by John Brown on the northwest corner of the hamlet's four corners.

By 1815, licenses are required for all inn and tavern keepers to legally serve and manufacture alcohol. Some think the fee of $5 — close to $100 in today's money — is highway robbery.

It is a pretty (but well-spent) penny in those times. With all of the stagecoaches now coming through the hamlet's four corners, business for the *Mendon Hotel* is better than good, and there won't be any competition until 1822 when the *Cottage Hotel* officially first opens its doors.

Later, the September 4, 1880 edition of the *Rochester Express* will report:

> *In former years, before the advent of the railroad, the village was of much more importance than at present. Two large stage houses glared at each other from opposite corners, and the time has been and is still commented on by toothless manipulators of the tobacco weed, on empty dry goods boxes and tobacco pails, in front of the grocery stores, when as high as 14 stagecoaches have been counted in close proximity to the four corners.*

It is a stated part of the innkeeper's license to responsibly treat the needs of stagecoach passengers, drivers, and their horses. Herds of livestock of all kinds on the hoof driven by *drovers* also come through town on a regular basis, and they, too, must be fed and tended.

Horses are kept in the barn behind what is now the Mendon Post Office until 1896, when his thriving business demands that owner Thomas "Yankee Tom" Finucane build a new stable just north of the *Cottage Hotel*.[7] The money he spends on materials and local craftsmen proves to be a good investment.

The barn, to this day, still stands.

Daily stage lines run in upstate New York beginning in 1804. But it is not until 1817 that the first stagecoach line run by Sam Hildreth comes hastening into the hamlet on its way from Canandaigua to Niagara Falls. The stage comes twice a week, taking three days to complete its route, and costs $2 one way, or around $47 in today's currency.

Mendon hamlet is never listed in written rosters of stagecoach lines. Then, as now, it is considered a small stopping place, perhaps not overly worthy of special attention.

---

[7] The original barn is renovated in 2020 by Hilary and David Stott, owners of the *Cottage Hotel* (legally renamed *The Cottage Hotel of Mendon* in 2005).

DISTANCES.	
	MILES.
From Canandaigua to East-Bloomfield,	9
West-Bloomfield,	5
Lima,	4
Avon,	7
Caledonia,	8
Le Roy,	6
Batavia,	11
Pembroke,	14
Williamsville,	16
Buffalo,	10
Niagara Falls,	20
	110
From Canandaigua to Rochester,	30
Lockport,	63
Lewiston,	20
Niagara Falls,	7
	120

FOUR DAILY LINES OF COACHES;

Leave the regular Mail Coach Office, in Canandaigua, for	Utica.
Three do. for	Buffalo.
Three do. for	Rochester.
One do. for	Warsaw.
And one on Tuesdays, Thursdays and Saturdays, for	Newtown.

1831. **C. H. COE & CO.**

DISTANCES.	
	MILES.
Geneva,	16
Seneca Falls,	11
Cayuga,	3
Auburn,	9
Syracuse,	25
Fayetteville,	8
Chittenango,	7
Vernon,	17
Utica,	17
Total distance,	**113**

[8]

Despite its hardships, riding in a stagecoach is both a necessity and a luxury. Its benefits go far beyond fast travel. In Mendon hamlet, a natural stop for stages from four directions, the experience is one that is greatly anticipated.

As historian Arch Merrill describes it:

> *The coming of the stage was an event in any village. It brought the mail, the news of the outside world and all kinds of passengers; politicos ready to talk issues at the drop of a beaver hat; businessmen in broadcloth, backwoodsmen in homespun, an occasional British globetrotter "slumming" in crude*

---

[8] Richard F. Palmer, *Stagecoach Days*, (November 11, 2017), https://stagecoachdays.blogspot.com.

young America; itinerant evangelists, fancy women, and concert singers; adventurers and emigrants bound for the West.[9]

The stagecoach reigns as a mode of intra- and interstate travel in Upstate New York for most of the 1800s.[10] Even after the opening of the Erie Canal in 1825,[11] stagecoaches continue to be a primary form of public transportation, especially during the four to five winter months when the canal is closed.

It's noted that cholera victims begin arriving in Rochester via The Erie Canal, and it is not long after that an epidemic sweeps through Mendon claiming 14 lives. According to the 1890 edition of the *Mendon Cemetery*:

In July of 1832, the cholera scourge visited the little hamlet being brought by a stage driver from Rochester. During this epidemic the greatest excitement prevailed throughout the community, and the people were frequently awakened at night by the sound of the

---

[9] Arch Merrill, *Stagecoach Towns* (Louis Heindl & Sons, Rochester, NY, 1947).

[10] Route 64 is surveyed in 1797 but is yet to be made into a truly passable route. It is not until the early 1840s that railroads and Erie Canal packet boats supplement public conveyances.

[11] When the Erie Canal opens on October 26, 1825, the novelty of touring on packet boats increases the need for stagecoaches.

workman's hammer upon the coffin of a victim who had probably been taken during the day previous.[12]

**Liberty Coach in Mendon Hamlet in front of
the Mendon Grange Hall (former Presbyterian Church)
selling War Bonds in 1918**
(Courtesy: Diane Ham.)

As you might imagine, the advent of the railroads also dramatically changes the nature of travel in the hamlet and across the entire country. A *Lehigh Valley Railroad* depot built in 1982 in the hamlet brings more visitors than can be counted. Stage lines continue to be a necessity, especially in rural areas, as a means of reaching rail depots, the Erie Canal, and to travel between growing cities.

---

[12] Daniel Allen, *In the Mendon Cemetery from 1825 to 1890*, (J.W. Watkins, Mendon, NY, 1890).

By 1848, the writing is on the stagecoach inn wall—aside from "Tally Ho" or "coaching" clubs that tour the Finger Lakes in coaches specially built for leisurely excursions,[13] this form of travel is nearing its end. By 1918, except for lone places in the West, the last of the stages will be replaced by *gasoline wagons*, railroads, steamships, and packet boats along the Erie Canal. Contrary to popular speculation, though, it is the motorcar—not the railroad—that is primarily to blame for the stagecoach's final exit from the landscape.

The railroad in the hamlet is destined for extinction, too. The depot will be torn down in 1952 and 20 years later the rails pried up and hauled away. The right-of-way will be turned into walking and equestrian trails[14] as part of the nation's evolving *Rails to Trails* movement of the 1990s.

Much to local sorrow, especially for people like Russ Mahrt and his cousins who grew up there, the *Mendon Hotel* will be sold to Gulf Oil for a gas station and close its doors for good in 1957. It will be intentionally burned down, exiting the hamlet in

---

[13] Richard F. Palmer, *Traveling to the Thousand Islands by Stagecoach*, Thousand Islands Life, Volume 18, Issue 8, August, 2023.
[14] The local *Lehigh Valley Trail* system for hiking, biking and equestrians was established by The Mendon Foundation—a nonprofit land trust chartered in 1993.

"a blaze of glory" as a demonstration of local firefighting techniques.[15]

Without the constant hustle and bustle of the stagecoaches and trains, Mendon hamlet returns to being a "don't blink or you'll miss it" country crossroads. For many years it is even without a traffic signal. (When one is installed, it is said that local farmers will choose to ignore it.)

Nostalgia for the days of the stagecoaches is stronger than ever—not just for hamlet residents—but for travelers passing through. There's something timeless about the hamlet that the many changes it has endured will never erase.

That the *Cottage Hotel*, our revered stagecoach inn, manages to survive with its basic personality as an old-time saloon intact is also something of a minor miracle. Two hundred years later, it's still a welcoming watering hole where people from all walks of life can gather and find entertainment, comfort and community.

Mendon hamlet, as you have just seen, has never been just a "One Horse Town."[16] As Tom Midney,

---

[15] This exciting event was witnessed by Rosemary (Heckman) Lewis when she was eleven years old. "The whole town came out," she recalls. "It was amazing!"

[16] Hear an original music track about the *Cottage Hotel* by Johnny Bauer at:
https://johnnybauer.com/track/1240920/one-horse-town.

an out-of-towner who is drawn here year after year, puts it:

> *I return to The Cottage feeling it is the best thing that ever happened to me. And because it always feels just like 'my home away from home' — I never leave without a big smile on my face.*

We'll drink to that, as we're pretty sure those arriving by stagecoach at the *Cottage Hotel* did back in the day too!

Snowbound Stagecoach[17]

---

[17] Richard F. Palmer, *Stagecoach Days*, (December 25, 2012), https://stagecoachdays.blogspot.com.

Chapter II

How to Build a Lasting Legend: The Construction of the *Cottage Hotel*

For a moment, let's travel back to 1819.

George S. Stone and his older brother, Jeremy, stand at Mendon hamlet's crossroads watching the stagecoaches come and go. They can see that business is booming at the *Mendon Hotel* across the street. *Plenty of room for competition*, they conjecture.

Four-horse stagecoaches had been passing through town since 1810. But in 1817, Sam Hildreth puts Mendon hamlet on the map when his organized stagecoach line from Canandaigua to Buffalo makes its first appearance. A steady stream of visitors has been arriving ever since.

A year later, the Stone brothers purchase undeveloped land on the northeast corner of the crossroads, hoping that the $1,000 they've paid for the property (the equivalent of almost $23,000 today) will prove to be a good investment.[18]

They've already observed that those traveling on stagecoaches are not the only potential customers. By law, the proprietors of inns and taverns must take care of stage drivers, stable hands called *hostlers*, and the ever-present *drovers* that herd cattle and other livestock from town to town.

Admittedly, *drovers* are a rough bunch. Most likely they will bed down in the stable with the horses, but they too work hard and must be well fed. Although clearly of a different social status, they will be welcomed as warmly as the rest of the guests. No doubt they will have some wild tales to add to the entertainment at the tavern's communal table!

Visitors do tire of having to share their sleeping quarters with strangers, sometimes four or five to one of the larger beds. But this is common practice,

---

[18] The 4 1/2 acres in Lot 30 where the *Cottage Hotel* will be built is purchased in 1818 for $1,000 from John W. Cady and Maria C. Cady of Johnstown in Montgomery County, New York, before Mendon is annexed from Ontario to Monroe County. The deed is later recorded in Monroe County on October 31, 1928. Note: today it will cost you upwards of $60,000 for one acre of land near Mendon hamlet.

for rooms are scarce and stagecoaches usually arrive full of ten or more passengers.

The two-story *Cottage Hotel* will have nine bedrooms, while the three-story *Mendon Hotel* across the street offers 10 upper sleeping rooms. No doubt both establishments will find ways to squeeze in a few more customers.

It's possible that John E. Tomlinson, the owner of the *Mendon Hotel*, may have been the one to suggest a new inn to accommodate the overflow from his own business. By the time the *Cottage Hotel* opens for business a little over two years later, it will be a common sight to see up to 14 stagecoaches lining the streets.

Now it's time for the Stone brothers to start bringing their dream of a new stagecoach inn and tavern to fruition.[19] First things first—a foundation must be built. The raw materials of sand, stones, and limestone are readily at hand, but they must be gathered and hauled to the site.

The right kind of sand is easy. It's plentiful and can be found in the run-of-the-bank gravel pit just up

---

[19] According to Mendon Historian, Diane Ham, the previous owner, John W. Cady, lived in Johnstown in Montgomery County and probably did not live on the property in Mendon hamlet. "Construction of the *Cottage Hotel* most likely would not have begun until at least 1819."

the hill from what will become the *Cottage Hotel*. The same is true for limestone, which will be broken into chunks and burned in a lime kiln, then slaked with boiling water. This creates a chemical reaction that turns the limestone into a powder that will then be mixed with the sand to make a soft mortar.

> *The mortar is composed of one bushel of fresh stone lime to eight or nine bushels of clean sharp sand. As the strength of the building depends on the goodness of the mortar, it is very important that sand of the first quality should be obtained. Yellow sand or any sand that contains clay should be rejected.*[20]

When the last of the glaciers retreated some 13,700 years ago, they left behind geologic features unique to this part of western Upstate New York. *Kames* are mounded hills of sand and gravel. *Eskers* are rough winding ridges of sand and gravel, and *Drumlins* are more oval, egg-shaped hills consisting of rock debris, compacted clay, silt, sand, gravel, and limestone.[21]

---

[20] D. T. Greatfield, "Cobble Stone Buildings," *New Genesee Farmer and Gardener's Journal*, Volume 2 no. 5, 1841. (Bateham & Crosman, Rochester, New York), 66-67.
[21] Another geologic feature of note in Mendon are *Kettles*—depressions in the ground formed by the outwash of buried ice that form *Kettle Ponds* or *Kettle Lakes* (like Devil's Bathtub in Mendon Ponds Park) when filled with water.

Why are these important? Simply put: they are composed of the *till*, or sediment of the glaciers—all materials needed for stone foundations and structures.

Field stones (or *rubble*) and heavy rounded stones known as *cobblestones* or *roundheads* left behind by the glaciers are plentiful[22]. Despite their abundance, gathering these stones requires effort. It's grunt work, to be sure, but has to be done before building can begin.

What's needed are men with the strength, ability, and enthusiasm to work with stone. These might be neighbors or local masons. Or perhaps the Stone brothers themselves will pitch in and do the work themselves. No one really knows for sure.

By the early 1820s there are also craftsmen arriving in the area to work on the Erie Canal who might be called upon for their manpower and expertise.[23] The majority of these workers are immigrants from Wales or Ireland who gain competence as they build wells, foundations, pig cotes, and other settlers' needs throughout Monroe, Ontario, and

---

[22] Smaller, rounder stones created by the grinding action of the waves of Lake Ontario are also available and become especially prized by masons, but these are some 30 miles away from Mendon hamlet.

[23] Work on the Erie Canal began in 1817 in Rome, New York and was completed in 1825.

Livingston counties and *The Cottage's* foundation might have been one of these.

These masons will also build quite artful homes and barns in the hamlet in the 1830s. Of the 1500 structures built of cobblestones in the United States, 90% will be built within a 75-mile radius of nearby Rochester.

As you might imagine, farmers find stones of any kind to be a bit of a nuisance. Field stones along with *cobblestones* are unearthed as Mendon farmers plow their fields. These must be removed prior to planting their crops and before their plows are dulled or broken. *Rubble* might be used for foundations or to build drystone fences to separate their pastures. Mostly it is set aside in piles at the edges of their fields, making it an easy harvest. Children and women are often employed to collect stones from the fields, and many a farm hand or gatherer complains of sore hands that may soon require bandaging.

Stones are hauled by horse- or oxen-drawn wagons on flat, rough sleds called *stone boats* to where needed. Due to their heaviness, this is best done in winter or very early spring, when the ground is still frozen or firm. They are sometimes sorted for size using thick wooden planks with holes cut in them or sorted with a *beetle ring* made of iron. Then the work begins.

But now, be careful—there's no railing—watch your head, and let's take a walk down the steep, narrow plank pine steps into the basement of the *Cottage Hotel* and take a gander at its walls.

In this photo you can see how irregular stones were cemented in place by mortar, and topped by a 1 1/2 foot wide axe-hewn pine floor joist to form the foundation of the building.

The photo on the next page on the left, shows how repairs might have been made to eroded mortar. The photo on the right also shows how different sized stones were used.

It's clear that these weren't sorted for size or chosen for aesthetic purpose; but then again they weren't intended for public display, only for strength and function.

Cottage Hotel Cellar Walls, 2022

It's somewhat slap-dash work compared to the finely-wrought exteriors of the 10 cobblestone structures that still exist in Mendon hamlet, but by gum it gets the job done — despite freezes, floods, and a multitude of dancing feet above it, 200 years later that foundation still holds firm.

Last, just to give you another glimpse of the pine plank floors — on the next page is a view looking up from the basement ceiling that also shows the hand-hewn floor joist.

And here's what those same floors look like from above in the interior of *The Cottage*, with their beautiful, aged patina

Once the foundation is in place, it's time for the Stone brothers to build what will become the *Cottage Hotel*. The structure is described from various sources as:

A two-story, side-gabled building with post-and-beam construction. It has a low-pitched roof and two interior ridge-end chimneys. The floor joists are made of huge logs, with hand-hewn beams in the cellar. The floors are composed of pine planks.

Facing south, the five windows on the ground floor and the six windows above contain two double-hung shuttered sash fenestrations throughout, as do those on the east and west ends. The asymmetrical south side facing Victor-Mendon Road (Route 251) has a projecting pedimented portal (today's front entrance).

Like the Mendon Hotel across the street on Pittsford-Mendon Road (Route 64), The Cottage sports a handsome front porch with a railed balcony on its second story. There is also a lean-to on the west side.

In 2023, the Cottage building in its entirety consists of 2,025 square feet.[24]

There may have been some financial incentive to get the job done quickly. With more and more

---

[24] Edited and expanded from *Early Mendon Building Summary* by Mendon Historian Diane Ham, originally written by Diane in association with John G. Sheret (structure examination), Ermina Malin (deed search), and Langdon Clay (description).

stagecoaches arriving daily, the *Cottage Hotel* will certainly be a welcome addition to the hamlet.[25]

Here's a sample from Thomas ("Yankee Tom") Finucane's account book. Business seems to have been fairly steady from 1891-1893 — steady enough to enough to warrant the building of a new 30' x 40' two-story barn just north of *The Cottage* a few years later. Until the new barn is built, horses for the stagecoaches will be kept in a barn located behind the house next door.

```
      February 1891

1 Week          39.75
2 Week          52.20
3 Week          29.00
4 Week          42.30
Total Feb    $164.25

February 1892
1 Week          36.50
2 Week          42.25
3 Week          45.20
4 Week          47.25
Total Feb    $171.50

February 1893
1 Week          70.00
2 Week          65.00
3 Week          77.00
Total Feb    $299.00
   Board        80.00
Total        $379.00
```

```
March 1891
1 Week          70.50
2 week          49.00
3 Week          37.20
4 Week          50.00
Total Mar    $206.70

March 1892
1 Week          40.00
2 Week          30.50
3 Week          27.75
4 Week          39.00
5 Week          39.25
Total Mar    $176.50

March 1893
1 Week          98.25
2 Week          79.75
3 Week          98.50
4 Week          89.50
5 Week         105.50
Total Mar    $471.75
   Board        70.00
             $541.75
```

---

[25] It is purely conjecture, but it is possible that *The Cottage* may have operated as a tavern soon after its construction (most likely after 1819), and prior to becoming a licensed stagecoach inn in 1822. Unfortunately, to date there is no documentation for this.

The barn is completed on May 15, 1896 at a total cost of $407.91 for 1,320 square feet.[26]

```
The following appears in an account book kept by Thomas
Finucane owner of the Cottage Hotel in the hamlet of
Mendon. The book was found in a barn behind the cobblestone
house on the Mendon Ionia Road across from the former
cobblestone academy (later firehouse) by Fred & Dorothy
Barben when they purchased the farm on which the cobblestone
house stood.

The barn described as being constructed still stands just
north of the Cottage Hotel on the east side of the Pittsford
Mendon Road.

1896 Cash Paid for Building Barn size 30x40 Post 16 ft
Commenced April 22 1896    Finished May 15 1896
1896 To Humphrey & Holdridge  Honeoye Falls
        for siding $20.00 per 1000
        for flooring $18.00 per 1000
        for shingles $250.00 per 1000     $141.00
        for stalls $20.00 per 1000          17.50
1896 To Al Nye Mendon
        for frame jocye? rafters
        and other rafters                   99.00
1896 for digging and building wall          34.96
        for carpenter work  Chas. Peachey   34.00
                            Jim O'Brien     22.70
                            Edd Root        22.75
                       Leonard Bainbridge   12.00
                            Lambert Houck    3.00
                            Will Eckler      3.00
                            Frank Peachy     2.00
1896 for nails & extras to Ben Dolbeer      16.00
        Total Paid                        $407.91
June 18th 1896 Paid in Full - Thomas Finucan
Oct 29 1896 to paint    John Finucan     $ 15.00
                            Dock Hill      1.00
                            Gus Hill       4.00
1896 Total for lumber                     257.60
        for wall                           39.16
        for carpenter work                 99.45
        for nails                          16.00
        Total                            $407.90
June 18th Paid in full Thom. Finucan
Oct 29 For paint                           15.00
        For painting                       11.00
```

**Thomas Finucane Account Book
for construction of the barn next to the Cottage Hotel**
(Courtesy: Mendon Historian Diane Ham.)

---

[26] When renovated in 2020 by Hilary and David Stott, old circus posters will be found and a beam from the barn will be used to replace the footrest at the bar.

Here are some vintage photos of The Cottage courtesy of Mendon Historian Diane Ham. First, a rare photo of *The Cottage* in 1918.

And another of *The Cottage* in a postcard dated 1925. See the wagon wheels in the barn to the left?

On the next page is a photo taken in 1960 that appeared in the Thursday, August 22 *Honeoye Falls Times* showing the excavation for the installation of gas mains by Rochester Gas & Electric, bringing cooking and heating gas to Mendon hamlet for the first time. It's another good look at the handsome balcony that will be torn down shortly thereafter when owner Mary Elizabeth Heckman deems it unsafe for her children to play on.

Below is a 1978 photo looking south on Pittsford-Mendon Road (Route 64), with the barn, *The Cottage*, and the remnants of Howard ("Ike") Stanley's filling station in the foreground.

Here is the barn in 1994, prior to its renovation:

(Photo by John G. Sheret.)

And here is what *The Cottage Hotel* and the adjacent renovated barn looked like in 2022![27]

(Photo by Karen Mireau.)

---

[27] *Cottage Hotel* photos above, unless otherwise notated, are courtesy of the archives of Mendon Historian Diane Ham.

As we sit and have a cold one at the bar, it's hard not to ponder the history beneath our feet. Just think of the tremendous energy that went into excavating and then building those cellar walls! If only they could speak and tell us the stories of those who built them.

In the words of Paul S. Gordon ("Buzzy") Bronson[28] former owner of the *Cottage Hotel*, now a natural stone mason and artist:

> *So when you see some stone*
> *be sure to admire*
> *the pleasure it gives you*
> *as you warm by that fire*
>
> *Or when you see some stone*
> *that makes you feel good*
> *perhaps in a fence, in a field*
> *or a wall in the wood*
>
> *Give thanks to the men*
> *who were laying their claim,*
> *to the land with the stone*
> *by no other name*

---

[28] Excerpt from : *The Stone Poem* by Paul S. Gordon ("Buzzy") Bronson, July 22, 2000,
https://www.statementsinstone.com/special-words.

Chapter III

Burned-Over but Never Burnt-Out: Give Me That Old Time Religion

The "Burned-Over" District
Genesee Country in Western Upstate New York
(1830 Federal Census Map)

There's something about the very ground we walk upon in Mendon hamlet that has always attracted the out-of-the-ordinary.

We've seen our fair share of radicals and revolutionaries—from renegades to rascals to rough-and-ready rovers—not to mention our brave, intrepid, sod-busting, forest-clearing pioneers.

We've also been blessed with determined dreamers—the righteous, the visionary, the far-seeing, the free-thinking, and the unabashedly spiritually-minded. From the 1700s on, social and religious leaders, Native American and otherwise, have each had their heyday here in the hamlet.

In August of 1820, as the walls of the foundation for the *Cottage Hotel* are likely being finished, those in our country are just beginning their quest for women's equality and the right to vote.

It will be another 100 years before the 19th Amendment is ratified, but nearby on Quaker Meeting House Road, *The Society of Friends* (more popularly known as *Quakers*) hosts a wide range of forward-thinking lecturers. Suffragette Susan B. Anthony, African American evangelist and reformer Sojourner Truth, poet John Greenleaf Whittier, and abolitionist Frederick Douglass[29] all speak there at one time or another.

It's likely that people in the hamlet will go to hear these famous orators and this certainly gives those at our local watering holes something new to chew on. Although it will be another 40 years before the Civil War attempts to settle the issue of slavery, the tide of public opinion is slowly beginning to turn, thanks in good measure to those brave enough to speak out against injustice.

---

[29] Frederick Douglass, who published the abolitionist newspaper *The North Star* in Rochester, New York, was also a "station master" on the Underground Railroad.

In Rochester, a central hub of the *Underground Railroad*, Frederick Douglass joins forces with supporters of women's rights to combat prejudices of all kinds. Known stops on the *Railroad* are in Mendon Ponds at the farm of Reverend Henry Quimby[30]; and in Fishers at the Fisher Homestead, as well as other unofficial sites. Some say there may have been a tunnel between the *Cottage Hotel* and *Mendon Hotel* that was part of the *Underground Railroad*—a rumor yet to be proven—but it's not unlikely that hamlet residents may have assisted runaway slaves in finding their way to freedom.

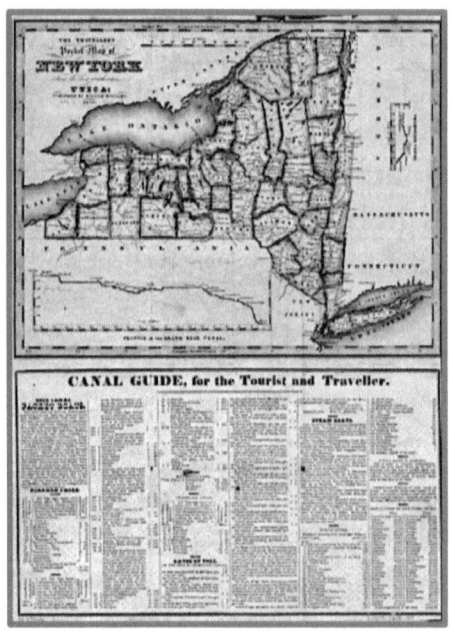

The Travellers Pocket Map of New York, 1826
(Courtesy: Library of Congress.)

---

[30] Reverend Quimby was a *Hicksite Quaker* and founder of the Rochester Anti-Slavery Society.

The Erie Canal, christened in 1825,[31] accelerates economic development in New York State, making it possible to travel quickly from the Atlantic Ocean to the Great Lakes and beyond. There's no doubt that a new world is dawning. Some come to western Upstate New York seeking riches. Some seek adventure. Others find the opportunity to break free of old ways of thought.

People of all faiths ablaze with enthusiasm for revivals and emotional preaching pour into the area. The steady stream of passionate believers, prophets, and mystics gravitating here soon grows to a fever pitch. Churches pop up like mushrooms after a rain. Some begin calling the region the *Psychic Highway*.

Evangelist Charles Grandison Finney dubs western Upstate New York the *Burned-Over* or *Burnt-Over District* because people seem to be on fire with new ideas.

Or are they just plain bonkers?

---

[31] The Erie Canal's nearest shipping port was in Pittsford, four miles north of the hamlet. Good transportation opened up new realms of financial possibility, but mostly for communities to the north. In bypassing the hamlet, the Erie Canal made sure that Mendon stayed agricultural.

Shakers, Quakers[32], Millerites, Universalists, Perfectionists, Theosophists, Seventh Day Adventists, Jehovah's Witnesses, Spiritualists (as well as other shorter-lived religions) all come calling. Over 30 sects, cults, crusades, original philosophies, and religions are spawned in the *Burned-Over District*. They join existing Baptist, Methodist, Catholic, and Lutheran congregations (among others) in or near Mendon hamlet. [33]

Upstate is also the site of a number of experiments in Utopianism, such as the Oneida Community, which boasts an idyllic life of free love, group marriage, and communal property. There are numerous Fourierist colonies (one exists in Bloomfield) based on the economic and social ideals of French intellectual Charles Fourier.

Pseudo sciences such as Phrenology[34] and Mesmerism[35] briefly make their appearances.

---

[32] As mentioned, members of *The Friends Society* were also called *Quakers*, although this was considered a derogatory term at the time.

[33] The establishment and history of early hamlet churches has been well documented by Mendon Town Historian, Diane Ham.

[34] Phrenology, which measured mental traits by the measurement of bumps on the skull, was developed by Franz Joseph Gall in 1796 and introduced in the U.S. in 1822. It was mostly discredited by 1840.

[35] Developed by Franz Mesmer in 1779, the theory of "animal magnetism" or the laying on of hands as a method of healing, continues to influence alternative medicine.

Theosophy and the occult practices of the Swedish theologian, scientist, philosopher, and mystic Emanuel Swedenborg also have their vogue, as do Freemasons, numbering up to six million members worldwide and still practicing in Mendon.

The *Cottage Hotel* (2 stories), and the *Mendon Hotel* (3 stories, below), mid-1920s

(Photos: Honeoye Falls-Town of Mendon Historical Society.)

And there they are, our hamlet regulars (right where we might have been) — sitting at the bar at the *Cottage Hotel* — smack dab in the weird whack-a-doodle epicenter of it all!

When *The Cottage* opens its doors for business in 1822, the hamlet is already a bustling community of several hundred inhabitants. It boasts two general stores, a blacksmith shop, a steam-powered flour mill and sawmill (both on Irondequoit Creek), an apple and peach drying house (later known as the *Springwater Inn*, now called *Ye Olde Mendon Tavern*), a coal and lumber business, and now two licensed stagecoach inns — the *Mendon Hotel* and the *Cottage Hotel*.[36]

Aside from all the *brou-ha-ha* and excitement of being a part of the *Burned-Over District*, visionary thinking is really nothing new — it has always been a part of the landscape in Upstate New York.

In 1799, Handsome Lake[37], a charismatic and controversial Seneca Indian prophet and religious leader began receiving profound visions from the beyond. From these he developed a moral code

---

[36] Diane Ham and Anne Bullock, edited by Julia P. Dickinson, *History of the Town of Mendon and Village of Honeoye Falls, 1838-2000*, (Honeoye Falls-Town of Mendon Historical Society, January 2000).

[37] Arthur C. Parker, "The Code of Handsome Lake, the Seneca Prophet," 1913. https://www.sacredtexts.com/nam/iro/parker/index.htm.

blending Quaker values of compassion with traditional Iroquois beliefs such as clairvoyance and spiritual revelation. Handsome Lake will become well known throughout Upstate New York and his prophecies said to have a direct influence on Mormon doctrine.[38]

And so, the dramatic scene has already been set.

In 1823, thanks to a timely visitation by the angel Moroni, the future prophet Joseph Smith, Jr. will find and unearth "The Golden Plates" at Hill Cumorah in Palmyra, 17 miles south of the hamlet.

Soon Joseph will translate their inscriptions (who some think to be pictograms of the Seneca Indian language)[39] into *The Book of Mormon,* and *viola*! the Mormon religion is off and running!

Location, location, location! Just adjacent to the hamlet lives future Mormon leader Heber Chase Kimball, a blacksmith and potter, later renowned as the maker of *Mucker-Pucker Ware*. He is best friends

---

[38] Although his rise to power was full of contradictions and he was opposed later in life, Handsome Lake's work revitalized the Iroquois belief system. His teachings in *The Good Word* (Gaiwi'io) are still recited in Iroquois longhouses.
[39] Thomas W. Murphy, "An Insufficient Canon: Popol Wuj, Book of Mormon, and Other Neophyte Scriptures," (Mormon Association Meeting, 2022.)

with Brigham Young,[40] whose parents' land borders his own family's at Tomlinson's Corners.

It's easy to imagine the two, both originally hailing from Vermont, helping each other on their family farms, rubbing elbows at the general store and post office, or maybe frequenting either of the two taverns in town—that is, before they embrace the Mormon religion, which frowns upon the public (emphasis on *public*) drinking of alcohol.

Brigham Young   **Heber Chase Kimball**
*(Courtesy: Church History Library,
The Church of Jesus Christ of Latter-day Saints.)*

It may or may not be a tall tale, but Brigham already has a reputation for favoring a tipple or two. In the 1970s, local hamlet farmers (who were then in their seventies and eighties) often told me stories of

---

[40] Brigham Young (1801-1877) died in Utah, having married 56 wives, and sired 57 children.

Brigham Young getting drunk and falling into ditches on his way home from the *Cottage Hotel*.

> 2/4, Brigham Young
> to 1/₂ ℔ Shin tea 8/ — 50
> to 1/4 ℔ pepper 2/b — 8
> to 1/4 ℔ allspice 3/- — .9
> " 1/₂ Gallon Lamp Oil 8/- — 50
> to 2 tumblers 1/— — 25
> " 1 sett cups & saucers 3/b — 3/
> " 1 tea pot 2/- — 25
> " 2 platters 2/b — 63
> " 1 Shin silk 6 — 6
> " 1 pint wine 4/ — 16 2

Brigham Young's Grocery Bill
Note the last item of '1 pint of wine'
(no doubt for purely medicinal purposes)

Brigham Young is destined to succeed Joseph Smith, Jr. in 1847 as the president of the Church of Jesus Christ of Latter-day Saints. His best friend, Heber C. Kimball, will later become fourth in

---

[41] An account book housed at the *Honeoye Falls-Town of Mendon Historical Museum* for the general store operated by Dr. Milton Sheldon shows purchases on credit by Brigham Young on October 2, 1829.

seniority of the original *Quorum of the 12 Apostles* as well as *First Counselor* to Brigham Young.[42]

Pretty sweet work, I'd say, for two country boys from the hamlet 'hood'!

It wasn't long before then that Brigham had arrived in Mendon in 1828 with his wife, Miriam Angeline Works Young[43] (the first of 56 wives), and their three-year-old daughter, Elizabeth. As the bill of sale on the prior page shows, he came into the hamlet for supplies, where he had a personal account at Dr. Milton Sheldon's general store.

He'd been trained as a master carpenter, metallurgist, and glazier, decent skills to have in early America. At the back of his parents John and Abigail "Nabby" Howe Young's farm at the corner of Cheese Factory and Mendon-Ionia roads, he built a chair and basket factory over spring-fed Trout Creek.[44]

---

[42] The Church of the Latter Day Saints was renamed the Church of Jesus Christ of Latter-day Saints in 1838. Not easy work being a prophet: Joseph Smith and his brother, Hyrum, were assassinated in Illinois in 1844 by an angry mob.

[43] Miriam Works Young (1806-1832) died of tuberculosis and was cared for by the Kimball family. She is buried in a small cemetery along Boughton Hill Road in Mendon.

[44] Heber C. Kimball (1801-1868) was later baptized into the Church of Latter Day Saints in Brigham Young's millpond, as were all Mendon Mormons prior to migrating west.

But there are . . . problems. Young is seen in a somewhat less-than-saintly light by his neighbors.

As a letter to the *Rochester Historical Society Publication Series* from Mendon resident John P. Lynn reveals:

> *Brigham was considered by his yeoman neighbors a sort of vagabond, a 'ne'er-do-well,' who would stop in the middle of any job, to argue the Scriptures, particularly as to their authority for minute differences of faith and practice. He was an attendant of the Baptist Church in the building that, until recently, stood upon the hilltop just south of Mendon Village. Whether he was an actual member of that Church is uncertain, and if he were, it was principally for argumentative purposes, never being able to agree with his brethren on the proper hardness of a shell. He was something of an Evangelist and, until he found the 'true faith,' wandered from sect to sect with more activity than welcome.*[45]

George W. Allen, who knew Young when he lived in Mendon, reported that:

---

[45] Letter from Mendon resident John P. Lynn, August 11, 1026, to the *Rochester Historical Society's Publication Series*. John G. Sheret, "Brigham Young: Carpenter and Cabinet Maker," *Crooked Lake Review* (Fall 2006-Winter 2007).

> *Brigham in his habits was essentially lazy, so far as labor was concerned, and an unprofitable hand to employ. He would shirk the hard and most laborious work, if possible, and would surely cut the day short at both ends of it and render some plausible excuse of family sickness or religious engagement as a reason for his absence. He had an appetite for dainties and delicacies and would generally indicate to the housekeeper where he worked, such food and drink he desired, accompanied with a very persuasive request that they be provided for his use while he worked there.* [46]

Apparently, Joseph Smith, Jr., the future founder of Mormonism, is no angel either. In 1816, Joseph, then age 10, and his family move to a farm near Palmyra, New York. His father, Joseph Smith, Sr., long suspected of being involved with counterfeiting back in Vermont, is thought to be a dishonest man. Neighbors are unsympathetic to the family, whom they consider barely literate squatters.

Joseph Smith and his family live in a place and time where many believe in crystallomancy, divining, or "scrying"—an ancient form of divination (from

---

[46] J. Sheldon Fisher, "Brigham Young as a Mendon Craftsman: A Study in Historical Archeology," *New York History*, Vol. 61, no. 4 (October 1980), Cornell University Press, 447.

'descry,' meaning to discern). When the Smiths lose their farm due to nonpayment of rent, legends of buried treasure in the glacial drumlin hills near Mendon afford young Joseph and his father an irresistible opportunity.[47]

Joseph Smith, Jr.
(Courtesy: Community of Christ.)

By placing special chocolate-brown "peepstones" or "seer stones" about the size of a large hen's egg in their hats (intended to block ambient light) and peering into them during proper phases of the moon, the Smiths contend that they can locate hidden gold and treasure.

---

[47] "The use of divination and magic ritual to discover buried treasure is part of a belief system wherein subterranean spirits control precious metals that can be captured by a knowledgeable magician." Clay L. Chandler, "Scrying for the Lord: Magic, Mysticism, and the Origins of the Book of Mormon." https://www.dialoguejournal.com\wp\content/uploads/sbi/issues/V36N04.

Although Joseph Smith grows up in a time when scrying is a common and acceptable form of folk magic, in the end it is all trickery and chicanery. Burying stashes of "treasure" that they will "find" and dig up in front of the eyes of their customers allow father and son to convince others of their visionary talents and to eke out a meager living.

Joseph's involvement with magic and mysticism begins early. He is 14 in 1820 when he has his first waking religious experience—just two years prior to the *Cottage Hotel* opening its doors. Much like a skilled magician, young Joseph is said to have a naturally charismatic and dynamic character, with the noetic ability to convince others to see what he wants them to see.

In 1826, when crystallomancy is deemed illegal in New York, Joseph Smith is brought to trial as "a disorderly person and an imposter"[48] and fined the amount of $2.68. Nonetheless, his first vision will lead to his discovery of the "Golden Plates" at Hill Cumorah and to publishing *The Book of Mormon* in 1830 at the ripe old age of twenty-four.

---

[48] Gordon A. Madsen, "Joseph Smith's 1826 Trial: The Legal Setting" https://byustudies.byu.edu/PDFLibrary/30.2MadsenJosephSmiths-12a5c181-05a1-4e48-b7a4-2d039c4c16f0.pdf. In 1830, Joseph Smith is arrested on similar charges, but acquitted.

The translations of those plates, inscribed with markings only Smith can decipher (with the help of special "spectacles" made of two conjoined seer stones), is the subject of much conjecture. Whether the translations are channeled directly from God, from the spirit world, from pictograms adopted from Seneca Indian traditions, plain ol' black magic, or entirely a fiction from Joseph Smith's imagination, remains a constant and lively source of controversy to this day.

Liberal Advocate.

Volume II.   Rochester, April 14, 1832.   No. 8.

Mormonism is said to have taken deep root in the Baptist church, in the town of Mendon, in this county. A number were re-dipped on Sunday last. The preacher said that he should never die, but be translated, after the manner of Enoch, and that in eighteen months Mormonism would be the prevailing religion; and, that in five years the wicked were to be swept from the face of the earth. When we see the degradation to which weak human nature has been reduced of late, we cannot wonder at such fanatical extravagance.

(Courtesy: Uncle Dale's Readings in Early Mormon History, 1832-1833.)

Whatever the source, Joseph Smith develops a religious cosmology that is highly complex and creative for someone said to have only three years of formal education. In an interview for *The Saints'*

Herald in 1879, his first wife, Emma Hale Smith, says quite plainly:[49]

> *Joseph Smith could neither write nor dictate a coherent and well-worded letter, let alone dictate a book like the Book of Mormon. And, though I was an active participant in the scenes that transpired, and was present during the translation of the plates, and had cognizance of things as they transpired, it is marvelous to me, a 'marvel and a wonder,' as much so as to anyone else.*[50]

Some say it is Smith's genius for rallying others around his ideas that leads to the early success of Mormonism, or that it is the enthusiasms of those drawn to the spiritual intensity of the times that play a greater part in Smith's ability to easily convert others to his original thinking. No doubt there are many influences at play. By 1833, 65 members from both Methodist and local Baptist churches have been dunked into Trout Creek and baptized in the Mormon faith.

Not all Mendonites are pleased by this startling exodus from their devoted folds, and none seem to object when Brigham Young leads the Mormon

---

[49] The LDS church reports that Joseph Smith may have had up to 40 wives, including Helen Kimball, the daughter of Mendon hamlet native Heber C. Kimball.

[50] Joseph Smith III, "Last Testimony of Sister Emma," (*The Saints' Herald*, Vol. 26, no. 19, October 1, 1879), 289.

migration to Kirtland, Ohio that winter. (Rumor has it that Mormons are stoned by the residents until they leave town.) In a now no-longer-startling act of rebranding, the LDS church later names Smith "The American Moses."

Joseph Smith addressing members
of the Quorum of Twelve Apostles in 1843-44
From L-R: Hyrum Smith (Joseph Smith's brother),
Willard Richards, Joseph Smith,
Orson Pratt, Parly P. Pratt, Orson Hyde,
Heber C. Kimball, and Brigham Young
(Public domain photo.)

We must now fast forward almost a century. Beginning in 1937, a grand theatrical pageant held every July enacts scenes from the *Book of Mormon* at Hill Cumorah in Palmyra, just a few miles from the hamlet.

In 1957, it is reported that 100,000 people from all over the world attend the event. The spectacle will close down in 2019, most likely a casualty of the Covid pandemic, but many local folks remember it as magnificent entertainment—with hundreds upon hundreds of actors, live music, imaginative costumes, and sets.

Mormon Pageant Sets New Mark In Attendance

PALMYRA, Aug. 3 — For the last time this year, Hill Cumorah tonight was transformed into a color-splashed setting for a dramatization of the saga of Mormonism.

Approximately 100,000 persons attended the three performances of the 16th annual "America's Witness for Christ" pageant, produced by memebrs of the Church of Jesus Christ of Latter-Day Saints. Last year's attendance figures hit a record high of 75,000.

Ontario County Sheriff Earl Thompson estimated the closing night attendance at more than 40,000, despite a threat of rain.

(Rochester Democrat and Chronicle August 3, 1957.)

In 2003, "All About Mormons," an irreverent animated *South Park* television episode,[51] sparks the idea for a musical: *The Book of Mormon*. Produced in 2011 by the *South Park* creators, it parodies the Hill Cumorah pageant. The play is now one of the longest-running comedies on Broadway.

Joseph Smith
(Courtesy:
https://southpark.fandom.com/wiki/Joseph_Smith.

---

[51] Clip of *South Park*, Season 7, Episode #12. See more links to this episode in *Resources* at the end of this book. https://www.youtube.com/watch?v=W4NemVO4JL0.

I hope none will take offense to these revelations. Aside from Spiritualism, of all the cults and movements of the *Burnt-Over District* mentioned above, the LDS church is the only one to prosper to this day. It remains one of the most powerful and affluent religious organizations, with over 16 million members and 30,000-plus congregations worldwide.

☙ ☙ ☙

It's a marvel, isn't it, to think that it had its origins in and around Mendon hamlet? What was the scuttlebutt, I wonder, by those sitting at the bar at the *Cottage Hotel* the day Joseph Smith first stumbled upon and translated those "Golden Plates" . . . ?

Chapter IV

All Aboard!
Tales of Rails & Trails
& the 63-year Run
of the *Black Diamond Express*
"The Handsomest Train in the World"

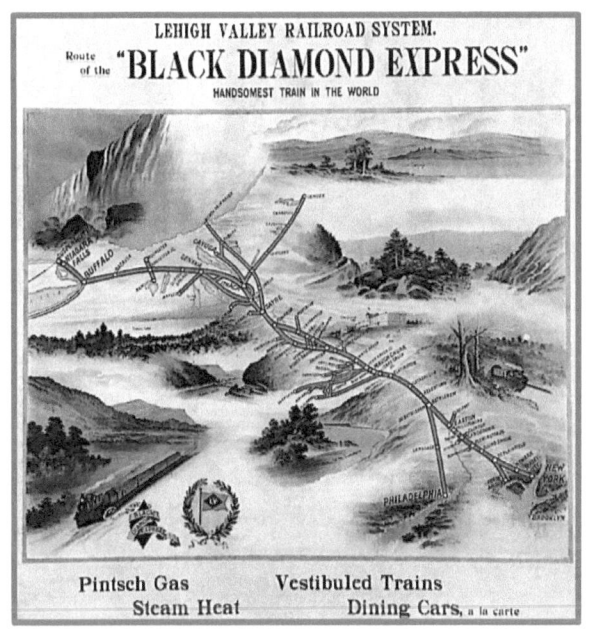

Black Diamond Express **Poster, c. 1900**
(Courtesy: Lehigh Valley Railroad Historical Society.)

All is relatively serene in Mendon hamlet these days, but when the *Lehigh Valley Railroad (LVRR)* establishes a railway depot here in September of 1892, daily life takes a much more dramatic turn.

Suddenly, the dream of traveling to destinations only seen in books or magazines is as simple as packing your bag, buying a ticket from Clive Harmon (Mendon's first station agent) in the depot only a few steps north of the *Cottage Hotel*, stepping onto the platform, and boarding one of the local passenger trains that stops daily in the hamlet. Unlike the "name trains," *locals* stop at every station along its route.

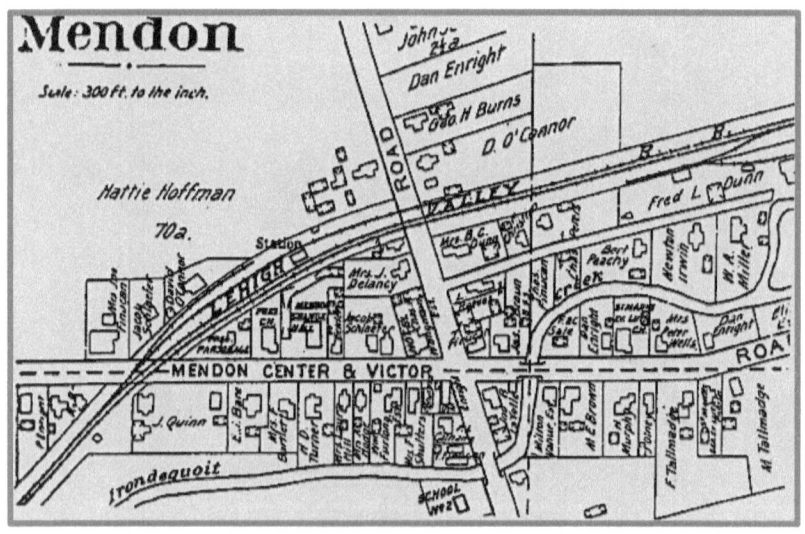

Mendon Plat Map 1924
(Hopkins Company, Philadelphia.)

The *Lehigh* is good for business. Being so close to the depot, both the *Mendon Hotel* and the *Cottage Hotel* (owned by Thomas "Yankee Tom" Finucane), will benefit from incoming travelers, as well as those who make the long, dusty, and sometimes dangerous trip on horseback or by coach.

Perhaps while waiting for the train, people might stop at *The Cottage* for a hot meal, a tankard of ale, or to slake their thirst for some tidbits of gossip. There's no doubt that the *Mendon Hotel* just across the street will attract customers, too — perhaps more well-heeled ones — for the *Cottage Hotel* is more of a humble inn, perhaps first built to accommodate the overflow from its fancier neighbor.

There is a bigger price to pay for all this modern convenience. For the next 80-plus years, the quietude of our previously bucolic countryside is shattered as local trains stop to exchange mail sacks and packages or pick up passengers or freight. Express trains barrel their way through the hamlet at speeds of up to 80 miles per hour. Whistles shriek and warning bells clang as they cross two sets of mainline tracks at the north and west of the hamlet's four corners. Can you imagine?

As author and historian Paul S. Worboys so vividly describes it:

> *Day and night since its arrival in September of 1892, up to a dozen passenger trains and a goodly number of freights rattled the bejeebers out of the little place — Sunday church sermons and the family china were forever at risk. But the compliant populace appreciated a little excitement now and then and soon took to setting up railhead*

businesses, commuting to schools, jobs, and shopping, visiting friends and relatives, not to mention having their best penmanship of the King's English hauled away on the mail car.[52]

To give you an idea of how many trains passed through Mendon (in bold) on a daily basis, here is a schedule from 1894, versus the one next to it, which was the last schedule issued in 1960:

TRAIN ARRIVALS AND DEPARTURES IN A DAY
AT ROCHESTER JUNCTION - FEBRUARY, 1894

A.M.
#	Route		Time
#166	Rochester to Rochester Junction	Ar.	4:10
#3	**New York to Buffalo**	Ar.	4:20
#167	Rochester Junction to Rochester	Dp.	4:23
#168	Rochester to Honeoye Falls	Ar.	8:55*
#5	**New York to Buffalo**	Ar.	9:17
#169	Honeoye Falls to Rochester	Ar.	9:20*
#170	Rochester to Rochester Junction	Ar.	9:45
#146	**Buffalo to Sayre**	Ar.	9:48
#171	Rochester Junction to Rochester	Dp.	9:50
#172	Rochester to Honeoye Falls	Ar.	10:45*
#2	**Buffalo to New York**	Ar.	10:50
#147	**Sayre to Rochester**	Ar.	10:55
#173	Honeoye Falls to Rochester	Ar.	11:40*

P.M.
#	Route		Time
#174	Rochester to Honeoye Falls	Ar.	4:45*
#175	Honeoye Falls to Rochester	Ar.	5:00*
#13	**Sayre to Buffalo**	Ar.	5:06
#148	**Rochester to Sayre**	Ar.	5:25
#176	Rochester to Rochester Junction	Ar.	7:10
#1	**New York to Buffalo**	Ar.	7:15
#177	Rochester Junction to Rochester	Dp.	7:18
#178	Rochester to Rochester Junction	Ar.	7:55
#4	**Buffalo to New York**	Ar.	8:00
#179	Rochester Junction to Rochester	Dp.	8:05
#180	Rochester to Rochester Junction	Ar.	9:05
#6	**Buffalo to New York**	Ar.	9:10
#181	Rochester Junction to Rochester	Dp.	9:15

Before...
The Lehigh Valley Railroad opened through Rochester Junction and to Rochester on September 1, 1892 and to Honeoye Falls on November 20, 1893.

And later...
The Honeoye Falls branch was extended through Lima, Livonia Center to Hemlock and opened for passenger service on August 5, 1895.

The new Rochester Junction station opened January 2, 1896 and the BLACK DIAMOND EXPRESS was inaugurated May 18, 1896.

TRAIN ARRIVALS AND DEPARTURES IN A DAY AT
ROCHESTER JUNCTION - NOVEMBER, 1960

A.M.
#	Route		Time	
#7	New York to Suspension Bridge	Pass	4:50	The Maple Leaf

P.M.
#	Route		Time	
#8	Suspension Bridge to New York	Pass	11:55	The Maple Leaf

And Later...
*Rochester Junction was not acknowledged on the last public timetables in effect from May 25, 1959 on.

The last passenger trains on the Lehigh Valley Railroad (The Maple Leaf) ran on February 3, 1961.

---

[52] Paul S. Worboys, "Haulin' the Mail: A Slice of Nostalgia in Mendon, New York," *Mendon-Honeoye Falls-Lima Sentinel*, August-September 2012, revised August, 2023.
[53] Archives of Paul S. Worboys, *Lehigh Valley Railroad Timetables, 1894 and 1960.*

Those in the hamlet didn't know it at the time, but life was about to get even more exciting.

The *Black Diamond Express*, 1896-1959
(Courtesy: Lehigh Valley Railroad Historical Society.)

On May 18th of 1896, the Lehigh's twin signature passenger trains—#9 westbound from New York to Buffalo, and #10 rolling east out of Buffalo—make their respective maiden runs to standing ovations.[54] Both are named *Black Diamond Express*—so called because the engines burn clean-burning hard "black diamond" anthracite coal. The *Black Diamond Express(s)*[55] soon become favorites of honeymooners bound for the romance of Niagara Falls and beyond. The trains quickly acquire the apt nickname *The Honeymoon Express*.

---

[54] Each train left at noon and arrived at their destinations around 10 p.m.
[55] A short film from 1900 of the *Black Diamond Express* can be viewed at:
https://www.youtube.com/watch?v=jVvabY7Y7fw.

The *Black Diamond Express* is widely advertised and becomes known as *The Handsomest Train in the World*. Since the *Diamond* is an *express*[56], it does not stop in Mendon hamlet or other diminutive burgs. The newly established Rochester Junction (five miles to the west) is the place to go to ride into or out of Rochester[57].

Black Diamond Poster
(Courtesy: Lehigh Valley Railroad Historical Society.)

---

[56] Although the term *'Express'* was dropped in 1915, it still only stopped at primary stations.
[57] For several years, Rochester's LV depot has been the wildly popular *"Dinosaur Bar-B-Que."*

And indeed it is! The sumptuous interiors of the cars, designed with refined Victorian opulence and elegance, provide maximum luxury and comfort for its passengers. As the *Rome Daily Sentinel* reports:

> *The eye is pleased and the brain soothed by the most artistic combinations of colors and mural decorations, hangings, and upholstery. There is not a trace of gaudiness to be seen; everything is rich and quiet, and therefore enduringly effective.*[58]

In its early years, the *Black Diamond Express consists*[59] are composed of four cars: two day coaches, a dining car (with world-class chefs) and one "Pullman Palace" parlor car[60] with an observation end. All are staffed with attendants wearing uniforms with the *Black Diamond* name and signature logo.

Each car is outfitted in polished Mexican mahogany with plate glass viewing windows, and Empire-domed ceilings in white and gold.

---

[58] *Rome Daily Sentinel*, March 24, 1885. Provided by Richard F. Palmer.
[59] With engine and tender, each consist measured 388 feet in length and weighed 492 tons.
[60] The *Pullman Car Company* was the dominant maker of quality railroad passenger cars, be they coaches, sleepers, diners, or parlor cars.

Long-burning *Pintsch*[61] gas and electric lighting illumine cars and vestibules and there is running water in the lavatories. The parlor car features separate changing rooms for ladies with a designated maid, lounges, writing tables, easy chairs, a private lavatory, and a library stocked with current newspapers and magazines. In the summer of 1934 *Black Diamond* cars become air conditioned — quite a luxury in those days.

Dining Car on the *Black Diamond Express*
(Courtesy: Commons.Wikimedia.org.)

---

[61] Pintsch gas, invented in 1851 by Carl Friedrich Julius Pintsch, was compressed fuel gas made of naphtha or petroleum products.

Kitchen on the *Black Diamond Express*
(Courtesy: Commons.Wikimedia.org.)

Viewing the awe-inspiring scenery from New York City to Buffalo from such surroundings must have been thrilling!

Although the cars are comfortably steam heated, travel during the winter months may have been even more exhilarating. As one mechanical engineer tells us:

There are few more impressive spectacles in this world than a powerful locomotive laboring through a heavy snowstorm. To the observer beside the track it looms up through the gloom tremendous and awful. The locomotive seems the embodiment of the death angel, moving swiftly and noiselessly. The snow has muffled the whir of the rolling friction of the wheels on the rails, and the train glides by like the insubstantial pageant of a dream. With its black breath, its snorts of fire, its hoarse voice, it is truly Apollyon, the destroying angel, and the man must be unimpressible indeed who does not feel a thrill at its advent.[62]

Train passing through Mendon in Winter
(From the private collection of Jackson Smith, Toledo, Ohio.)

---

[62] *Rome Daily Sentinel,* March 24, 1885. Provided by Richard F. Palmer.

Mendon Lehigh Valley Depot, circa 1910
*(Courtesy:
Honeoye Falls-Town of Mendon Historical Society.)*

**Eastbound train passing Mendon
showing the trackside mail catching post
slightly visible to the right of the telephone pole**
*(From the private collection
of Jackson Smith, Toledo, Ohio.)*

From the 1830s on, mail delivery becomes an important function of the railroad, with specially outfitted *Railway Post Office (RPO)* cars designated to sort mail *en route*. Delivering the U. S. mail by rail is big business for both railroads and stagecoach lines, with contracts worth hundreds of thousands of dollars a year.

Marguerite Olive Alexander of Mendon hamlet remembers her duties from 1950-1953, transferring mail (and her children) in a little red *Radio Flyer* cart to and from trackside to the post office:

> *My job was to haul a bag of first-class mail from Mendon's post office to hang on a trackside catching post. At 9:00 a.m., a passenger train, with a Railway Mail car behind the locomotive, sped through the hamlet.*
>
> *About noon, a mail clerk on the famed Black Diamond Express threw off a bag of incoming Mendon mail. I watched where it landed in the weeds while also making sure both trains snatched the outgoing mail into the car. If they missed and the bags fell by the wayside, I would collect both bags for delivery to the post office.*[63]

---

[63] See more of her fascinating story in the *Rochester Democrat and Chronicle* article, "My Life, My Words," September 19, 2012. Marguerite will pass away on April 5, 2016, at age 94. She is buried in the Mendon Cemetery.

In 1952, Mendon's depot is torn down, forcing Marguerite to seek shelter during inclement weather in a hexagonal cement railroad kiosk. It is barely the size of a telephone booth but fitted with a tiny potbelly stove for warmth.

Though it might seem like a pedestrian way to earn a living, collecting the mail can be downright dangerous, even deadly. On one occasion in 1938, the hamlet mail clerk's mother, Mary Schlaefer[64], and Robert Slaght, the station agent's 16-month-old boy, who was with her, were both killed by the *Black Diamond*.

Mrs. Schlaefer misread the speed of the oncoming train while crossing the tracks. Although she was able to throw the toddler out of the train's path, sadly, as the train's impact killed Mary, little Robert died of a fractured skull sustained in the tumble.[65]

Following World War I, and especially after World War II, passenger service declines as cars, buses, and plane travel become more popular. Mendon passenger service ends even earlier, in the mid-1930s.

---

[64] Mary Schlaefer and her husband, Jacob Schlaefer, owned and operated the *Mendon Hotel*, along with their daughter Lillian, from 1890 to 1909.

[65] Paul S. Worboys, "Haulin' the Mail: A Slice of Nostalgia in Mendon, New York," *Mendon-Honeoye Falls-Lima Sentinel*, August-September 2012, revised August 2023.

One of Mendon's grade crossings, above,
looking south on Pittsford-Mendon Road

*(Photos from the private collection
of Jackson Smith, Toledo, Ohio.)*

Looking east toward Mendon Depot
and the crossing guard tower (both left of center)

Increased automobile traffic causes controversy in 1939. A proposal is made to split the hamlet's four corners with a bridge and highway overpass over the bumpy grade crossings near the tracks, which causes long waits for drivers. As one hamlet resident, who lived here all his life, recalls, "I remember as a boy having to wait for those darn trains to pass through, sometimes hundreds of cars, just so that I could get to the gas station to buy my candy."

(Rochester Democrat and Chronicle January 29, 1939.)

The plan is ultimately defeated, but not before dividing citizens. Most object to the idea—one that would abolish the *Mendon Hotel*, affect business at the *Cottage Hotel* and other hamlet shops, and create dead-end streets at the intersection of Routes 64 and 251.

And so the familiar rhythm of the trains continues to be part of daily life for those in the hamlet. Russell ("Russ") Mahrt, who was five years old in 1946 when his parents, Frederick and Gertrude Mahrt, and his aunt and uncle Edward and Winifred Butts, bought the *Mendon Hotel* in the hamlet, remembers one of his favorite activities was going out to the tracks north of the hotel to watch the trains go by.

His interest in trains was inspired by his maternal grandfather, Richard Lake (1880-1966), who lived at the hotel for several years, and was a *tower keeper* for the New York Central Railroad — someone who threw the switches that allowed the trains to move from track to track. When he was about 5 or 6, his grandfather allowed young Russell to help throw the switches. "It was a moment I'll aways treasure," he says.

Around age 10, Russ and friends like Dennis "Denny" Dunn, Steve Habecker, Bob Kneale, Jeff and Nick Feldman, Joey Rappel, Jimmy Porter; and older boys like Howie Stanley, Jr., Jabout, Borrman, and Russ's cousins Judy, Jim, and Jackie Butts, would play pickup baseball games in the lot between the barn next to the *Mendon Hotel* and the Lehigh tracks. Kids being kids, they would always pause in the middle of a game and watch with fascination as the trains went by.

Russell ("Russ") Mahrt in 1953, age 10
(Courtesy: Russell Mahrt.)

"We'd make a competitive game out of counting the cars when the freights came by throughout the day, and wave to the engineers, who often waved back," Russ says.

Rosemary (Heckman) Lewis, whose parents owned the *Cottage Hotel* for several decades, remembers that she and her friends would stand by the tracks and wait for the caboose. They'd then yell "Chalk! Chalk!" and the men would throw them three- to four-inch pieces of chalk, which the men probably used to write on the railcars. The girls would use them for drawing.

Rosemary and her best friend, Holly Feldman, would often trek through the fields to where the train trestle crossed Irondequoit Creek.

One time Holly and I were walking along the tracks on the trestle when she fell down and got her foot caught in the ties. We tried and tried but couldn't get it out and, wouldn't you know it, a train was coming! We finally left her shoe there and got off the tracks, just in the nick of time!

Another time at that same bridge, we decided to go down the banks to underneath the trestle. There were snakes there that lived in the fine grey gravel, but we bravely made our way to the big stones below were you could sit comfortably. Big mistake! A train came by and showered us with sharp stones and choking dust. It was scary and stupid. If our mothers only knew!

The last chime whistle of the *Black Diamond Express* is heard echoing through the hamlet, when on May 11, 1959, both east and west runs close a glorious chapter of Mendon history. It is most certainly the end of an era, marked by moments of tragedy as well as splendor. Many an eye will moisten at the loss of the *Black Diamond Express*.

The *Lehigh Valley Railroad* officially ends passenger service in 1961, when the last of its name trains, the New York-Toronto *Maple Leaf*, makes its final run in the middle of the night, without even pausing at Rochester Junction. In 1976, relative tranquility returns to Mendon, when bankruptcy permanently derails the *Lehigh Valley Railroad*. Freight service will continue until March 31st of that year.

The tracks through the hamlet are pulled up in the late 1970s and, in the 1990s, the right-of-way becomes part of the nation's evolving *Rails to Trails* movement. The local *Lehigh Valley Trail* system for hiking, biking and equestrians is established by *The Mendon Foundation*—a nonprofit land trust chartered in 1993.

Mendon Lehigh Valley Trail Map
(Courtesy: The Mendon Foundation.)

Some people find novel uses for the abandoned trails. Back in the mid- to late '80s, a cadre of up to 20 friends, (a core group that included "Cagney," Joe, Yaca, and Dave) rode the old railroad sidings from Henrietta to Mendon hamlet on their three-wheeled all-terrain vehicles (ATVs). Going top speed, it took them about half an hour to get to the *Cottage Hotel*. As Cagney tells us:

> *We'd do this in all kinds of weather. When we got to The Cottage, we'd be covered with dust and dirt and brambles. The bartenders would look us up and down like we were from*

another planet, but thankfully, they'd serve us anyway. We'd slake our dusty throats with a mason jar or two of beer, then be on our way, sometimes stopping at Ye Olde Mendon Tavern before making it home before dark. Those were the days!

Nowadays, the hamlet is the start and finish point for the annual *Black Diamond Express Race the Trail* run, which attracts fans and participants from all over the country. It is supported by local businesses like *The Cottage,* now named *The Cottage Hotel of Mendon.* Proceeds from the event help fund the maintenance of the *Lehigh Valley Trail* and other community properties managed by *The Mendon Foundation.*

಄ ಄ ಄

It's an admirable tribute to that long-gone era, but still seems a far cry from when the adventure of train travel first ignited our small-town imaginations. Nostalgia for those days in the hamlet will have to suffice for now.

(Courtesy: The Mendon Foundation.)

Chapter V

Last Call for Alcohol!
Prohibition Comes to Mendon Hamlet

(From the private collection of Karen Mireau.)

How dry I am, how dry I am
It's plain to see just why I am
Oh, how I call for alcohol
And that is why so dry I am[66]

Are you Wet or are you Dry? That is the question in the spring of 1876, when no new liquor licenses are granted in Mendon hamlet due to concerns "aroused by the evils of intoxication."[67]

---

[66] Irving Berlin, chorus to song "How Dry I Am," from the Broadway show *The Zeigfield Follies of 1919*.
[67] *History of Monroe County, New York 1788-1877* (Everts, Ensign & Everts, New York), 835.

Both public and private drunkenness were already on the minds of many of those in the hamlet. It was not unusual during those times for people to drink alcohol regularly and to excess—and from a very early age.

In his book *From the Stagecoach to the Pulpit*, published in 1847, hamlet resident Elder Hiram K. Stimson documented a childhood spent drinking and carousing. His father, Samuel Stimson, was a tailor and for a time kept a tavern in Lima. Samuel later owned "a small whisky grocery, obtaining his stock from one 'S' who kept a hotel and store in the village of East Mendon."[68] Unfortunately, Hiram's father was a chronic drunkard, and soon acquired a sizable debt to 'S' which he could not pay.

Samuel Stimson expected his son to work off his debt to the hotel. This prompted young Hiram to slip out of town on the first stage and take a job on an Erie Canal boat at 1 1/2 cents a mile with board included. He then worked in 1824 as a stagecoach driver between Albany and Schenectady until age 23, when Hiram became ill and was urged to come back home to Mendon. He tells this tale of Christmas, 1828, which I relate here in its entirety because it so clearly describes the controversy surrounding alcohol and gives us a truly unique

---

[68] The identity of "S" may refer to Ezra Sheldon, Jr., who is listed as owning the *Mendon Hotel* in East Mendon (now known as Mendon hamlet) in 1815.

glimpse of life in the hamlet at that time. Hiram later became a Baptist preacher.

> *Then a friend . . . who was acquainted with me from a child, knowing all my reckless habits, spoke up: "Boys, Hi (Hiram) is right; I have a mind to see how many will join in 'kegging' up for a month? All that will, step this way, and I will take your names; and a month from tonight all meet at my house, to talk over the matter and see how we can stand it."*
>
> *Twelve put their names to a simple pledge not to drink for thirty days, at the end of which time we were to meet at the residence of General Cady, a man of wealth and highly respected, though he had long carried on the distilling business in that town. This was the first temperance effort in East Mendon.*
>
> *At the expiration of the thirty days we met at the General's house. The community had in the meantime become not a little excited on what they called the "cold water question." That unhistorical, but not altogether uninteresting group, is worthy of a moment's scrutiny. There were old men who had "followed strong drink" from childhood — blear-eyed and red-nosed. There was the temperate drinker, expressing his opinion that "a little was for health." There were the*

young men and youth of the place, looking on curiously to see what would be the upshot of the "cold water" movement.

One man said he put his name down on Christmas and had kept his pledge until that last day, but would not suffer again as he had during the month for the best farm in Mendon; and he had stopped on his way there and improved his liberty by taking a drink. He felt better. This man died a drunkard in Mendon.

I was called upon to express my views. I said I had been in a commingled state of mind and feeling during the last thirty days. The first ten days, everything went like dragging a cat by the tail, hard pulling, with much squalling. But for the last twenty days everything was changed for the better. Wife was better; little boy was better; neighbors were all changed for the better; and the world seemed to be made on purpose to make me and everybody else happy. I knew of but one thing as a drawback to keep us from all being happy—the devil in the shape of whisky. Forty more added their names that evening, some for a month, others for a year. Ethan Allen, a young man about my own age, joined for "ninety-nine years." I was not to be outdone by him and put my name down for one hundred. [69]

Strong views about alcohol are not confined to Mendon hamlet. The national debate escalates and soon politically divides the nation. It leads to the passage of the 18th Amendment in 1917[70] and, two years later, to the creation of the *Volstead Act*[71], intended to enforce Prohibition.

As the *Cottage Hotel* had been happily satiating our craving for alcohol for over a hundred years prior to Prohibition, it might have appeared to be a bold 'thumb nose' to continue to do so after the country went officially dry. The hamlet has always been a magnet for renegades, rumrunners, and visionary thinkers.

Thanks to the *Mullan-Gage Act*,[72] further enforcement of Prohibition had already been in effect for a

---

[69] Elder Hiram K. Stimson, *From the Stagecoach to the Pulpit*, (R. A. Campbell Publisher, St. Louis, 1874), 70.
[70] On December 18, 1917, the 18th Amendment, prohibiting the sale or creation of any beverage with alcohol above 0.05%, is passed in both chambers of Congress, and is ratified on January 16th, 1919.
[71] The *National Prohibition Act*, or *Volstead Act*, is passed to enforce legislation of the 18th Amendment on October 28th. The country goes dry one year later, as specified by the 18th Amendment, on January 17, 1920.
[72] On April 5th, 1921, the *Mullan-Gage State Liquor Enforcement Law* goes into effect. It is an attempt of the State of New York to enforce Prohibition, making violations of the

year, but this doesn't deter those in the hamlet. A loophole allows farm districts to preserve their crops over the winter. Hard cider and apple jack, the natural results of fermented apple juice, are not illegal—nor are grapes and grape juice. (It's no wonder grape crops quadruple during this time.) Medicinal and religious uses of alcohol are also given a free pass.

It's beer or "liquid bread" that is at the heart of the problem. After all, wheat, hops, and other grains do not ferment on their own. But even this has a remedy thanks to an even more stringent restriction—the New York State liquor tax law passed in 1896, better known as the *Raines* law.

Thankfully for stagecoach inns, there is still a place to wet your whistle—an explicit loophole in the *Raines* law allows lodging houses with ten rooms or more to provide guests with drink as long as it is served with complimentary meals seven days a week. This leads to abuses in some saloons such as offering a brick between two pieces of bread or sandwiches made of rubber as a "free meal," but we have no evidence to suggest that this was done by hotels in the hamlet.

There are other obstacles to consider.

Volstead Act also violations of state law, requiring state and local state and local police to enforce federal law.

In May of 1897, Edward Strong, then owner of the *Mendon Hotel*, is taken to task for hauling a hen house onto his hotel property and turning it into a quasi-dwelling — all this *coop-la-la* in order to keep his liquor tax certificate. His intent was to circumvent the *Raines* law requirement that two-thirds of homeowners within 200 feet of an establishment give their written consent. For some, this is considered a stroke of absolute genius. (Predictably, the chickens acquiesce and scratch out their approval.)

Strong's efforts fail to hold muster, however, especially after it is learned that nine members of his family, plus one boarder, occupy all but one of the rooms in the hotel, — yet another violation of the *Raines* law. It also doesn't help his cause that four years earlier, Strong had been convicted of selling liquor without a license.

Books & posters of the times
(Courtesy: Library of Congress.)

Earlier, in March of 1897, the election of town officers in Mendon and the subject of the excise tax brings out voters in record numbers, the largest poll ever other than presidential elections. The two hotels in East Mendon (our hamlet) "came out of the battle with colors flying" to the detriment of three saloons in other parts of the Village of Mendon. To the dismay of many in Honeoye Falls the majority voted to remain "dry."

There's no doubt that there is big money in black market booze. Moonshiners, wildcat breweries, and bootleggers abound, including at least one admitted rumrunner in Mendon hamlet.[73] With violations of the *Volstead Act* becoming more commonplace, Congress adopts what becomes known as the *Jones Law* (or *Five-and-Ten law*) in 1929, increasing penalties for first offenses to five years in prison, a $10,000 fine, or both. This ups the ante for violators, for this law also makes it a felony not to report suspected offenders.

Throughout Prohibition, regular raids in Rochester are reported, and at least one along Fairport's main street, but there is little to suggest that Mendon hamlet is subject to much harassment.

---

[73] He may have been telling me an embellished tale, but hamlet native Frederick Martin ("Fred") Garling (1903-1991) once confided to me (with a mischievous smile) that during Prohibition he had been a *rumrunner*, as he called it.

On one occasion, though, in 1931, "dry agents" visit the hamlet and seize two half-barrels of beer from owner Ernest Ehrenberg at the *Mendon Hotel*. What they actually did with the beer is anyone's guess, but the *Cottage Hotel* is spared such a humiliation. On May 6, 1932, padlock orders are issued against the *Mendon Hotel* and seven other downtown Rochester establishments for dry law violations.

Dry Agents Visit Mendon, City Places

Two Rochester drinkeries and one at Mendon fell before the onslaught of a group of Rochester prohibition agents yesterday. Agents reported the places were:

Mendon Hotel, Ernst Ehrenberg, proprietor; two half barrels of beer.

Saloon, 685 Maple Street, Norman J. Ritzenthaler, proprietor; two half barrels of beer.

Saloon, 258 Spencer Street, John Rendsland, proprietor; two half-barrels of beer.

Agents early yesterday morning raided Louie's Chop House, 240 Verona Street, and said they seized 14 pints of whisky, two quarts of gin, and three half-barrels of beer. Joseph Manger was arrested as proprietor.

Padlock Orders Issued Against 8 More Places

Eight more restraining orders against places in which prohibition agents charged the dry law had been violated yesterday brought the total of temporary padlock orders filed in United States Marshal Joseph Fritsch Jr.'s office to 15 for the week in Monroe County.

Among the orders was one for the Mendon Hotel at Mendon. The others, all in Rochester, included: 510 Portland Avenue, George and Charles Reinhardt; 1065 Hudson Avenue, Joseph Koszlowski, Stanley Zodzniski and Elizabeth Chlebowski; 263 Portland Avenue, Marion Lambert, Alex Lambert, Don Fass and Della Appleton; 784-786 Maple Street, Ernest Hetzfield, Henry and Fred Kodisch, Daniel Sloan and John A. Coak; 2122 Main Street East, Charles Burley and Rocco Rinando; 10 Owen Street, Thomas Dean, William Carroll and James Vonglis; 455 Lewiston Avenue, Edward Hollenbeck, Dudley Harmon and Alvah E. Belcher.

It's not reported how long these establishments stayed closed, but a little over six months later,

---

[74] Rochester *Democrat and Chronicle*, December 31, 1933.
[75] Rochester *Democrat and Chronicle,* May 6, 1932.

jubilant celebrations are held by taverns and cocktail lovers all across the country when on December 5, 1933, Prohibition is officially repealed by the passage of the 21st Amendment.

Thus ended a difficult chapter in American history and removed at least one worry from those owners operating taverns in the hamlet of Mendon. As evidence, a few days later, on December 15th, owner Ernest Ehrenberg is promptly issued a new liquor license for the *Mendon Hotel*.

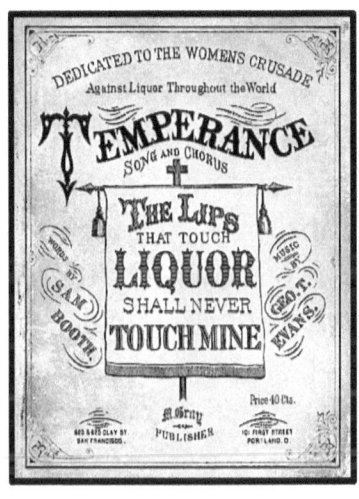

(Courtesy: Library of Congress.)

The full history of the Temperance movement is far too complex to outline here—and there are others who do this much more precisely. But there is a thread in this story that is easy to forget—that is, of the women of all races who stepped into positions of leadership on both sides of the question and for the first time helped forge national policy.

It's no coincidence that women's right to vote is ratified the same year as Prohibition, or that Prohibition, Abolition, and Suffrage are intricately linked. Although there were many disagreements, each movement served to help strengthen the other, using similar arguments to foster peace and social justice.

In the end, *The Noble Experiment* or *The Great American Experiment* as it was called, was destined to fail. Not all women or men believed in or tolerated legislating personal habits or morality.

Fortunately for us, we've never had to sing, "How Dry I Am" in the hamlet, and since *The Cottage Hotel of Mendon* (a business now again officially owned by a woman), continues to indulge our inclination to knock back a few now and then . . . life, as they say, is pretty damn good.

(Courtesy: Library of Congress.)

Chapter VI

Yo Ocarinas!
The Lost Factory of Mendon Hamlet

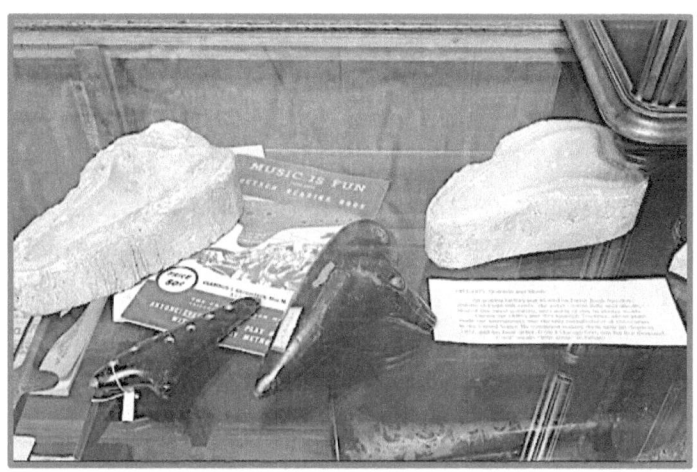

**Rudolph Teschner ocarina display
at the Honeoye Falls-Town of Mendon
Historical Society Museum**
*(Courtesy: Honeoye Falls-Town of Mendon
Historical Society Museum.)*

Who of us at the *Cottage Hotel* would ever guess that in 1878 an immigrant from Germany would build and operate the first ocarina factory in the United States—right here on a farm in Mendon?[76]

And what the heck *is* an ocarina, anyway?

---

[76] What follows is a consolidation of a college paper written in 1980 and a four-part guest column for P. J. Erbley's *News & Notes from Hither and Yon* that appeared in the *Mendon-Honeoye Falls-Lima Sentinel* in 2023.

I certainly had no clue until one wintry February morning in 1978 when Mr. Fred Garling[77], a Mendon farmer then in his late '70s, walked in and sat down near the *Bevador* at the end of the *Cottage Hotel* bar.

It was Fred's habit after working in his fields to refresh himself at *The Cottage*. It was here, with a glass of his favorite rosé, that he would begin ruminating about his childhood in the hamlet. On this occasion, he remembered paying pennies for an *ocarina*, or *carnival whistle* as he called it made of fired clay. Wistfully, he smiled and said, "I will never, ever forget its lonesome, bird-like sound."

Ocarinas, I soon learned, were among the most ancient of musical instruments — existing in Central America from pre-Columbian times. Shaped like a sweet potato, they came to be called by that name after being introduced in Europe where its Italian derivation from *oca*, 'a goose,' and perhaps the Latin *avis*, 'a bird,' attests to both its shape and bird-like tone.[78]

There are many such businesses in small-town America that flourish and die without a trace, but

---

[77] Frederick Martin ("Fred") Garling (1903-1991) was well known in Mendon hamlet for his disarming smile, his kindly wit, his gentle humor, and his generosity.
[78] A Peruvian word, *occa*, 'the same,' also signifies an edible root.

this particular enterprise completely captured my imagination. How could one earn a living in the industrious days of the late 1800s manufacturing clay flutes?

It would be two years before I could unravel the mystery of the actual site of the factory and the kiln where the ocarinas were fired, but this was an enigma worth searching out.

☙ ☙ ☙

In 1877, Rudolph Teschner traveled to Europe where he saw an ocarina in a Vienna museum. Found in the ruins of Pompeii, it was a crude instrument made of clay with a mouthpiece and four finger holes for playing a variety of notes.[79]

Returning to his family home in Rochester, Teschner made his own version, an instrument with eight holes, but was very disappointed that his prototype did not play. One night, the idea to change the ocarina to ten holes—an octave and a third—came to him.

Was the answer revealed in an insightful dream? No matter, it worked! In 1878, after successful

---

[79] Modern *carnival whistles* were made by Guiseppe Donati of Budrio, Italy, beginning in 1860, in sizes ranging from soprano to bass, 17 years before Mr. Teschner discovered the instrument in Vienna.

testing, Teschner made 200 instruments and set about introducing them to the world. Traveling mostly by train, he visited wholesale houses from New York City to California. He made a triumphal Mendon return through Mexico and the American southland, his efforts having been quite successful.

In 1885, Rudolph Teschner and his wife, Frederica, bought thirty-two acres from the estate of Orpha Lloyd[80] at 267 Parrish Road. The private property is now occupied by a charming white frame house and several well-preserved barns.

Ocarina molds
(Courtesy: Honeoye Falls-Mendon Historical Society Museum.)

Rudolph Teschner was a lucky man. The indispensable element for durable ocarina production was a ready source practically over the

---

[80] In 1941, Florence T. Keenan, Teschner's daughter, sold the property to Thomas O'Brien and his wife. Successive owners were Albert ("Alby") Thomas and his wife, and Fred and Dorothy Ray. It is now owned by David Friedlander.

hill from his home. The majority of the putty-like clay used in making his ocarinas was obtained from *Factory Hollow*, a milling complex (mostly powered by Honeoye Creek waters) near West Bloomfield. We can only guess, but this ready source of clay may have originally led him to purchase the farm on Parrish Road.

Once there, Teschner called upon Frank Forsyth, an East Bloomfield carpenter, to build his shop. Forsyth reports that, "It had two stories. The clay grinding rig and machines were downstairs and the upper floor was for storing. It was a good substantial building."[81] It must have been well crafted as the structure was later moved to an adjoining building lot and remodeled into a home.

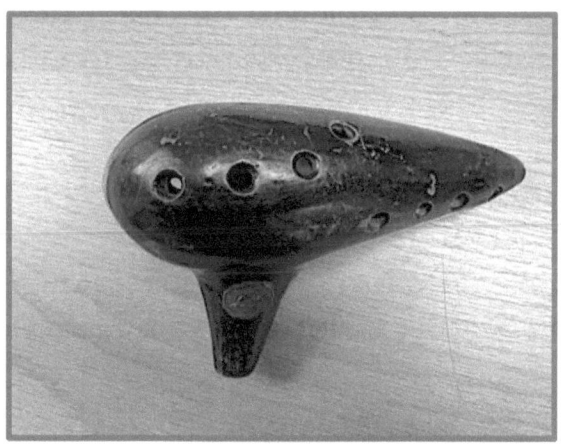

A typical Rudolph Teschner ocarina
(Courtesy: Honeoye Falls-Town of Mendon Historical Society Museum.)

---

[81] Bill Beeney, "All Around the Town," column in the Rochester *Democrat and Chronicle*, October 4, 1951.

Former location of Rudolph Teschner's ocarina kiln at 267 Parrish Road in Mendon
(Courtesy: David Friedlander.)

Rudolph's ocarina factory used six to eight tons of clay each year, from which nearly 20,000 instruments were fashioned.[82] Almost poetically, in May 1920, he completed his last order—5,000 ocarinas for a Chicago firm—three months before his death.

Thanks to Fred Garling's original clue, and to David Friedlander,[83] the current owner who acquired the farm in 1997, we now know precisely where the ocarina factory was situated. As David reports:

---

[82] Teschner's first instruments were painted yellow, but later he painted them black, and made them in 32 sizes, running from high C to low C, or four octaves.

[83] David Friedlander is Deputy Chief of the all-volunteer Mendon Fire Department, better known nowadays as *Mendon Fire.*

I'd been told there had been some kind of factory on the farm when we bought it. I didn't give it too much thought then, although I used to wonder when I would find bricks while mowing on the highest point of the property. I now know that these bricks were most likely left over from Rudolph Teschner's kiln. The whole hill is sand, and there are two rectangles, about a foot deep and 15-20' x 25-30' still visible at the edge of the woods where clay was dug.

Ocarina clay pits
filled with water in winter
(Courtesy: David Friedlander.)

After Rudolph's death, the factory was abandoned. Sadly, since no family members or property owners took an interest in restoring the kiln it deteriorated over time and almost became lost to local memory. Fortunately there were those (aside from Fred

Garling) who still had first-hand knowledge of the factory. J. Sheldon Fisher, founder and curator of Valentown Museum of nearby Fishers, New York,[84] recalled the Teschner house auction on Parrish Road where he observed "a five to six-foot pile of ocarinas and plaster of paris molds" that remained after Teschner's death. Mr. Fisher salvaged several ocarinas at that time, too.

Ward Parrish (1899-1989) and his sister, Rena Parrish (1890-1982), both of Ionia, also knew the Teschner family since their grandfather and uncle had a farm across from the factory. Mr. Parrish not only helped the Teschners build the addition to their home, but he also moved the factory to the east of the barns. Miss Parrish was a good friend of Florence, the Teschner's only child, remembering that Rudolph and his daughter shared an interest in the violin.

Rena Parrish agreed that the manufacture of ocarinas, in "a great many shapes and sizes," was indeed a curious occupation. But the Teschners (who apparently hired help to work their farm) made a good living at it, having "very large orders from all over the country." She said that Rudolph

---

[84] J. Sheldon Fisher (1907-2002) was a friendly, vigorous seventy-two when we met, and a legendary regional historian. He became famed for rooting out Western New York artifacts (and was made an honorary Seneca Indian for his efforts to preserve their culture).

"... never liked to play for people and I never heard him play. But I did hear him test them for sound." She added that the Parrish siblings possessed at least one example.

(Courtesy: Honeoye Falls-Town of Mendon Historical Society Museum.)

Strangely, most contemporary histories of the ocarina fail to mention Rudolph Teschner at all.

Here's what we do know:

In 1911, Teschner is listed in the International Directory of Music Industries[85] as a manufacturer and distributor of "occarinos."

The ocarina, being easy to play, soon becomes popular, and business is good. Good enough for Teschner to petition the United States Congress for a return to higher tariffs on imported musical instruments.[86]

1918 Wurlitzer Catalog #110
(Courtesy: Illustration collection of P. J. Erbley.)

---

[85] Frank D. Abbott and Charles A. Daniell, (Presto Publishing Company, 1911).
[86] Rudolph appealed to a return to the *McKinley Tariff Act of 1890*. His objection was to the *Wilson-Gorman Tariff Act of 1894* which lowered tariffs from fifty to twenty-five percent for importers of musical instruments.

Whether or not Rudolph's appeal has any direct effect, his wish is granted a year later by the passage of the *Dingley Act* of 1897, which brings back new duties on imports.

The lower tariffs may have almost put Rudolph out of business, although his only competitor in America at the time is Heinrich Fiehn, a German manufacturer who markets his now highly collectible ocarinas through the catalogues of *Sears, Roebuck & Co.*, and *Montgomery Ward & Co.*

With the coming of *Rural Free Delivery*, catalogues from the major mercantile companies were essential in the houses (and "outhouses") of rural America
(Courtesy: Illustration collection of P. J. Erbley.)[87]

---

[87] With many thanks to Paul S. Worboys for his editorial assistance and generosity in providing images from his private archives.

Teschner distributes his own ocarinas through John Howard Foote, a musical instrument dealer with shops in Chicago and New York City, as well as through the Rudolph Wurlitzer Company.

When Rudolph dies on September 1, 1920, obituaries appear from coast to coast—from the Rochester *Democrat and Chronicle* to the *Santa Maria Times* in California.

After his death, the popularity of ocarinas continues to soar. Ocarina-only concerts become the rage in the 1930s, with Wilson Junior High School hosting one here in the Rochester area. In 1988, Soviet musicians tour the U.S., featuring the ocarina as one of their traditional instruments. A stop in Corning makes sure that ocarina enthusiasts will have a chance to hear their local sweet potato played with an international flair.

Feature films such as "*The Good, the Bad, and the Ugly*" and "*The Road to Singapore*" (with Bob Hope, Bing Crosby, and Dorothy Lamour) highlight ocarina songs and players. Even the scarecrow in "*The Wizard of Oz*" gets into the act, with ocarinas accompanying his song, *If I Only Had a Brain*.

Many years will pass until attention returns to Rudolph's ocarinas. Bill Lane,[88] and the late

---

[88] William ("Bill") Lane has been involved with the *Honeoye Falls-Town of Mendon Historical Society* for over 28 years. In

writer/historian John G. Sheret, share a pivotal moment in the late 1990s when they happen upon a cardboard box of ocarina molds that John knew had been stored in the upstairs portion of the *Honeoye Falls-Town of Mendon Historical Society Museum*.

This marks a turning point in the preservation of Mendon's fascinating ocarina history . . . though not exactly right away.

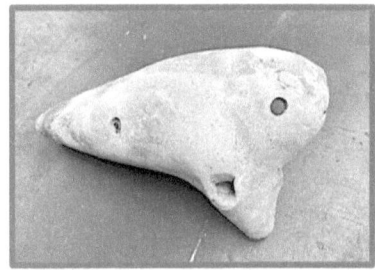 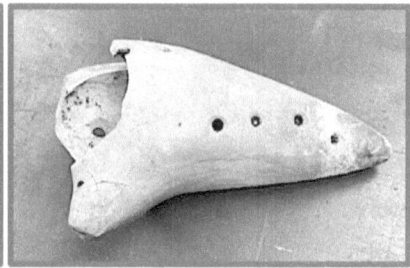

Examples of Unfired Ocarinas
(Courtesy:
Honeoye Falls-Town of Mendon Historical Society Museum.)

As Bill Lane recalls, it is not until 2007 that they will acquire museum-specific software and begin cataloguing the objects in the museum's collection.

In the meantime, the 1990s are particularly good years for the ocarina. In the world of classical music, György Legeti's *Violin Concerto* features four soprano ocarinas, an avant-garde novelty at the

---

addition to being interim Museum Curator, he is currently chair of the society's board of trustees.

time. And who could ever anticipate that ocarinas would become an obsession for video game players?

Nintendo 64 aficionados recall with great zeal *The Legend of Zelda: Ocarina of Time*, the best-selling action-adventure game of 1998, where the hero has to learn thirteen ocarina melodies in order to progress in the game. Interest in ocarinas spikes and, since that time, the game continues to inspire sales. Hail ocarinas!

A decade later, ocarina fans are again rewarded when Apple releases *Smule Ocarina*[89], making it possible to play the ocarina on your iPhone and share your music with others around the world. It is now one of Apple's all-time favorite music apps.

There is no doubt that Rudolph Teschner was an inventive, enterprising man—rather like an

---

[89] https://apps.apple.com/us/app/ocarina/id293053479.

American "Rumpelstiltskin," although instead of spinning straw into gold, Teschner made his fortune fashioning and firing up our humble native clay into beautiful, soulful, musical instruments.

Our story now comes full circle back to Mendon and the *Cottage Hotel* where, almost a century after Rudolph Teschner began his enterprise and Fred Garling first told us his tale. To see one of Rudolph's ocarinas up close, visit the *Honeoye Falls-Town of Mendon Historical Society Museum*. There, you can view ocarinas and molds, as well as miscellaneous printed items, such as ocarina-related instruction and music booklets.

ଔ ଔ ଔ

Rudolph Teschner, wherever you may be, hopefully you will be comforted to know that your creativity and entrepreneurship will not be forgotten here in the hamlet. May you rest in peace and inspire others to create something marvelous from Mendon's humble and magical ground.

Chapter VII

Let's Go Honkey Tonkin':
Our Local Watering Hole Finds its Mojo

"Hey Ma? Can You Come and Get Me?"
Cottage Hotel Telephone[90]
October, 2022
(Photo: Karen Mireau.)

July 7th is "National Dive Bar Day."

Some people might be inclined to call our venerable *Cottage Hotel* a "dive," or if they're in a more generous frame of mind, a "hole in the wall." Those

---

[90] The perfectly preserved original dial telephone (remember those?) is still on the wall near the entrance to *The Cottage Hotel of Mendon*.

who are especially polite will probably describe it as a plain ol' "townie pub."

There's no doubt that *The Cottage* qualifies as a classic country joint, an old-time neighborhood-style saloon where local folk can relax, toss back a few (okay, on occasion maybe more than a few) and be themselves.

But anyone who has an inkling of what the *Cottage Hotel* really is would never call it a "dive" and intend it as a slur. It would be used only in the most loving, respectful definition of that word.

Fact is, *The Cottage* was once officially given an even more preposterous nickname by a lady that drove up in a limousine and demanded that her driver go in and check it out. He exited and dubbed it *The Five Star Dump*. Local people found this more than hysterical. T-shirts were made and are rumored to be worn to this day by people like Tommy Dunn.

You may have noticed recently that dive bars have become very trendy and chic. There are a lot of imitators out there, but as we all know, the *Cottage Hotel* is the real deal.

The term "dive," you might recall, originated in Prohibition, when thirsty customers seeking a drink or two had to duck into speakeasies hidden below street level. Of course, it also came to have references to other illicit pleasures, though it's not for us to go down that road here. (You'll have to use your own imagination.)

Some say that because some consider it a dive, that there is an element of danger at *The Cottage* that makes it even more appealing. Admittedly, it has a slight whiff of intrigue, where no bunkum or bullshit is tolerated. There's certainly been times at *The Cottage* when it wasn't unreasonable to worry about getting stabbed by an jealous motorcycle mama or to have to suddenly run for cover as bar stools flew like bats-out-of-hell across the room in the middle of a fist fight.

Okay. These things *may* have happened, but they were momentary blips in the continuum—far and few between.

Musician Paul Strowe, who has played regularly at *The Cottage* for over 50 years, can vouch for this. "In all that time, I've never witnessed anything but a minor skirmish here and there," he says. "For the most part, the atmosphere at *The Cottage* has always been one of peaceful coexistence and of just being with good friends and having a great time."

And after all, it's places like *The Cottage* that host the local *Little League* teams, the softball and bowling leagues, the fish frys, the spaghetti suppers, the quilting bees. They're the ones that put on weddings and funerals for their regulars and celebrate everything in between.

If that's *dive*, then I say, "Dive On!"

In its best sense, a dive is a place where there is no pretext of class—where everyone is on equal footing no matter what their station in life. It's a place where even outsiders can belly up to the bar, be warmly welcomed, and made to feel like they've come home to roost.

**Yup. It's electronic,
but there's still a dartboard!**

That's our proud 200-year-old tradition—and one of the *Cottage Hotel's* many true claims to fame. Since 1822, it has been almost exactly what it is today: a comfortable, unpretentious place where people from all walks of life can rub elbows and tie one on if they choose—without being shamed or blamed the next morning.

**Decals on the *Cottage Hotel*
Ladies' Room Wall**

Whatever you might call it, you and I both know that *The Cottage* has what most wanna-be bars, dive or otherwise, lack — and that is . . . character. And as you also know, character is something you simply cannot buy or manufacture. It just plain *is*.

It may not be glamorous and it may not have changed much over the years — but thank heaven for that and all the things that make up *The Cottage's* sometimes shabby but homespun heart and soul. We've got good cheap drinks, friendly bartenders, and a jukebox chock full of country songs (as well as contemporary tunes) just to name a few.

All in all, it's the kind of down-home energy embedded in every square inch of the place that keeps us coming back for more.

It's deep within the still slightly smoke-scented walls; in the comforting sound of the tap swooshing open to fill your mason jar with draft beer; in the patina of the old, slanted pine plank floors; in the mismatched no-frills wooden bar stools; in the deer mounts, license plates, album covers and stickers plastering the ceilings and walls.

Yet another extraordinary thing about *The Cottage* — one that has probably kept it from going completely downhill from time to time — is that for the most part it has been run by women. They might not have always been on the masthead or in the ads in the local paper; but trust me, either behind the scenes, tending the bar, or working the door, it's been feminine power that has kept *The Cottage* on its path as a comfortable place to sidle up to even in the middle of the day to nurse your beloved *Cream Ale*.

Front Door Vignette

Jacky (Muzdakis) Fisher, then only 24 years old, was an anomaly when she first took on the daunting task of owning *The Cottage* as a young woman, the only *single* woman to ever do so. Downright brave and amazing if you ask me! After Jacky married Baird Fisher, another steadfast hamlet regular, they happily managed *The Cottage* together for another 15 years.

Owning a bar is not an easy business. If you look at the history of the owners of *The Cottage* in Appendix I at the back of this book, you'll see that the majority of them have been married or long-term couples. More than a few male owners have publicly recognized their wives or female business partners as the force behind their success.

Working with a partner takes drive, loyalty, persistence, and I daresay, a whole lot of patience but according to those who have frequented *The Cottage* through the years, couples like the Fishers, the Heckmans, the DiNardo-Marinellis, and the Stotts, did and do so now in grand style.

At this point, a woman is at the helm of *The Cottage*. Along with her husband, David, Hilary Stott has held *The Cottage* together through a rollercoaster of thick and thin. They have brought it to a place of near perfection by preserving the best of its historical aspects while improving things to keep *The Cottage* contemporary.

People come from miles around, as they always have, to eat home-style comfort food like the *Cottage Burger*, soak up the atmosphere, and hear local bands. Those who have had the good fortune to stumble upon the hamlet and *The Cottage* on their own are often tempted henceforth to make it their "best kept secret" even though Mendon hamlet has always been considered as being, (please excuse my belated mother's French), "way out in East Bumfuck."

And the joke on all the scoffers, disparagers, and people who've looked down their noses at *The Cottage* over the years as a country dive, is that Mendon hamlet is now considered the most affluent suburb of Rochester.[91]

To its credit, Mendon has a long tradition of resisting total gentrification. The horse farms and hiking trails and all-out phenomenal natural beauty of the landscape, formed eons ago by the glaciers that many in the hamlet have fought so hard to preserve and protect, is what makes it so special and rare. Once gone, these old stagecoach hotels and the beautiful, idyllic fields cannot be replaced—and those who have fought to preserve and protect them truly deserve our respect and gratitude.

---

[91] Suburb? Most of us would laugh at that definition. After all is said and done, we know at heart that we're still *country*.

But call it a dive? Sorry. We still have to take exception to that one!

As a 200-year-old stagecoach inn and tavern that has been treasured by thousands of people through time, I think I can speak for anyone who has ever stepped foot in the *Cottage Hotel* and fallen under its special spell—that we simply wouldn't trade its history and hospitality for any fancy, hi-falutin' joint in the world!

Chapter VIII

The Big Chill:
The Cottage's Beloved *Bevador*
Gets a Facelift

(Courtesy: Thermo Scientific.)

Nothing reminds those who return to *The Cottage* of the good old days more than our iconic *Bevador* beer cooler. Tucked into the right-hand corner behind the bar, there it stands—a steady beacon always ready to welcome you like an old friend when you walk in the door.

The *Bevador*, as you might expect, has its own illustrious history.

From the early 1900s, the Jewett Company manufactured refrigerators in their Buffalo, New York plant. By the '30s, they were a well-known household brand. The *Bevador*, with its unique cylindrical shape (as well as its larger twin brother, the *Beerador*), quickly became a national American icon for beverage storage.

(Courtesy: Thermo Scientific.)

Resembling a bottle of beer, the original *Bevador*, including its distinctive cap, stood 7 feet 6 inches tall by 4 feet in circumference. Both the *Bevador* and *Beerador* featured hammered steel finishes, glass doors, neon lighting, and four to seven adjustable rotating shelves. From the beginning, it was billed as a "merry-go-round" for beer. All that was missing was the carousel music! (Well, that and maybe a few horses.)

Both models proved to be true workhorses, though, when it came to beverages — the *Bevador* holding 11 cases of beer, and the *Beerador* twice that amount. As early newspaper advertisements touted, ". . . its Forced Draft cooling unit assures quiet, dependable operation and uniform cooling of every bottle," keeping things appropriately chilled with their "self-contained general electric twin cylinder compressors."

What could be better? In 1939, you could have your very own *Beerador* for $595, with half down and two years to pay to boot. The *Bevador* was only $455. Such a deal! Today, fully restored, a *Bevador* will run you ten grand (or maybe more) for one in original working condition.

In 1959, the *Beerador* was to find another, perhaps more medicinal, use when the Greek government bought 43 slightly modified versions and rebranded them as "Blood Bank Refrigerators." With all the beer that has coursed through *Cottage Hotel* patrons' veins through the years, we might have predicted and patented that novel idea.

 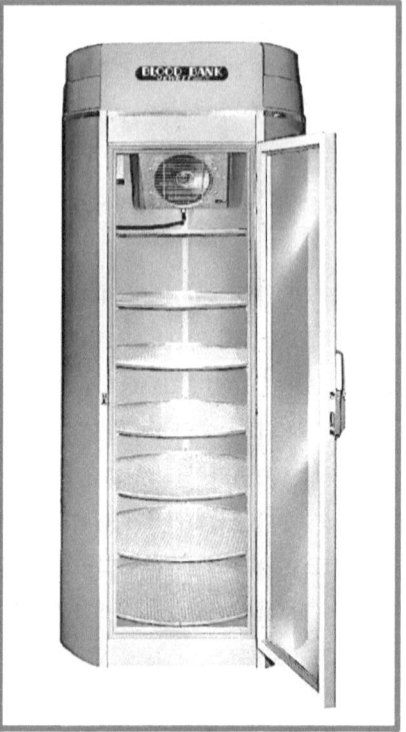

(Courtesy: Thermo Scientific.)

Although it's not certain when the *Bevador* first made its debut in the hamlet, it was already there in 1950 when *The Cottage* was purchased by Albert "Al" and Mary Elizabeth Heckman.

In this rare photo from that time period on the next page, you can see the *Bevador* all dressed up as a bottle of Genesee lager. The guy (in what we *hope* is a Halloween mask) looks like he may be full of a few too many "Gennys" too.

The *Bevador* remained that way until sometime around, or maybe just after, the Heckmans sold *The*

Cottage to Robert F. "Bob" Clifford in 1972, at which point it was painted brown to resemble a short-neck *Labatt Blue* label.

Lucky for us, our *Bevador* passed muster when in 1972 Paul S. Gordon ("Buzzy") Bronson took over management and restoration of *The Cottage* and decided to keep the *Bevador* in place. Buzzy says there might have been a critical moment when the *Bevador's* fate was on the line, but thankfully reason prevailed. "It's still the best beer cooler on the planet," he admits.

The *Bevador* in the 1950s
(Courtesy: Mendon Historian Diane Ham.)

The *Bevador*'s life as a Labatt bottle continued under John Urquhart ("Burdock") Ross's ownership of *The Cottage*. Musician Walt Atkison remembers Burdock taking extra special care of the *Bevador*:

> *Burdock was always tinkering and fidgeting with the Bevador. He'd cobble it together when it went on the fritz so it wouldn't go completely downhill and he was always worried it might need extensive repair.*

In 2005 Hilary and David Stott purchased *The Cottage*, and at that point they freshened up the *Bevador* with a nice dark green Heineken logo.

Cottage Hotel of Mendon **owner Hilary Stott in 2005 with the** *Bevador* **painted as a Heineken bottle**
(Courtesy: Hilary Stott.)

Caged Alpha Monkey Label
(Courtesy: CB Brewers.)

Says Hilary:

> *That lasted until Mike Alcorn from CB Craft Brewers[92] turned the Bevador into a monkey cage with the Caged Alpha Monkey bursting out! This was his staple product and The Cottage was known to sell more kegs than any other bar, ever. That was his thank you to us!*

In 2016, after many years of diligent and uninterrupted service at The Cottage, it appeared that the Bevador was on its last legs. Hilary was given the tragic news by repairman Don Mutch that it simply wasn't worth restoring.

---

[92] *CB Brewers*, formerly *Custom Brewcrafters*, was the second oldest craft brewery in Western New York. It closed its doors in 2019.

She immediately objected. "It's just not right," she argued. "The *Bevador* is not mine! It belongs to everyone at *The Cottage*. People come here and they want to see things that remind them of the good old days, and our *Bevador* is one of them."

And that, as they say, was that!

Somehow they managed to lift the 1050-pound *Bevador* over the bar using steel poles (even when empty, it's a lot heavier than it looks) and transport it to *Mantique and Oddities Etc.* down the road in Bloomfield, where Pat Falin patched it up and made it as good, if not better, than new. The *Bevador* was then given a new coat of chalkboard paint in a dignified steel grey color, much like the original models.

The *Bevador* poses with then *Cottage Hotel* Manager Michelle Harrington, October, 2022

According to David Stott, the cost to restore the *Bevador* was . . . (are you holding onto your barstool?) . . . a whopping $6,000 . . . but more than well worth it, according to the Stotts, just to have the *Bevador* back on track!

Our *Bevador*
2022

Almost everyone who has ever been to *The Cottage* has fond memories of the *Bevador*. Patty Gotham, who often came to *The Cottage* as a teenager back in the '60s and '70s, and still stops at *The Cottage* on her way home from time to time, says, "I was fascinated by it. It was such an unusual thing because most coolers were ones you had to bend down into to get a beer. This caught your attention from the get-go."

Cottage fan Tom Midney notes that the *Bevador* is one of the first things he associates with *The Cottage*. "It's iconic. To me it's a symbol of the great times we've all had at *The Cottage*."

And so, our cherished *Bevador* chugs on, keeping our favorite beers icy cold, and our special *Cottage* memories warm. Hopefully future generations will continue to be inspired by its undeniable charm.

Chapter IX

Fearless Leaders:
Owners, Managers, & Lessees
Through the Years

The Cottage Hotel, circa 1954
"The Friendly Inn" by Martin de Wolfe
(Painting from the archive of Rosemary (Heckman) Lewis.)

A local watering hole, no matter how large or how small, how fancy or how ordinary, is a sacred space.

It's where we come to unburden ourselves of the drudgery of our daily lives, to catch up on local gossip, to ponder the state of the universe. If it's a good local bar, a true neighborhood bar, it's somewhere you can connect with others, let loose, and be yourself without judgment.

The *Cottage Hotel* has always been such a refuge, in great measure because of the owners and the managers who oversee those in the kitchen and behind the bar. It's they who create an atmosphere of trust and comfort that gives them license to tend to our world-weary souls.

A complete timeline of owners of the *Cottage Hotel* dating to 1822 can be viewed in Appendix I at the back of this book. What follows are recollections and first-hand accounts of owners of *The Cottage* for the past 70+ years. Many were legendary characters in their time — and for various reasons.

---

[93] From: *Sesquicentennial Souvenir Program and History, 150th Anniversary Celebration,* (Town of Mendon, August 14th-18th, 1963), 52.

Albert Thomas ("Al") Heckman & Mary Elizabeth Heckman

Mary & Al Heckman
(Courtesy: Personal collection of Rosemary (Heckman) Lewis.)

Al & Mary Heckman
(Courtesy: Mendon Historian Diane Ham.)

When Albert Thomas ("Al") Heckman sold the Rochester bakery he'd inherited, he and his wife Mary Elizabeth Heckman, wanted a quieter, safer place to raise their two children, Tommy and Rosemary. And so, on June 29, 1950, they purchased the *Cottage Hotel* from August Van Castiles and Martha Van Castiles.

The family, along with friends, Dell and Earl Woodard, moved to Mendon hamlet and for many years they all lived together on the top floor of *The Cottage*.

Photos show that they had a very comfortable apartment with a fireplace in the living room and pretty curtains at the windows. You can see swatches of the charming hand-painted retro wallpaper from the 1930s, when the Van Castiles and their six children lived there.

"The wallpaper was in what served as the liquor closet when I lived there," Rosemary Heckman remembers. "It was a place my mother always kept padlocked 'to keep the employees honest' she said."

The Heckmans were well known for their love of family and their compassion for others. Later on, after their friends the Woodards had left, they sometimes rented out a room to local people who were down on their luck and needed a place to live.

Al and Mary were universally admired in the hamlet as genuinely nice people; even though according to some, Al may have imbibed a tad too much from time to time, and it was Mary who ran the show.

As Rosemary (Heckman) Lewis recalls:

> *My mother was definitely in charge. She was good at delegating. She did all the hiring and firing and did the accounts. She was the primary bartender at night, too. Her nickname was, "The Queen." She was a force of nature!"*
>
> *She was quite a beauty with natural dark red hair and very blue eyes. She was the "Lilac Queen" one year in Rochester and "Miss General Motors" where she had worked for a while. She was very smart. She had wanted to be a nurse, but never graduated from high school due to having typhoid fever.*

Rosemary's memories of her father are equally vivid.

> *My dad was handsome and quite a character, too. He had a great voice, as did my mom. He loved to sing songs like "My Wild Irish Rose" and "Shine on Harvest Moon." He was an alcoholic who almost died of bleeding ulcers, but he quit drinking and smoking at age 50, and lived in good health until age 89.*
>
> *My parents always looked out for other people. When people were in trouble or needed money, my dad would give them something easy to do and then make them feel like they had done him a huge favor. He allowed people to keep their dignity, and*

never needed recognition. I loved that about him and I learned a lot from him.

Longtime hamlet resident Dick Joint grew up with Rosemary. They went to 1st grade together in the one-room schoolhouse at The Mendon Academy until Mendon schools were centralized — then they would ride the #2 bus to Honeoye Falls. He remembers the family well.

I can picture them right now. Al was tall and slender. With her bright blue eyes and red hair, Mary was a very attractive older woman — she appeared that way to me even at age eighteen. They were very sociable people. I think Mary was the only bartender they had in the evening. After a few, Al would get to singing like an opera singer, while Mary would play the jukebox and dance with all the old guys.

Al and Mary owned *The Cottage* for 22 years, still the record for all *Cottage* owners in recent history. It was undoubtedly a tough business, but they stuck with it and made it a success, all the while raising a family — and for that we must give them a huge round of applause!

Robert F. ("Bob") Clifford

**Robert B. Clifford, Robert F. ("Bob") Clifford, Tom Clifford, Gerry Clifford
1955**
(Courtesy: Fred Seager.)

Robert F. ("Bob") Clifford[94] owned many well-known restaurants in the Rochester area, including the famous *Maplewood Inn* in Pittsford.

Although it was primarily a neighborhood tavern, somehow *The Cottage* caught Bob's interest. In 1972, after his retirement, he purchased the *Cottage Hotel* from Al and Mary Heckman for $75,000.

---

[94] Robert F. ("Bob") Clifford (1909-1991) owned 11 restaurants in the Rochester area, including the *Cottage Hotel*. He died on January 4, 1991, at age 82.

But it was never about the money. The final business statements from the Heckmans show that they had never earned more than $57,000 a year from *The Cottage*. Now that he was retired, Bob saw *The Cottage* mostly as a place he could go and meet people and shoot the breeze.

Bob was well known to be a shrewd businessman. When he bought *The Cottage*, he began charging only a nickel for a draft beer. Although he wasn't making much, he didn't care—it was a tactic that had successfully won the steady loyalty of customers at the *Maplewood Inn*, and it worked equally well, if not better, in Mendon hamlet.

As John Bronson, a former bartender at *The Cottage*, as well as a friend of the Clifford family, tells us:

> *Bob was a clever, soft-spoken, understated guy who was an astute judge of character. He had a good read of people. No matter what kind of restaurant he owned, he figured out what his constituency wanted and then gave it to them.*

Fred Seager, who ate dinner with the family almost every Friday night, describes Bob as a someone who always had to have something to do.

> *He loved to drive fast cars—he preferred Chrysler 300s—and he definitely knew how to run a business. He had a generous nature,*

> too. When cigarettes in his machines went from 26 to 30 cents a pack, Bob would tape pennies to the packages so that his customers wouldn't have to pay the difference. He also had a sentimental side, unusual for men of that era. When my father was dying, he was at my side with me, crying tears of grief.

There was a slight *kerfluffle* when Bob bought *The Cottage* from the Heckmans. *The Cottage* at that time had a water problem. It had two cisterns in the basement and a well, but because the gas station next door had a leak, they couldn't drink the well water. The Habeckers next door complained that the tainted water was draining into the creek. To keep the peace, the Heckmans put in a sewage treatment system that cost them close to $1,000, quite a bit of money at the time. It required the periodic adding of chemicals and constant checking to keep it running properly.

When Al Heckman sold *The Cottage*, he did so impulsively. Mary Heckman was not happy with the deal and her relationship with Bob Clifford soon soured. Bob, in an angry state, locked the whole place up, including the storeroom where the water treatment controls were housed. Mary Heckman failed to inform him that without the chemicals *The Cottage* would soon begin to stink — but she knew it wouldn't take long before Bob figured that out.

As mentioned, Bob's signature restaurant had been the *Maplewood Inn*, which served a $2.99 strip steak, a $3.99 filet, and reportedly had only one cash register. It had been a smash hit in Rochester for many years. When he sold the restaurant in 1968, he signed a non-compete clause with the new owners, Gordon Haggett, his wife, and Haggett's brother Pat J. Mammano—an agreement that would quickly cause trouble.

The deal was that Clifford wouldn't operate a restaurant within 50 miles of the *Maplewood Inn*. *The Cottage*, of course, was only eight miles away as the crow flies. Even though he assured the new owners that it was just a tavern and that he wouldn't be serving food, the new owners of the *Maplewood Inn* threatened to bring suit.

"Hah!" Clifford quipped at the time, "Should they prevail, I'll take a vacation. I could use some rest anyway."

Unconvinced and undeterred, the new owners persisted and secured an injunction granted on May 26, 1972. Suddenly, Bob was in a position where he was forced to either sell *The Cottage* or lease the business to someone else.

And there, just upstairs at the *Cottage Hotel*, sat Buzzy Bronson.

Paul S. Gordon ("Buzzy") Bronson

Paul S. Gordon ("Buzzy") Bronson
(Courtesy: Paul Bronson.)

Talk about being in the right place at the right time.

That year, local real estate developer, Paul S. Gordon ("Buzzy") Bronson, who built and orchestrated upscale housing subdivisions in the Mendon area such as *Fox Hollow, Langpap, Partridge Hill, Thornbush,* and *Architecture 83,* was running his construction business from rooms above the *Cottage Hotel*—space that he was renting for $100 a month.

Buzzy was more than lucky. Bob Clifford happened to be his best friend, Gerry's, father. "Bob was a true mentor to me," Buzzy acknowledges. "He pretty much taught me everything I know about doing business, and the bar business in particular. And like Bob, I saw potential in *The Cottage*."

They made a handshake deal—Bob kept the building and Buzzy took over the business at *The Cottage* for $467 a month on a triple net lease, one where Buzzy paid for the interest, taxes, utilities, and any upgrades. "Bob told me, 'You'll make that much from the pinball machine.' It was a steal of a deal. Heck, I would have paid that much for the office space."

Buzzy immediately started making changes to the interior of *The Cottage*, although he was careful to retain and subtly improve the original "saloon" feel of the circa 1822 building. Years earlier he had remodeled *Thirsty's* bar in Pittsford, using heavy barn wood on the walls so that you couldn't put a fist through them. (This might tell you something about what occasionally went on there with some of the clientele.)

Luckily, *The Cottage* walls were made of sturdier stuff. He crafted and laminated the cherrywood bar top and later put in booths where a 12-foot long shuffle bowling arcade game once took up valuable seating space. Thankfully, he kept the *Bevador*. "It would have been a crime to get rid of it," he says.

He also built the 8' x 10' raised platform at the back of the bar that became the music stage, with ample room for a four- to six-piece band.

Buzzy took Clifford's ongoing business advice to heart. He replicated his mentor's brilliant strategy of charging only 5 cents for a draft beer (one that usually cost a quarter) as a way of building a base of loyal customers. This worked well although soon enough Buzzy raised the price to 10 cents, which actually brought in a little revenue. In the first year, Buzzy tripled the income made by the previous owners. Both Bob and Buzzy were astonished. "We were going through 20 kegs a week!"

Buzzy hired Louis, a German cook who made homemade soups and old country favorites like sauerkraut and bratwurst, and began serving Zweigle's Hots, as well as steak sandwiches and what is now renowned as the *Cottage Burger* (with French fries, of course) to satisfy the ever-growing lunch crowds.

The classic *Cottage Burger* that originated with Buzzy was made with a 1/3 pound mixture of Jacobson's ground sirloin and ground chuck (similar to fine Angus), cooked medium rare, and served on a DiBella's brioche-style bun. The buns were buttered and grilled on the flat top, something Buzzy claims made all the difference.

> *We served ketchup, mustard, relish, and Bermuda onions with the burgers, of course. I didn't have a "special sauce" per se, but I did make my own Greek-style hot sauce that was a knock-off of the kind used at Nick*

Tahou's, using ground beef, Tabasco, red chili sauce and my secret ingredient — cinnamon. This was ladled on top of the burgers if people wanted it.

Buzzy also continued the traditions of weekend fish frys (using flounder instead of haddock), and spaghetti suppers — all of which endeared him to hamlet residents. For one summer, he put a charcoal burner outside the building. Hamburgers and hots were passed to customers through the front window on Pittsford-Mendon Road.

Buzzy is rightly credited with building the music scene in Mendon hamlet. He brought in down-home bands like the *Swamp Root String Band*, consisting of "some RIT guys and a female fiddler who played bluegrass-style music" and who enticed families (with their kids and babies) to *The Cottage* on Friday nights for a dollar-a-pop cover charge. *John Mooney* who, thanks to Buzzy, got his start at *The Cottage*, became a regular performer, as did Jeff Williams and the *Earl Weems Revue*.

The music lineup started drawing people from Rochester, Pittsford, Victor, Canandaigua, Naples, and even further out in the Finger lakes. Every night, Buzzy's best friend, Gerry Clifford, who'd owned *Thirsty's* in Pittsford since 1968, had to pass by *The Cottage* on his way to his home in Mendon. He'd see that *The Cottage* was always packed and correctly surmised that Buzzy was doing three times the business that he was in Pittsford, a much more affluent town closer to Rochester.

"Sometimes Gerry would close *Thirsty's* early and come hang out at *The Cottage*," he says. "I had great managers, too," Buzzy remembers, "and Gerry kept stealing them for his own place."

As Buzzy is known to quip, "Where the ducks go, the hunters follow." He also continued the tradition of "Ladies Nights" at *The Cottage*. Nickel beers and discounted cocktails for the young women meant big business, because after a certain hour the price would go up. "By then the guys would be let in and they would buy their girls their drinks at full price. It was a win-win for everyone."

Another strategy he initiated was to occasionally give away free shots of peppermint schnapps[95], especially on *Euchre Card Nights*. "Now," says Buzzy, "nobody can drink just *one* shot of schnapps. After the free one, people will naturally buy shots for each other — at $1 a pop. I think a 32-ounce bottle of schnapps cost us $2, so you do the math."

> *Food was another loss leader. We pretty much sold our food at cost, which is what Bob*

---

[95] That tradition would be carried on by future owner, John Urquhart ("Burdock") Ross, who also would bring a bottle of schnapps up on stage and pour musicians shots between music sets. This *Cottage Hotel* (and the *Mason Jar*) ritual began with the band *Slipton Fell*.

Clifford had taught me, but it was great because it brought people in the door even during the day, especially when local construction workers were rained out.

On the weekends, there were lines of people out the door and it was pretty certain that our capacity was way beyond what the Fire Marshall would allow. But it was all great fun! Our only real problem was parking. People who lived nearby were getting upset that people would park just anywhere and throw trash around and the Town of Mendon complained.

It was Gerry Clifford who said to me, 'How can you have a parking problem? You have no parking!' He was right, we didn't. It was the town's problem. All the local businesses were grappling with it. Somehow we worked it out by making a deal in which the streets outside The Cottage were cleaned up on a regular basis. In reality, having that much business was a problem you wanted to have.

In 1975, Buzzy bought the historic *East Bloomfield Inn*, another historic stagecoach inn not far from *The Cottage*. Suddenly, he thought about selling. "Between my contracting business and new ventures, *The Cottage* was now a distraction," Buzzy says. "It was time for a change."

John Urquhart ("Burdock") Ross

John Urquhart ("Burdock") Ross
(Courtesy: Steve Anderson.)

John Urquhart ("Burdock") Ross[96], once an executive at Dun & Bradstreet, lived in the hamlet across the street from *The Cottage* and had been a regular for many years. He thought it was "a hell of a business." Every year he would plead with Buzzy Bronson to sell him *The Cottage*, and every time Buzzy promised he'd give him first crack at it when he was ready.

---

[96] A book-length tribute to Burdock can be found in the poetry collection, *Tell Me Again | That the Dead | Do Dream* from Azalea Art Press at www.Lulu.com.

In 1975, he and Burdock, along with their mutual attorney, John Redmond, came to an agreement. For $20,000 (as reimbursement to Buzzy for physical improvements), and a triple net lease of $2,177.50, Burdock became the sub-lease owner.

To his credit, Burdock, like Buzzy before him, was not a fan of disco music which was popular then, and he encouraged many young up-and-coming rock, bluegrass, and acoustic musicians to make their debut at *The Cottage*. There was usually a show every weekend night, but musicians would often come and spontaneously "jam" during the week as well. There were also Tuesday *Mug Club* nights, which featured musicians such as Paul Strowe.

Burdock and John Redmond would subsequently team up to run another music club, the *Mason Jar* in Henrietta, a venue that was also a hub for great music, but quickly gained a reputation as a magnet for drug users and dealers. John Redmond was known to boast that he had access to the best cocaine in town, "even better than the local judges," and that he rewarded high revenue achieving bartenders with ample supplies of coke.

This seems a somewhat shocking admission now, but in the 1980s it was a sign of the times, and to be a supplier of this popular party drug was, to some, a badge of distinction. As many were to discover, the addictive nature of cocaine, and especially crack cocaine, could become much more than a momentary pleasure—it could become an uncontrollable and sometimes deadly choice.

Burdock managed both the *Mason Jar* and *The Cottage* from 1975 until his own tragic and untimely death in 1981. Without Burdock's energy, the *Mason Jar* quickly went downhill and eventually out of business.

"He really had a passion for *The Cottage*," Buzzy Bronson recalls. "But he was also a guy who liked to party. I asked him before he bought it whether he really wanted to be in the bar business. It's tough. You have to be careful. It pretty much takes over your life."

Buzzy saw Burdock as a very sincere person, "completely down to earth, but a square peg in a round hole," Buzzy observed then. "He was friendly, and everyone, I mean *everyone*, liked him. It was really sad for all of us when we learned that he was gone."

Many people in the community mourned, and still mourn, the loss of Burdock, whose happy-go-lucky enthusiasm for life was contagious. He is remembered as a very kind and generous person, a fatherly figure who often helped young people, even strangers, cope with their troubles, or give them a chance to try out their artistic talents.

Musicians, especially, benefitted from his willingness to let others take center stage.

Dick Joint, a hamlet resident who has been with the Mendon Fire Department for almost 60 years, recalls:

> *Burdock was a really good guy, a smart person who was good with figures. He was very well-respected here in Mendon. He was also a little on the eccentric side. People said that he kept a goat in his kitchen, although I never actually saw it. One time, though, I remember watching him work on the roof of his house. It just over the bridge, a few doors down from the Cottage on the opposite side of the street. He had tied himself to a rope that went over the roof and then was hooked to a car on the other side just in case he slipped off. That was something to see!*

Keith Baker, of *Paulsen, Baker and Garvey*, a popular band that often played at *The Cottage*, saw Burdock clearly as someone "who created something he'd dreamed of . . . and who was able to live his dream."

Like many of us, Keith never suspected what was to come. When Burdock took his own life on October 19th of 1981, it shocked and shook those who knew him to their core. That great grief was one that brought many of us together at the time and continues to inspire us to be grateful for the good things in our lives.

After Burdock's death, despite ups and downs, *The Cottage's* basic character as a *Cheers*-type gathering place continued on through the years. Even so, to this day, the spirit of *The Cottage* is still suffused with the aura of that devastating tragedy. "He lived like a rock star, he died like a rock star, because he *was* a rock star," avows his good friend and house mate, Hendo.

As musician Steve Anderson, guitarist, and songwriter for *Slipton Fell*, so poignantly reminds us in the song by the same name: *(You'll Never Feel Alone) at the Cottage Hotel*,[97] the memory of Burdock will never be forgotten.

(Courtesy: Steve Anderson.)

---

[97] To learn about original songs written about the *Cottage Hotel* by Steve Anderson, Keith Baker, Johnny Bauer, and Jeff Williams, see Chapter XIII and *The Cottage Hotel Songbook,* Azalea Art Press, 2023, at www.Lulu.com.

Ann (Ross) Chaintreuil & Renier Chaintreuil

**Renier Chaintreuil,
L-R - John Chaintreuil, Ann (Ross) Chaintreuil
& Alexander John Chaintreuil, 1980.**
(Courtesy: Ann & Renier Chaintreuil.)

After Burdock's death, the lease to the *Cottage Hotel* passed directly to his estate.[98] As the estate administrator for her brother, Ann (Ross)

---

[98] Ann Chaintreuil, a partner in *Macon, Chaintreuil & Associates*, and later the architectural firm, *Chaintreuil Jensen Stark*, designed the stage shell for The Eastman Theatre, the year-round *Dancing Wings Butterfly Garden* at the Strong Museum of Play, and one of the eight *Architecture 83* homes at Partridge Hill in Mendon—as well as many other significant structures throughout the U.S.

Chaintreuil's name was never on the lease itself. Due to legal reasons, Ann and her husband decided not to assume ownership of the business. They continued the terms of the lease that existed between Bob Clifford and Buzzy Bronson under the auspices of Burdock's estate.

This later proved to be a sound choice when at one time they were sued due to a traffic incident involving someone who had left the bar under the influence. "We were able to defend our position by having no interest in the bar business," Ann says.

For a number of years after Burdock's death, *The Cottage* had some rocky moments. An unfortunate series of temporary managers/owners allowed the physical site of *The Cottage* to deteriorate, and according to some, the drugs and partying were out of control. Ann, who then was juggling family obligations and a partnership in an award-winning architectural firm, didn't have time to be involved in its day-to-day operation.

As Ann remembers it:

> *My husband and I had three little kids, careers, and family stuff happening, and this lease situation became a constant liability for us with lack of payment on either side of the sub-leases. Bob Clifford soon discovered that we were the most reliable people in this lineup of interested persons and four years later*

when the Bronson lease expired, he offered to sell us the property. We purchased it in both our names (Ann and Renier Chaintreuil) in 1984 for $90,000 and Bob Clifford took back a mortgage. The purchase enabled us to select a tenant or lessee we felt comfortable with to operate a bar/food business. Aside from obvious monthly rent payments, it was stipulated in the lease that the tenant maintain the property, obtain appropriate insurance coverage, etc.

After the Clifford mortgage was paid off, we sold the business in April of 2005 to Hilary and David Stott for $230,000 and took back a $135,000 mortgage for 15 years. The profit on that sale and the mortgage interest received went towards our three children's college educations.

In summary, my overall feeling was one of great relief to be out of this situation. Often the lease would go unpaid. Sometimes the lessees would not get the required insurance stipulated in the lease and, out of an abundance of caution, we would be forced to make the payments ourselves.

John's untimely death, combined with not knowing what I was getting into, caused enormous monthly stress. Once The Cottage was sold, that went away.

Even so, in some ways it was difficult for Ann to let go of *The Cottage* because of its connection to her brother.

> *I did, and still do have, an emotional pull to The Cottage because of John. I loved my brother, but unfortunately I was not really integrated into that part of his life . . . it was fun to see all the action when he invited me to visit The Cottage, but it was not in my comfort zone. I really didn't understand where my brother was during this phase of his life, but I do know one thing for certain — John loved that bar, and he loved the people and the kids that hung out there.*

Until the business and property were sold to Hilary and David Stott in 2005, the sub-lease of *The Cottage* remained in Burdock's name. It then continued to pass from owner to owner.

Jacqueline ("Jacky") Muzdakis Fisher & Baird Fisher

Laid-back landmark Jacky Fisher, owner of the Cottage Hotel, is on a first name basis with most of her customers and tries to keep the rustic flavor alive.

Jacky (Muzdakis) Fisher
(Democrat and Chronicle, November 7, 1994.)

In 1982, Jacky Muzdakis and her partner Baird Fisher were regulars at *The Cottage*. Neither were particularly happy with the way things at their local watering hole were headed.

Jacky, who was tending bar on *Mug Club* nights at the time, decided she'd like to take a shot at being an owner.

Ann Chaintreuil got personally involved:

I remember a wild trip to New York City with the very young Jacky. The liquor license had been removed from the Cottage Hotel for some infractions . . . I cannot remember if it was someone serving a minor or cleanliness or health issues. But whoever was managing The Cottage Hotel after John's death had caused the license to be rescinded. In that time period I did not know who to trust. But I took a chance on Jacky.

Jacky wanted to become the new owner of the business, but we could not clear the license. So we went down to New York for a presentation to the governing authority. As two young and very professional women, we convinced the liquor board to give us a chance. I had no idea she was the youngest person to ever hold a license. But if my memory serves me well, I knew we had hit a home run with this interview, and we celebrated a bit before coming back to Rochester.

I felt very empowered by the experience. After everything I had been through with my brother's death, being in the middle of this lease, the mismanagement of the business after John's death, being responsible for a sub-lease on a property that was failing, and trying to run my own architectural practice, I felt I had finally found a young responsible

145

woman who wanted to start her own business and run The Cottage Hotel. And after this trip, I felt she would be successful.

And so, in 1982, at age 24, Jacky Muzdakis became the youngest person in New York state to receive a liquor license. She acquired a lease from Ann Chaintreuil, as administrator of her brother John Ross's estate, for $2,177.50 a month, and managed *The Cottage* with her sweetheart, Baird Fisher, whom she married in 1985.[99]

Jacky and Baird added more music to *Fisher's Cottage Hotel* menu on weekends. There were no "Ladies Nights" but they continued the tradition of the Tuesday night *Mug Club* that Burdock had initiated.

A bartender who worked for Jacky and Baird then remembers that people would come in at 7:00 p.m. with $5, chug down that much beer at a nickel a mug, and then leave at 8:00 p.m. when the price per mug rose to two bucks.

Jacky was on a first-name basis with her customers and she became so friendly with them that she

---

[99] Jacky and Baird married in 1985 and Baird's children, Jeremy Fisher and Megan Fisher, came into the household. Jacky and Baird then had a daughter, Lindsey Fisher, in 1986. The family lived together just a few doors down from *The Cottage* on Pittsford-Mendon Road.

could sometimes predict what they would order. She filed to rename the business *Fisher's Cottage Hotel* in February of 1992, and that remained the official name of *The Cottage* until the triple net lease was sold to Louis C. ("Lou") DiNardo for $30,000 in 1998. It then became *Lou's Cottage Hotel*.

> *We ran the business with our friends and family for 16 years. It was an amazing time. Our customers and patrons were the absolute best ever and our employees were top notch. We've kept these friends for over 40 years. That's it . . . that is our legacy!*

Louis C. ("Lou") DiNardo & Nancy Marinelli

Lou's reign is often remembered as being one wild party. One bartender, who worked for Lou at *Lou's Cottage Hotel* from 1990-2000, tells us this:

> *We always had a good time, but Lou was a rough and abrasive character. I couldn't tell you the words that would come out of his mouth. His famous quote when he'd serve up the chicken wings was 'One f-ing order of wings. And one f-ing napkin.' This always got a laugh, because of course you can't eat wings with just one napkin!*

---

[100] Photo courtesy of Deb and Tim Smith. The original sign was given to Hilary Stott.

Working for Lou and his partner, Nancy Marinelli, could sometimes be stressful. "The two of them were like oil and water," he says. "They had terrible, tumultuous fights and would scream and yell at each other. I often had to tell them to 'take that stuff outside' so that the customers wouldn't hear them."

Yet another (anonymous) witness to Lou's style tells us:

> *He wasn't the most pleasant person to deal with. He was a patron of The Cottage long before he owned it. When he did, he treated it more like his own living room. His rules were law and it was his way or the highway!*

"Lou's days definitely had a lot more testosterone," Chris Carosa, publisher of the *Mendon-Honeoye Falls-Lima Sentinel*, admits.

> *The Cottage had an undercurrent of danger back then. I was in my twenties, and that atmosphere appealed to the demographic of my college friends, who had all lived together in a dorm at Yale (coincidentally called 'The Cottage').*
>
> *Back then, playing pool at The Cottage was our priority. We'd come in the back door and put our quarter on the edge of the pool table if it was crowded, then grab our beers in*

> mason jars, and play until we lost, which wasn't often. We weren't pool sharks, we just loved to play.
>
> Later, when I got married in the hamlet, naturally we all went to The Cottage to celebrate. It felt like karma. From then on anyone coming to visit would always stop there. It was the kind of place you always felt welcome, even if you were from out of town.

Fish frys and spaghetti supper nights continued to cater to the local crowd, and the specialty, the *Cottage Burger*, (a tradition that started with Buzzy Bronson) was one that they made sure stayed front and center. Nancy Marinelli, Lou's partner and co-manager, described the oval-shaped burger as "a cheeseburger with lettuce, tomato, mayo, a secret sauce, hot sauce, and horseradish."[101] It sold back then for $4.75 on a hard roll.

Chris, who is the self-described "world's premier hamburger historian"[102] confirms that it was and still is the best burger he's ever tasted. "With all the fixings, at a 1/2 pound and more, it's almost too big

---

[101] Quote from Nancy Marinelli, *Rochester Democrat and Chronicle* article: *Escape Route* by staff writer Bennett J. Loudon, June 4, 2004.

[102] See Chris Carosa's award-winning book, *Hamburger Dreams: How Classic Crime Solving Techniques Helped Crack the Case of America's Greatest Culinary Mystery*, Pandamensional Solutions, Inc., 2018.

to eat!" He theorizes that it is the grill itself that imparts a subtle flavor to the meat. "Fortunately for us, the new owners have kept this tradition, and added even more comfort food to the menu."

Lou and Nancy, like many *Cottage Hotel* managers before and after them, were a power duo . . . and they ran *Lou's Cottage Hotel* together until Lou's death from cancer in 2004. Nancy would continue to run the business until it was sold in 2005 to Hilary and David Stott. Sadly, Nancy would pass away just a few years later, in 2009.

Hilary Stott
& David Stott

David & Hilary Stott
(Courtesy: Hilary & David Stott.)

As people soon discover, all things in Mendon hamlet are connected.

David Stott's family was in the video game business and *The Cottage* was one of his accounts. For over 20 years, until selling the business in 2012, he learned the bar business via his vending services. He learned what people did right — and also what they did wrong.

Hilary and David met at *Thirsty's*. They married in 2002 and soon began raising a family in Mendon.

They had always been fans of *The Cottage* and had high hopes of buying the business from Ann Chaintreuil but weren't having any success.

In 2004, they again tried to convince Ann to sell *The Cottage* to them, but she wasn't quite ready. As David recalls: "I called two weeks later and just happened to bring my daughter, Amanda (who was 1 1/2 years old at the time), along with me. Ann immediately fell in love with Amanda and I believe that because she could see our pure intent and energy as a family, she finally agreed to sell."

Before the paperwork was signed, it was rumored that someone had offered Ann $50,000 more. "We only found this out from Ann's husband after the papers were signed," David says. "Ann never mentioned it. She has the kind of integrity that she honored our verbal commitment." In April of 2005, Hilary and David Stott officially became shared owners of the legendary *Cottage Hotel*, with Hilary owning the business on a $1,200/month triple net lease, and David owning the property.

And it was definitely time for a major transition.

According to many, after Lou DiNardo died, *The Cottage* had quickly gone downhill. The era of casual drinking was gone and drug users had taken over. Hilary knew how tough addiction could be — she had wrestled early on with her struggles with alcohol. "Owning a bar definitely accelerated things," she says. "I came out of it after a year and a half, but I hit bottom hard and fast."[103] This served to intensify her strong vision for The Cottage.

> *We wanted it to be more of a family place. It was David's brilliant idea to put a Sno-Cone machine in the bar area. Every time a child came in, they would get a free Sno-Cone, and the sound of all these kids laughing and screaming in delight definitely changed the atmosphere for the better.*

Like owners before them, they faced a multitude of day-to-day challenges. First, the Stotts had to wrestle with ongoing water and sewage issues.

> *We dealt with extreme water treatment problems for years after taking over The Cottage as it continued to be piecemealed through the different ownerships. It made sense because no one wanted to invest the money if they didn't own the property. This situation resulted in a DEC-approved water treatment system costing $120,000, that also requires maintenance four times a year at over $3,000 per visit.*

---

[103] Hilary Stott continues to follow her path to recovery and to share her strength, experience, and hope with others who still struggle.

Hilary and David are committed to maintaining as much of the history of *The Cottage* as they can. In 2016, they repaired the iconic 1940s *Bevador* beer cooler that had been in the bar for as long as anyone could remember. (It set them back a cool six G's.)

Then, in 2020, they renovated the barn next to *The Cottage*, originally built in 1896. "We were able to save four of the horse stalls," says David, "but by that point everything else had deteriorated."

Every holiday, Hilary, David, and their family and friends decorate *The Cottage* to the hilt.

> *It's one of the creative things we like to do to make it fun for everyone. Family parties, reunions, anniversaries, graduations, birthdays – all are things we like to celebrate.*
>
> *One of the best things are the 'Cottage Babies' we've seen come in from the time they were infants and watch grow up. Bringing all these families together and making them feel welcome is what makes it all worthwhile.*

The Stotts have also instituted ongoing family-oriented events like *Trivia Night*. Every Tuesday, their good friend Steve Miller challenges the hamlet to test their powers of memory. Says Steve, "It accidentally became one of the most successful nights at *The Cottage*, and all because Hilary and

David were willing to take a chance and do something inventive.

In retrospect, it was fortunate that they bought *The Cottage* when they did instead of leasing it. With David as the property owner and as Hilary's landlord, that flexibility allowed them to stay open during any downturns and through the worst of the Covid pandemic. "We wouldn't be in business otherwise," Hilary says.

Hilary and David have now owned and managed *The Cottage* for 18 years. Hilary is also a partner in the *Penfield Pourhouse* and in the upscale restaurant *Mendon 64*, just north of *The Cottage* on Route 64. Mendon 64 was the site for several years for the *Mendon Music Festival*, which honored our local musicians.

Recently, the Stotts have also bought, rebuilt, and opened *Bumpa's* (the name the grandkids call David), a pizzeria next door to *The Cottage* where they hope to add a connecting patio to make it a more expansive outdoor dining space for everyone.

Over the years, there have been offers from others to buy *The Cottage* but whenever Hilary contemplates selling, it gives her pause.

> *My wish is that the next owners, whoever they might be, will support the history of this special place. It has been a labor of love for us,*

and I hope the same will be true for those in the future.

The Cottage has been in continuous operation now for over 200 years. We can't help but raise a glass to that, to all the owners through the years, and to the Stotts, who have preserved the original soul and spirit of the *Cottage Hotel* as a place for all of us to come together.

Chapter X

Behind the Bar: The Other Side of the Story

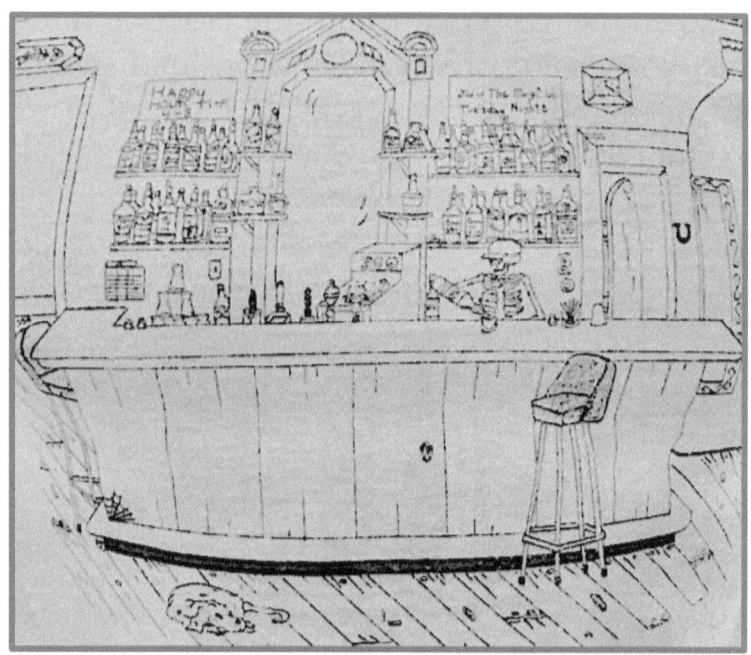

(Drawing courtesy of Kimberly ("Kim") Ormiston.)

When a person walks into the *Cottage Hotel*, what do they see?

They see the bar, some barstools, the line of beer taps, the liquor arranged neatly on the shelves, the antique mirror behind the cash register.[104] They might see the jukebox out of the corner of their eye,

---

[104] The antique *Cottage* cash register was given to a dealer when the Stott's purchased *The Cottage* in 2005.

note the location of where the bowling game once was, and (back in the day until 2010) the cigarette vending machine — also the pool table if that's their interest, and perhaps they may even notice the side door where the regulars come in.

One thing sure to get their attention right away is the bartender — for it is he (or she) that will soon be taking their drink order or making change for their "cigs" or a game of pool.

Bartending *looks* easy enough, but as anyone who has worked in the restaurant trade can tell you, it definitely takes a bit of skill. Books can tell you how to mix a drink, but there's an art to tending bar properly that can only be learned by jumping in feet first and taking control of that space — and usually, by proxy, that of the entire bar.

A piece of the original cherrywood bar on display at *The Cottage Hotel of Mendon* with an embedded dime[105]

---

[105] The original bar top was renovated by Paul S. Gordon ("Buzzy") Bronson in 1972, then replaced by Hilary and David Stott in 2020 with one built by local Mendon craftsman Steve Tubbs.

First and foremost, tending bar takes stamina. Standing on your feet for eight hours (a usual shift), lugging around 35-pound cases of beer, and sometimes having to physically remove customers from the premises, takes strength and endurance.

You also have to have enough dexterity to be able to pour speed shots from a height of two feet (for Tom Cruise-type drama), draw a draft beer with a perfect head (foamy, but not too foamy), and if you're really good fill five mugs simultaneously during *Mug Club*. In the midst of all this, you have to constantly two-handedly wash glasses to keep up with demand.

And consider this: before the advent of credit cards and digital cash registers, you had to add up drink prices in your head and quickly and accurately make change. (A lost art, to be sure.) If you're really sharp, you also develop an eye for trouble and defuse potentially explosive situations before they escalate.[106]

John Bronson, younger brother Buzzy Bronson, knows exactly what we are talking about. Between going to school and a rigorous schedule as a Division I soccer player, he tended bar on weekend

---

[106] If the owner is not present, the head bartender typically takes over as management, and what the bartender says, goes. That's a lot of responsibility for what you're usually getting paid a pitifully small hourly wage to do.

Any *Cottage Hotel* bartender will instantly recognize this setup behind the bar, the same as it was in the 1970s

nights at *The Cottage* from 1972-73. He also worked up the road in Pittsford at *Thirsty's*.

Who else would know better what it's like to look out on a busy band night at *The Cottage* and see a swarm of thirsty 18+-year-olds five-deep to the bar, all in various stages of inebriation trying desperately to get your attention? Or figuring out that the guy by the pinball machine is a hustler and, after the boss tosses him down the front steps, paying the jerk twenty bucks so he doesn't sue. Or denying a customer, who is already more than intoxicated, but who also happens to be a really good friend, beg (after last call) for one more round.

As John reminds us . . .

> *You have to have 'lizard eyes,' and be able to pivot and see what's going on at each end of the bar so that you can really serve your customers efficiently.*
>
> *In other words, you don't want to be 'a five-mile-an-hour bartender in a ten-mile-per-hour bar.' You have to really hustle. The upside to all this, of course, is that you never really get bored.*

Molly (Phillips) Babigian,[107] who has worked at *The Cottage* since she was 17 and tended bar off and on through the years, can certainly relate.

> *One night in particular we were really slammed. We were so busy I thought I would lose my mind. Just then, I looked out the window to see a party bus roll up! Forty more people got off the bus. It was so crazy, I just had to laugh. I'm not sure how, but we made it through!*

Hendo, who was the barback on Friday and Saturday nights, as well as bartending at *The Cottage* on Sunday afternoons, later became Assistant Manager at the *Mason Jar*. In both places, he witnessed just about every kind of excess you can imagine. "Woodstock had nothing on *The Cottage Hotel*," he says. "Remember, back then we had no

---

[107] Molly (Phillips) Babigian is the wife of Harout Babigian, son of current *Cottage Hotel* owner Hilary Stott.

cell phones and no internet. Drugs, alcohol, hormones, and the opposite sex—that's all we had to go with—and nobody had any shame!"

And as writers and hamlet dwellers Deb and Tim Smith so aptly report:

> *While closing time in Monroe County has always been 2:00 a.m., until 1990 closing time in Ontario County was 1:00 a.m. So if you were out in Victor partying hard on a Friday or Saturday night and heard that bell ring for last call, the question often asked would be, "What's the closest bar in Monroe County?"*
>
> *The answer of course was The Cottage, and the results were quite consistently crazy. If you could have set up a toll booth around 1:00 a.m. anywhere on the county line heading into Mendon, you could have made a fortune.*
>
> *So as all the Ontario County hardcores would converge, en masse, on The Cottage, the establishment would undergo a unique transition. There would be nights where just before 1:00 a.m. the Cottage might be almost empty, then suddenly, in a matter of minutes, the doors would be deluged with dozens of devoted but delusional die-hards and Dead*

Heads determined to drink down that last defining draft.[108]

Your corner seats await
(Note: one chair is always reserved in honor of John Wallman.)

Buzzy Bronson, who owned *The Cottage* from 1972-75, offered his bartenders and managers what was an innovative incentive at the time to do a good job. In addition to their $400 a week base salary, he would pay them an additional $50 if they

---

[108] Adapted from: "Skyler Smith's Tour of Mendon: The Cottage Hotel, Part II," *Mendon-Honeoye Falls-Lima Sentinel*, April 26, 2018, 2.

maintained a proper balance between revenue and bar costs. Says Buzzy:

> *We had great people working for us back then — Connie Alissa, John Bronson, Mark ("Coach") Dennis, Tommy Doggett, Deidre ("Deedee") Dutcher, Doug Foxall, Don Jeffries, Joe Polosi, Peter Silos, Erick Thompson, and Gus Yates are ones that you may remember among others at The Cottage.*

Like loyal homing pigeons, some are compelled to return to *The Cottage* from time to time. Here's former *Cottage* bartender, Don Jeffries, in 2023 with current owner Hilary Stott:

Doug Foxall, who managed the *Cottage Hotel* and tended bar days and evenings from 1974-75, vividly remembers the scene at *The Cottage*:

When you came in the door there was a bowling machine on the left. It cost a dime and six people could play at a time. Everyone loved it! They would play it even when the bands were on stage.

The concession guy who serviced the machines would come by every two weeks. There would usually be between $1500-$1600 in dimes and we could split the revenue. We had a running battle because he wanted to raise the price to a quarter. I told him that there was no way in hell! The locals loved it, and people came to The Cottage just to play that machine!

Of course there was the pool table, and the air hockey machine in the back and a pinball machine to the left of the bar, but it was really that bowling machine that everyone loved.

I'm not big on crowds, so I enjoyed the late morning hours when the farmers would come in and have a beer and a shot. They'd been in the fields since 5:00 a.m., so this was their quitting time.

I'd never worked in a bar before, but The Cottage was a very friendly place. Buzzy Bronson, who owned the place then, was a really creative guy. Once he started bringing music in like the Swamp Root String Band business really started to pick up. We also *began the tradition of serving hamburgers and that also brought people in the door.*

One thing I remember about the bar was when a kid from Pittsford who had just been out west came in and asked for an "Upside-down North Dakota Snowshoe." What the heck is that? I wondered. Turns out, it was a shot of Wild Turkey and peppermint schnapps. You'd lay your head back down on the bar and we'd pour the shot directly into your mouth! That certainly got people going! I thought it was so great that I later named my boat after it.

Deidre ("Deedee") Dutcher, whom *Cottage* regulars always affectionately called "The Dutchess," tended bar at *The Cottage* beginning in 1976. She was hired by Buzzy Bronson as a manager and ran *The Cottage* for close to a year before Burdock purchased it in 1978.

"Buzzy wasn't too impressed with my degree from the University of Rochester in political science," she says. "But he was in desperate need of a someone to fill that role due to the unexpected departure of his former manager."

She, too, has colorful memories of the bowling machine.

> Those who played it know that it used a puck to knock down the pins. If we were really drunk, we'd use a heavy glass ashtray instead. And, if we were really, really smashed we'd get someone to lay down on it and push them into the pins. We called this "body bowling."

As Manager, one of Deedee's responsibilities was closing things up at the end of the evening. She admits that after partying all night, she sometimes was a trifle too inebriated to walk up the steep stairs to the office.

> If I was too hammered, I would put the cash drawer into the oven, and then lock up for the night. Hopefully, I'd remember to get there the next morning before Louis, our cook, did—and before he started pre-heating the stove!

Deedee remembers only one serious managing misstep—and that was when she hired the band *Bahama Mama*[109] to play on Wednesdays during what she called "Hump Day Specials."

> *Bahama Mama was one of my favorite groups. I just loved all the guys in the band,*

---

[109] *Bahama Mama*, with Ron Stackman, Jim Schwarz, and Lou LaVilla, became the *Majestics* in 1980. Later, Rudy Valentino and Fitroy 'Brother' James joined the group, and together they gained national and international fame.

> *especially Ronnie Stackman. Unfortunately it turned out to be a horrible business decision. Bahama Mama was a reggae band, and the crowd they attracted didn't drink – they smoked pot. When the band went on break, they'd all go out to the parking lot to do a few doobies. The result was that we didn't sell any alcohol. They were a great band, but it was definitely not a good financial move on my part.*

Because the *Cottage Hotel* bar is a relatively short L-shaped one, with seating for maybe 10 chairs, it can sometimes feel like a bit of fishbowl when you're behind the bar. As Kathryn ("Katie") Miller, who began bartending at *The Cottage* in July of 2023 admits:

> *I've worked at the Cottage since 2018 but have been close to the Stott family even longer. I began as a dishwasher, then bussed tables, and then after Covid in 2022 I began serving. It took a while for me to say 'yes,' but after I turned 19, I moved up to being a bartender.*
>
> *I am so shy that I was a little scared at first to be behind the bar and have to talk to so many people. But now it's fun! The people at The Cottage are super nice, and the regulars are so friendly and loyal, that it makes it really*

> *easy. You get to know everyone really well, and they get to know you . . .*
>
> *It's fast-paced and hard work sometimes, but bartending has made other things in life easier. I now have the self-confidence to introduce myself to people. At The Cottage, it's less like a job and more like being with a big family. I leave work every day smiling, and I don't think many people can say that!*

As in any tavern, there are, of course, ongoing challenges. *Cottage* bartenders, both male and female, often witnessed and sometimes were subjected to some rather bad behaviors by customers.

Harout Babigian[110], who tended bar at *The Cottage* off and on for over five years, saw more than his fair share of drama.

> *The Cottage has never been a conventional place. People there get a little too comfortable — they tend to forget they are in a public establishment. Like the time I saw someone suddenly pick up a barstool and smash it into a guy's face, breaking his nose. As far as I could tell, it was unprovoked. Things like that could happen, though mostly late at night. You had to keep an eye out, be ready for the unexpected, and*

---

[110] Harout Babigian is the son of Hilary Stott.

break up fights and throw people out before they caused more damage.

His sister, Madison "Maddie" (Babigian) Trickey, who also tended bar as an adult, witnessed a lot of crazy happenings — including one memorable night when a very inebriated customer staggered up to the bar bleeding profusely. For some unknown reason he'd put his fist through the men's room mirror and someone had to chase him down Route 64 for the money to pay for the damage.

Sometimes, things got personal. Maybe a little *too* personal. As Sarah Jane Clifford reveals to us (and there is no pun intended):

> *One time while I was tending bar, I was standing in front of the large antique mirror in front of the cash register. I had on a tube top, and one of the regular patrons (I won't say who) reached over and pulled my top down to my waist.*
>
> *It was the '70s. Naturally, I was not wearing a bra, and the entire room got a pretty good look at my anatomy. Thankfully, I was a gymnast, and in pretty good shape, if I do say so myself!*

One bartender, who worked at *The Cottage* for many years with Jacky and Baird Fisher, and also during Lou DiNardo's time, tells us:

There were a lot of different characters who came into The Cottage. Most good, some not so good, but that was rare. There were also things that happened that were surprising, too. One guy, Tommy Dunn, who was a tree trimmer, would always walk in, slap his money down on the bar, and buy everyone a round. Every single time. You could count on it like clockwork. That was pretty amazing. I also remember walking in on customers having sex on the pool table in the back room. That was a whole lot more common than you might think.

**The new bar top, replaced
by Hilary & David Stott in 2020
& crafted by Steve Tubbs**

"That's why I never played pool there," quips Hendo, who as a bartender also saw his fill of "Full Montys" both at the pool table and the pinball machine.

Another bartender still gets misty-eyed when he recalls the night a female who had just turned eighteen came into *The Cottage*.

> *She walked in, turned to her girlfriends, and said loudly enough for everyone to hear: "The guy behind the bar with the moustache is mine!" That raised my eyebrows, as well as a few other things, I can tell you.*
>
> *Lucky me. I was the one with the moustache! After the bar closed, she invited me into the back room and we consummated her coming of age, so to speak, on The Cottage pool table. We had a couple of other trysts after that night, and before parting she gave me an engraved beer stein that said — you guessed it — 'The one with the moustache is mine.' I'll never, ever forget it!*

Although I never received an invitation as enticing (or satisfying) as this guy's, I do know what it was like to tend bar at *The Cottage Hotel*. In 1978, I was hired by Burdock as the day bartender. For the next two years while I was going to school, I worked there during the week, but I was also on call nights and weekends — mostly because I lived across the street and kitty-corner from *The Cottage*.

On my very first day, a man came in and told me that his wife had left him and that he was seriously considering suicide. I was barely twenty years old, had never tended bar before, and he was my first customer.

I didn't have anywhere near the kind of life experience to match that situation, and there wasn't any advice I could offer him, as perhaps a good and more experienced bartender might have been able to do. Somehow, miraculously, by the time he left he was in cheerful enough spirits to thank me for taking the time to listen to him.

The original bar top
(Courtesy: The Cottage Hotel of Mendon)

Somewhere along the way someone had told me that the key to being a good bartender was to be able to listen. Truthfully, all I had done that day was let him talk and that is what seemed to do him some good.

After that first rather intense day, working behind the bar at *The Cottage* seemed like a piece of cake. I loved being there, mostly because the people were so great. It was a tight-knit community from all walks of life: construction workers, landscapers, real estate developers, bankers, teachers, students, shop keepers, and farmers.

I especially loved the farmers.

They would come into the bar during the day to take a break from the hard work of tending their fields, dressed in their mud-stained Carter overalls and flannel shirts, remnants of cow patties still clinging to their boots. No one gave a rat's patootie then or would think to do so today.

Those hard-working men actively tilled hundreds of acres dating back through the generations to the town's origin. They'd politely order a draft beer or a 50-cent glass of rosé, leave a more-than-modest gratuity, smile, tip their caps, and be on their way.

Sometimes they would leave me baskets of apples or flats of strawberries as a tip—and one time Freddie Garling gave me a ladder-back chair he had made. They were as sweet and unassuming as could be. You'd never guess that they were millionaires, sitting on of what is now extremely coveted, uber-valuable Mendon land.

Just as in the television series *Cheers*,[111] when everyone came together at the bar, at *The Cottage* we could all agree on at least one thing—that it was "Happy Hour"—time to relax, to leave your cares behind, and to make a few toasts to life, love, and the pursuit of happiness. And all this in a place where "everybody knows your name."

As far as I can tell, this has never changed, and hopefully it never, ever will!

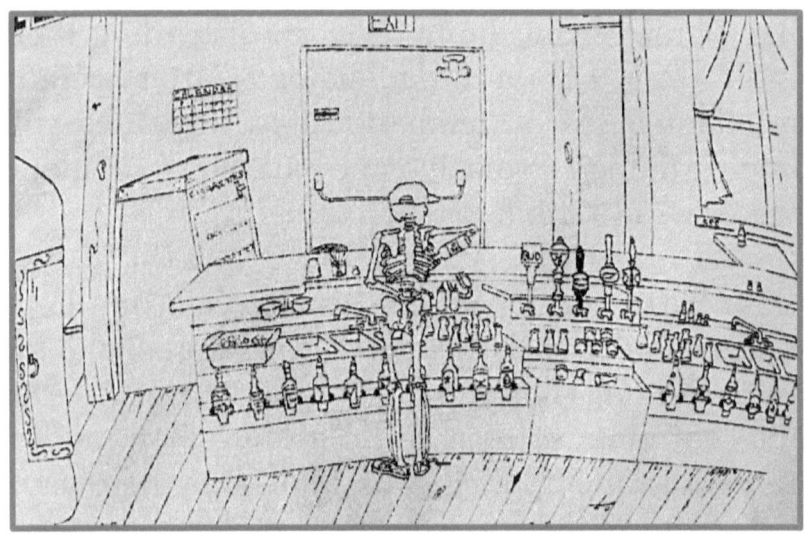

(Drawing courtesy of Kimberly ("Kim") Ormiston.)

---

[111] In Los Angeles, California, in the early 1980s, I worked for CEO Grant Tinker of NBC. Ironically, on my first day on the job, Grant and I watched the "rough cut" of the pilot episode of *Cheers* in his Burbank office. It instantly reminded me of all the regulars at the *Cottage Hotel*.

Chapter XI

Of Men & Women & Mason Jars: The Tradition of the *Mug Club*

**Classic *Mug Club* Mug
circa 1980s**
(Collection of Steve Anderson.)

It was 1980.

Female friends of mine, whom I'd met while working as the day bartender at *The Cottage*, were all interested in quilting. Somehow along the way we decided to form an old-fashioned quilt club. If I recall correctly, we called ourselves (somewhat lamely in retrospect) "The Sew 'n Sews."

We were a diverse and dedicated group of 8-10 women. I was the youngest, having just turned twenty. Others were from 30 to 60 years of age, from all over the Finger Lakes region. Some came from Mendon hamlet; others came from Canandaigua or Hemlock—quite a trek, especially in wintertime on those icy, hilly, deer-populated rural roads.

Around that time, Burdock had come up with the idea for the *Mug Club* using mason jars with handles on them and imprinted with the *Cottage Hotel* logo to serve draft beer. This became the template and the inspiration for the *Mason Jar*, another venue he developed later in Henrietta with his lawyer and business partner, John Redmond.

"The *Mason Jar* was like *The Cottage*," Bill Haywood says, "only bigger and crazier." Bill, who tended bar there until early 1983, often subbed at *The Cottage* on *Mug Club* nights when it became popular.

The concept for the *Mug Club* was simple—on Tuesday nights, once you bought your 16-ounce "mug" for $2, at 7:00 p.m. sharp, beer would start at a nickel a jar.

Steve Anderson, Burdock's good friend and lead guitarist and lyricist for the band *Slipton Fell*[112] was there from the beginning. "I went with Burdock to a restaurant supply house in downtown Rochester to pick out the mugs for the *Mug Club*. That was a really special moment. I really felt honored to be part of that decision."

Says Steve:

> *John always said the plan was to pack the bar before seven o'clock so that people could get their space at the bar and sell as much beer as possible. Then basically he would give it away for an hour. People would be so buzzed by then that they'd stay drinking well after the 8:00 p.m. deadline. Worked perfectly!*

At exactly 7:10 p.m., the price would rise to a dime, then to 30 cents at 7:30. The price would return to $2 a mug precisely at 8:00 p.m. According to first-hand reports, by that time pretty much everyone would be hammered. It didn't take long for the *Mug*

---

[112] From the time the band was in high school, *Slipton Fell* played regularly at *The Cottage* and were the inaugural act for the opening of the *Mason Jar* in Henrietta, New York.

Club to catch fire and soon after its success was duplicated at the *Mason Jar*. Regulars had their own special hook for their *Mug Club* mug on the wall at *The Cottage*. Artist Kimberly ("Kim") Ormiston even designed special *Grateful Dead* stickers for their individual mugs.

All-star hockey player Eric Kozlowski remembers those days and how popular the *Mug Club* was with his teammates and friends. "People would come from all around Rochester. Sometimes we'd buy 12 mugs at a time and fill them with beer at 7:00 p.m. for 60 cents," he says. "It was the best deal in the whole city..."

Our quilt club met on Mondays, but occasionally we would be there early on Tuesday *Mug Club* nights. We didn't mind having our drinks in plain mason jars, but the *Mug Club* mugs sure were cool. Everyone wanted one. Eventually, each of us had a *Mug Club* mug, even though we didn't always put beer in them.

Jacky Fisher also has fond memories of *Mug Club* days:

> *The neat thing about the Mug Club was that it brought in the kids, and they came back for more. Strategically, it was a great Burdock idea. I was one of the bartenders that worked it for him and I could fill five mugs at a time at the tap with one hand – a "girl record" for*

> *sure! We kept it up for a lot of years. The times changed; the laws changed . . . we all had to make changes . . . but it was fun while it lasted!*

Meanwhile, our quilt club had a marvelous time. We sat at what were the cozy booths near the windows across from the bar at *The Cottage* (ones later removed to make more room in the bar area), stitching our already-cut-out pieces of calico cloth together—cracking jokes, talking about our everyday lives, sometimes swearing as we inadvertently stabbed a finger with our needles, and drinking copious amounts of 'Tanqueray & Tonics' out of mason jars.

Once the quilt squares were completed (and you could see what started out as very even stitches become wobblier as the evenings wore on), we joined them together, added a border, and then gathered in the backyard of one of the farmer's wives with an antique quilt frame that had belonged to their great-grandmother.

We stood in the spring sunlight, passing our needles back and forth, stitching the quilt top to the backing. It really felt like we were back at the turn of the century, doing what women did then to create art, community, and winter warmth for their friends and families.

When the work of quilting was done, we took it back to *The Cottage*. With the blessing of Burdock, we sold raffle tickets for a dollar, then watched as our beautiful (or at least we imagined it to be so), completely hand-sewn quilt went to the person with the winning ticket—one that Burdock would ceremoniously pull from a *Mug Club* jar.

With our earnings, we paid our bar bill from over the many months it took to finish our quilt—all those mugs filled with gin and tonics added up—but it seemed like a completely satisfying exchange. Although we were a little sad to see our quilt go to a new home, we knew that the person would enjoy it. Everyone was happy.

Mug Club mug with Garfield image
(Courtesy: Chandler Coyle.)

There were successive variations of the *Cottage Hotel* logo on the mugs over time. During the years Jacky and Baird Fisher owned and put their personal stamp on *The Cottage*, the mugs and *Cottage* softball shirts sported a *Garfield* imprint. Garfield? As Jacky speculates, "I'm not sure why we did that, but I guess we're lucky we didn't get sued!"

The original mugs from Burdock's and the Fishers' times are now collectors' items. Like the illustration at the beginning of this chapter, they have a black logo saying "Cottage Hotel" on the front, with an image of farmers threshing their fields. The tagline below it says: "Beautiful Downtown Mendon." Others, like the one above, have simpler logos. They are probably faded by now, but if you have one, hang onto it!

And mugs aren't the only *Cottage* items worth collecting. Vintage *Cottage* t-shirts are another treasure that people have held onto, sometimes passing them down to friends and family. Burdock's friend and housemate, "Hendo," remembers going to pick out t-shirts for *The Cottage* and how everyone wanted one. *Cottage* fan Brian Lyons, who made a point of archiving *Cottage* t-shirts through the years, is good enough to share them with us here:

  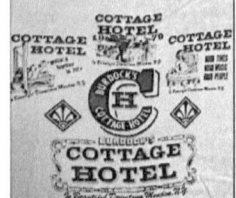

(T-shirt photos Courtesy: Steve Anderson)

The artwork seen on pages 158, 176, 184, and 185 is from an especially popular t-shirt designed by Kim Ormiston. "It was just something I liked to do at the time for fun," she says.

In the early '80s after John Ross bought the bar he sold t-shirts. People proudly wore them and eagerly awaited new editions.

I designed two of them. The first was a big hit. It was a caricature of the inside of the bar area with the bartender pouring a drink, with all the identifiable things the bar was known for at the time — like the spot on the bar top with the embedded dimes, the bottles behind the bar, the beer taps, the stacked shot glasses, and the old fashioned cash register.

It also included the Bevador (the Labatt bottle-shaped beer cooler to the right of the bar), and the trophy fish displayed in the overhanging doorway to the left of the bar. There was a dog napping in the corner. The dog was "Freckles" — Burdock's dog, an ancient English Setter. Freckles must have also been deaf because he slept through a lot.

In the spirit of the Grateful Dead who everybody loved at the time, the bartender, trophy fish, and dog were all in skeleton form. The bartender wore a baseball hat that said 'Houston,' as the bartender was meant to represent Craig Williams ("Sandman") who was working there at the time.

The back of the shirt showed the bar from the bartender's perspective, to include his view of the glasses, the drink mixing tools, the beer taps, the front door, the wooden booths, and the old cigarette machine with the pull knobs. The shirts sold out in a week.

The Cottage Hotel t-shirts in general were very popular and a new design usually sold out in a weekend, but this particular one was a very bright "Kodak" yellow shirt. It was Burdock's choice. I remember Burdock, Bud Simmons, and I went downtown to the shirt printing company and he picked that color, wanting to do an untraditional color for some reason. People were not crazy about the color but really liked the design. We ordered a second small batch in light blue.

The second shirt I did was a design of the Cottage Hotel mug which we all had for Tuesday night Mug Club. Beer was really cheap if you had a Cottage Mug and the pizza was free while it lasted. After a while some people started marking their mugs so they could leave them at the bar, ready for the next Tuesday. I recall painting some Grateful Dead Stickers for some of them. If I *remember, they started putting their mugs on hooks in the ceiling above the bar.* [113]

Designs for t-shirts continued through the years. (Let's not forget the *Five Star Dump* t-shirt that is still worn by Tommy Dunn!) And here's a few shirts that were made into a quilt for Hilary by Jessica Gottfried:

The merry tradition of the *Mug Club* continued until 2004. When Hilary and David Stott bought *The Cottage* in 2005, they searched every inch of *The Cottage*, but no mugs of any kind were to be found.

They decided at that point to change it up a bit and begin a new tradition. Now, on *Mason Jar*

---

[113] Kimberly ("Kim") Armiston is now a budget analyst for the federal government in Washington, D.C.

Wednesdays, you can get a 32-ounce mason jar of beer (twice the original volume of the *Mug Club*), mugs for only three bucks. Such a deal!

To this day, you'll notice that the lights strung above the bar at *The Cottage Hotel* are housed in mason jars. It's a respectful nod to those *Mug Club* days, thanks to the Stotts, who are intent on preserving the original personality of *The Cottage* as much as possible.

If you're out and about in Mendon hamlet, and you ask nicely, they might just serve you your beer or cocktails in a mason jar, just like they used to do. And if you've still got your *Mug Club* mug and can find (and still fit into) your *Cottage Hotel* t-shirt—lucky, lucky you!

(Collection of Steve Anderson.)

Chapter XII

Our Haunted Hamlet:
Ghosts & Ghoulies of the *Cottage Hotel*

Spooks & Specters
The Cottage Hotel of Mendon
October, 2022

Mendon hamlet has never been a stranger to what some consider fringe or out-of-the-ordinary ways of thought.

Let's not forget that the *Cottage Hotel* is located in what was known as the *Burned-Over* or *Burnt-Over District*, a section of western Upstate New York where people were once said to be "on fire" with religious revivalism. In the mid-1800s, over 30 sects, cults, crusades, original philosophies, and non-conformist religions were born here.[114] The advent of Spiritualism, with followers who believed (and still believe) in mysticism and our ability to speak directly with the dead, profoundly influenced people all over the world.[115]

And you may not be surprised to know that it had its start just a few miles from the *Cottage Hotel*!

On March 31st of 1848, Margaretta ("Maggie") Fox, age 14, and her sister Catherine ("Kate,") age 11, first heard and responded to "spirit rappings" in their home in Hydesville, New York, less than 20 miles from the hamlet. They convinced their older sister, Leah, that they were communicating with an itinerant peddler that had supposedly been killed and buried beneath the house.[116]

The sisters were no strangers to mediumship or clairvoyance. Their maternal great-grandmother,

---

[114] In the mid-1800s, Shakers, Quakers, Millerites, Universalists, Perfectionists, Mesmerists, Phrenologists, Seventh-Day Adventists, Theosophists, Jehovah's Witnesses, Spiritualists, and The Church of Latter-day Saints were but a few of the groups that first took root here.
[115] Over 100 Spiritualist churches exist in the U.S. today, with 300 in the United Kingdom, and hundreds more around the world.
[116] Unidentified remains were later found some six feet below the Hydesville cellar.

aunt and uncle, and others in the family had a history of occult experiences.

Even so, the Fox sisters fled Hydesville *tout suite*, but the spooky rappings followed close behind. For the next forty years, their elder sister Ann ("Leah") Fox managed their careers as mediums, making them international celebrities as Spiritualism spread like wildfire, both here and abroad.

**The Fox Sisters:
Margaretta ("Maggie") Fox,
Catherine ("Kate") Fox
and Ann ("Leah") Fox**
(Courtesy: Library of Congress.)

Arthur Conan Doyle (author of the Sherlock Holmes mysteries)[117] was a hard-core believer in Spiritualism, as were William James, Mark Twain, Marie and Pierre Curie, James Fenimore Cooper, Frederick Douglass, and western New York native, L. Frank Baum (author of *The Wizard of Oz*) to name a few. Even Queen Victoria consulted Spiritualist mediums and attended seances. It was estimated that by the mid-19th century from 4 to 11 million people followed Spiritualism in one form or another.

Oh, *Snap*!

Was it all a childhood prank gone terribly awry? The Fox sisters would be subject to strip searches, debunking, attacks by mobs, and endless disheartening attempts to discredit them.

Eventually they succumbed to the pressure. Both younger sisters descended into alcoholism. Maggie admitted publicly that it had all been a fraud — the rappings were caused by loud clicks practiced beneath their long skirts in their toe, ankle, and knee joints. Maggie immediately recanted her confession, but by then the damage was done. Leah, on the other hand, continued to defend

---

[117] Arthur Conan Doyle also wrote *The History of Spiritualism, Vol. I and II*, Cassell and Company, Ltd., 1926.

Spiritualism until her dying day.[118] Several years later, Kate and Maggie, having declined into poverty, would also be dead, but not before penning their own candid recollections.[119]. To this day, the movement they started lives on even more vibrantly than before.

The Fox Sisters findings may have been a hoax, but there's no doubt about it—the *Cottage Hotel* really is haunted. Based on my own and other people's experiences, I absolutely believe it to be so.

Often while I was tending bar during the day and especially during the dead of winter, for many hours I was often the only person on the premises. It was then that I would hear footsteps walk from one end of the upper floor to the other—abruptly stop—and never return.

Other times, I would clearly hear voices murmuring in the musty, gloomy basement—a place not many people ever visited. I could never make out their conversations, but I knew that they were meant for me, and for me alone, to hear. It always sent a chill up my spine.

---

[118] Ann ("Leah") Fox Underhill, "The Missing Link in Modern Spiritualism," (Thomas R. Lenox & Co., New York, 1885.)

[119] Reuben Briggs Davenport, *"The Death Blow to Spiritualism,"* (G.W. Dillingham Company, New York, 1897.) Ann ("Leah") Fox/Underhill/Fish died in 1890, Kate Fox/Kane in 1892, and Maggie Fox/Jencken in 1893.

A Spirit Stands guard at
The Cottage Hotel of Mendon
October, 2022.

And I'm not the only one to experience the eerie and the unexplained.

Rumor has it that back in the day, when *The Cottage* may have operated as a brothel, there was a young lady who tripped on her long skirts as she was coming down the back stairs. She fell and broke her neck, and it is said that from time to time you can still experience the faint scent of her lilac perfume in the back room.

Owner Hilary Stott tells about an experience that happened one Thanksgiving, when 15 people were in the bar. There was a deafening bang on the floor above and it was discovered that an entire shelf in the office had collapsed on the floor. The shelf had been completely solid and bolted to the wall. No one had been upstairs, and the sound was so loud that it was heard above all the music and chatter down at the bar.

Another *Cottage Hotel* bartender tells us this:

> *I was working by myself at night. Around 11:00 p.m. I heard a loud noise in the pool room. It sounded like a bagful of coins being slung across the floor. Goosepimples rose up and down my flesh, and the hair on the back of my neck stood up, but when I walked in to investigate . . . there was nothing there.*

Another tale is told about a man who rented a room upstairs at the *Cottage Hotel* in the late 1980s or early 1990s. He got so used to seeing apparitions appear and disappear in front of him, that it seemed totally ordinary to him.

Cottage patron Brenda Zimmerman Kessler has had several unexpected paranormal experiences. The first occurred when she'd stopped in for a lunch of a legendary *Cottage Burger*.

> *At the bar was a person sitting a few chairs down. (He was a young person, good looking.) Out of the blue, he said, "I left my*

body." There was silence. He then said, "You can do it, too!"

I said, "How?" He said, "I read this book, 'Journeys Out of the Body' by Robert Monroe." And he handed it to me.

I was intrigued. I read the book. I was a regular meditator and decided to do it. After six months of ardent trying, I was successful. In a state of wakefulness and sleep, you learned to wake yourself up. I learned to rev up my vibrations and enhance them.

I have had a handful of experiences since, one which was scary. One time, I went to fall back into my body, but was startled that I would get hurt and that nothing would stop me from hitting the floor, but I was fine.

I don't know if he was a real person or not, [120] *but he changed the shape of my life completely! Thanks to my experience at The Cottage, my two daughters have both had similar out of-body experiences.*

Brenda's second experience may have been even more profound.

---

[120] If by chance you are the young man in this story, please get in touch! We want to hear from you . . .

This was a waking dream or dream experience at The Cottage. I was standing in front of the swinging doors that led from the bar to the kitchen. It seemed like a regular dream, but it was so real!

There were two people on either side of the doors. One was Burdock, the other was shorter (maybe Bud Simmons or Craig Williams). Both were dressed in country gear with cowboy hats and boots. They were very non-threatening and they seemed welcoming. They said, "You can go through this door." They stepped aside and I went through the door and turned to the right.

> *I became awake. I knew, I felt, that I had transitioned to another dimension and the colors were the most vibrant I have ever seen. There was a giant pool with beautiful shimmering water and very inviting. I was mesmerized by the color and beauty and dove in and the experience overall was very pleasant.*
>
> *I realize now that the doors were a portal. It was a gift to open my mind.*

Kent Hughes, who has been coming to *The Cottage* since the '70s, has had a number of supernatural experiences there, too.

> *There was definitely some kind of energy around where the stage area was and is — other bands have told me this, too. There were times when certain songs were played that the electric would go completely out. Other times, they would feel it suddenly get icy cold up on stage.*
>
> *Sometimes, when I would walk from the bar to where the old stairs were and the pool table was located, I would encounter a cold wall of air that would be almost a 10-degree drop in temperature. As I walked on, the room would become as warm as it was before. It was totally real and totally mystifying.*

I played music and helped out at The Cottage from time to time, and when there was no one else there, I would hear and see things that just didn't make sense. In the basement, where I would sometimes need to go for supplies, I once saw something that should never have been there. It was an anomaly – some kind of form – and it made the hair on the back of my neck stand up. It made me never want to go down there again!

And of course ghosts and ghoulies are always present on *All Hallows Eve* at *The Cottage*.

"Ghould Rush" (*Gold Rush*) Members
Peg Dolan, George Botticelli, & Tom Price
at *The Cottage Hotel of Mendon*, Halloween 2003

"The Cottage always seemed to me to be an energy magnifier," says Kim Ormiston, the talented artist who designed many of *The Cottage's* iconic t-shirts. "It was both literally and metaphorically a crossroads where both the positive and the negative (whatever it was that fed it) would be intensified. Although I never experienced the paranormal, this energy always seemed to be present."

Kim is not alone in never having witnessed ghostly presences. Molly Babigian also regrets that the spirits have never shown themselves to her. "It's a sore topic for me! I am very open to the supernatural, and it seems like everyone else has had experiences but me. I'm actually a little bit upset about it!"

Indeed, her husband's parents, current owners Hilary and David Stott, were once visited by a medium and ghost hunter who found definite evidence of paranormal activity at *The Cottage*. Not at all surprising!

There are also others such as Pat Freeman, owner of *Ye Olde Mendon Tavern*, who have spoken openly and on record about their own up-close-and-personal experiences with the supernatural in the hamlet—but that, as they say, is a book yet to be written.

Chapter XIII

What a Long Strange Trip It's Been: Sex, Drugs, & Rock 'n Roll at the *Cottage Hotel*

St. Patrick's Day *Cottage Hotel* Ad
(Rochester Democrat and Chronicle, March 16, 1978.)

Okay, now we're getting to the *really* good stuff.

There are stories about things that have happened at *The Cottage* through the years. And then there are the stories . . .

Some of the hijinks and shenanigans that went on particularly during the '70s and '80s at *The Cottage*, may not be ones you'd want your children or grandchildren to know. But don't worry, your secrets are safe here — most of the tales are told here anonymously.

Part One
Dangerous Liaisons

First, let's talk about *Sex*.

Cottage owner Hilary Stott had always been curious about something. One afternoon, she felt called to stand up and ask the lunch crowd, "How many of you have had sex at *The Cottage*?"

> *I wasn't surprised to see that more than half the people raised their hands. There was a pause as everyone looked around and had a good laugh at seeing who their kindred spirits might be.*
>
> *But then a lone voice from the back of the room tentatively spoke out, saying . . . "Does that include the parking lot?"*
>
> *Many more hands shot up! That's when I knew for sure that all the rumors about sex at The Cottage were true.*

It seems that just about everywhere at *The Cottage* was a likely spot for *getting it on*, as they used to refer to it. The bar, the bathrooms, the back stairway before it was torn out, and no doubt the back bedroom upstairs all had their moments. Shocking, isn't it? Or perhaps not . . . it was in some ways a sign of the times that people felt open to "love the one you're with," but it also may have been a direct result of just one too many "*Alabama Slammers*"[121] or shots of *Wild Turkey*.

There is a plethora of risqué tales specifically about the *Cottage Hotel* pool table as being the site of spontaneous, or sometimes planned, romantic liaisons. These might happen almost any time of day, as the pool table was in the back room of the bar, and (somewhat) hidden from general view.

Not that it mattered, apparently.

For some, it was a challenge to kiss or be kissed (or otherwise) on *The Cottage* pool table. For others, to be "deflowered" there was a rite of passage. Although I never personally witnessed these phenomena, it was said to happen quite frequently — and there are more than a few people who will back this up.

Bands playing at *The Cottage* decidedly had an advantage when it came to secret places to party. There was a bedroom down the hall from the back stairway where the musicians would keep their equipment and hang out between sets. A number of

---

[121] An "Alabama Slammer" was a popular shot drink at *The Cottage* composed of vodka, *Southern Comfort*, orange juice, and grenadine which gave it (and you) a rosy glow.

people have said that this was also a well-known site for clandestine rendezvous.

"I personally had three or four encounters there between the ages of 18 to 21," one *Cottage* regular reports. "I had inebriated women hurling themselves at me left and right, but never hooked up at *The Cottage*," another musician confesses. However, according to other first-hand reports, this may have been a fabrication on his part intended to protect the innocent . . . or himself!

ಌ ಌ ಌ

Part Two
One Tequila, Two Tequila,
Three Tequila . . . Floor

Now, put on your party hats, and take off the one that says, *Just Say No*. It's time for some straight talk about *Drugs*.

Alcohol, naturally, was a big part of the scene at the *Cottage Hotel*, but so were drugs of all kinds and all manner of description. (If you've ever worked in the restaurant trade, you probably know this is true of most bars and bistros.)

For those of you unfamiliar with such things, in the beginning there was *grass* or *pot* or *Mary Jane*. Whatever you called it then, there is no comparison now — it was a version of marijuana considerably less potent than today. Back in the '70s and '80s, musicians who were on stage (the right back corner nearest the bathrooms), often saw joints being passed from person to person in full view and no attempt to hide them.

There were varieties of popular prescription drugs around, too, such as *Valium*, something just about everyone had access to (mostly from their parents' bathroom cabinets). Valium was a drug considered so benign back then that some people popped them like they did aspirin.

You didn't need a dealer to score 'uppers' like *Speed* or crystal methamphetamines. Same thing for 'downers' like *Quaaludes*. But by the late '60s and early '70s, mind-altering "shrooms" or *Magic Mushrooms*[122] became popular. Other psychedelics like *Acid*, or *LSD* and *Mescaline* also came more frequently into use during this time.

Steve Anderson, who has many such stories, shares this one with us:

> *I remember one crazy trip with Burdock and a guy named 'Grateful Tom' to Maine where*

---

[122] For the uninitiated, *Magic Mushrooms* contain psilocybin, known for the intense psychedelic and hallucinogenic effects caused when ingested. Psilocybin "shrooms" were legally banned in the '80s, along with heroin.

> we tripped our heads off at a Grateful Dead concert.

> It was a true "bad trip." We had planned to go to Boston for a show the next night but were so spaced out all we could think of was to drive the 14+ hours home.

By the '70s and '80s, snorting lines of *Cocaine* was definitely a thing, followed by smoking the far more concentrated *Crack*. As one veteran *Cottage*-goer attests, "It used to snow a lot, even in summer, at the *Cottage Hotel*."

Dealing marijuana and other drugs out of the back room or the kitchen at *The Cottage* seemed right as rain for some. It's how some (not all) bands supplemented their income from the door, how some (not all) owners cemented relationships with their employees and entertainers. "We often got paid partly in cash, and partly in coke," one musician confirms. "That was pretty standard."

The availability of drugs and the general party atmosphere at *The Cottage*, combined with lax attention to New York State's drinking age law (18 back in the '70s), made it a favorite of many adventurous high school students. It's why a certain crowd of people were drawn to *The Cottage* in the first place.

Alcohol, as you might expect, continued to prevail as the drug of choice at *The Cottage*, particularly with the advent of Burdock's Tuesday night *Mug Club*.

Fatal accidents due to drunk driving happened far more than we'd care to remember, typically at the curve heading north on Route 64. There were other bars in the area, but whether or not those accidents were directly a result of being at *The Cottage*, was often hard to pin down. Dick Joint, a 60-year member of the Mendon Fire Department who was often called to those horrific scenes, feels that many times those accidents could have been avoided.

Addiction is a terrible thing, *n'est pas*? Perhaps you know someone who has experienced it, or perhaps you have suffered it yourself. The truth is that drinking and drugs proved to be the ruin of many lives through the years. Although most of us came out of that time period sober and changed for the better, sadly some did not.

"You have to see things in context. It was a different time, with a different attitude towards drinking in particular. We just didn't realize the gravity of the problem back then," comments Deedee Dutcher.

As one musician also observes, "They were exciting times, with exciting new drugs, but nothing can stand that level of transformation before it fractures. And this is what I saw happen to many people. Some, particularly bar owners, lost everything."

Perhaps the most tragic casualty of this era for *Cottage Hotel* fans was the death of John Urquhart ("Burdock") Ross, who took his own life on October 19, 1981. It is a loss we continue to deeply mourn.

Those who spent time with him during his last days sensed an uncharacteristic cynicism in Burdock — always a positive, happy-go-lucky person who took care of everyone around him — but no one could have anticipated, or prevented, what was to come.

Those who knew him well would expect that Burdock would be the first to say, "The show must go on." So now . . . let's pause for a moment, give our thanks for all those, past and present, who have been a part of the spirit of *The Cottage Hotel*, and consider how the magic of the music made at *The Cottage* makes it such a special place.

෴ ෴ ෴

Part Three
Musical Magic (& Mayhem)

Live music has always been a powerful part of *The Cottage* buzz. Back during the Al and Mary Heckman era, when their son Tommy and daughter

Rosemary (Heckman) Lewis were teenagers, piano players would entertain revelers nightly.

> *"Jerky Bob" and "Goofy Bob" were our favorites. "Jerky Bob" probably suffered from cerebral palsy and had a tremor to his hands, but he played a mean piano, as did "Goofy Bob" who was, as his name would imply, just plain fun.*

Buzzy Bronson, who owned and ran *The Cottage* from 1972-1975, was responsible not only for ramping up the interior atmosphere of the bar, but considerably amping up the music scene in the hamlet as well.

> *We filled a niche that didn't exist. There was a guy we called "Wee Willy" – a delivery man who played fiddle – he was like something right out of the movie 'Deliverance' and just fantastic.*
>
> *One of our favorite bands was the Swamp Root Singers. On Friday nights we'd charge $1 at the door and we'd pack 'em in. It was a real cross-section of people – professors, beatniks, families, kids, babies – even around the bar area where everyone was smoking. Everyone loved it!*

The original band members of what became the *Swamp Root String Band* met as graduate students at

RIT where they would jam together in between their art and design classes.

One of their first gigs was playing at a tent party on Langpap Road. Buzzy approached the group, then composed of Brian Williams on bass and guitar, Sandra ("Sandy") Stark on fiddle, and Joe Rickard on guitar and banjo, saying that he liked their music so much he'd like them to play at *The Cottage* three nights a week . . . for as long as they wanted.

(Rochester Democrat and Chronicle August 24, 1975.)

As Brian Williams[123] recalls:

We said we'd take it! We spent every night for the next week putting together enough songs for an evening, then we debuted as the Swamp Root Singers. After Joe's wife, Marylou, bowed out of the band, I bought a bass fiddle at a junk shop and Molly Stouten, my girlfriend at the time, learned how to play it a key at a time. After a few gigs, we added more old-time hoedown and Southern Appalachian music to the mix.

Not many people locally were playing the kind of music we did, the folk music revival was in full swing, and we became somewhat of an overnight success. I had been working on my masters in ceramics but gave up my dream of starting a pottery shop because working the clay would take the callouses off my fingers. I then did a 180 and became a full-time musician.

We continued to play at The Cottage for two years, until 1975 when I was asked to join John Mooney's band, along with John and Robert ("Bobby") Weiner. We toured all over

---

[123] Brian also has an extra special connection to *The Cottage*. For a short time as a second job, he would perform until two or three in the morning, then clean the bar and prep the food for the next day's lunches when he worked as the short-order cook!

the country for about 10 years together. Everyone in the Swamp Root String Band went on to have professional lives as musicians, but it all began with Buzzy Bronson and the Cottage Hotel!

The Swamp Root String Band
Stephen Slottow, Margaret ("Molly") Stouten,
Brian Williams,
Sandy Stark, Joseph Rickard
(Courtesy: Brian Williams.)

ೞ   ೞ   ೞ

Buzzy, of course, was responsible for launching many musical careers, including that of legendary blues steel guitarist, John Mooney.

John Mooney
(Photo by: James Minchin III.)

When John was 15 or 16, he was looking for part-time work. I hired him to sweep up and clean The Cottage. Around that time his father bought him a steel guitar and he taught himself to play. At one point we auditioned him (like we did all the other bands), by having him try out and play for free to see if people liked him. They did! And that was the beginning of his musical journey, right here on the Cottage Hotel stage.

From 1975 until his death in 1981, Burdock continued Buzzy's legacy, bringing in talent sometimes four or five nights a week. Like Bronson, he's credited for supporting local artists and turning the hamlet into a destination for music lovers from all over Rochester, the Finger Lakes, and beyond.

ଔ ଔ ଔ

Walt Atkison (of *Walt Atkison & the Sun Mountain Fiddler*) was one musician who played at *The Cottage* on a regular basis, and who has vivid recollections of Burdock and *The Cottage*.

> *The way Burdock set it up we would play at The Cottage at least once a month on the weekends, and sometimes on Wednesdays. This worked well for everyone. People could anticipate our being there, and John would know what kind of crowd to expect. I probably played there over 40 times over a three-year span from 1978-81.*

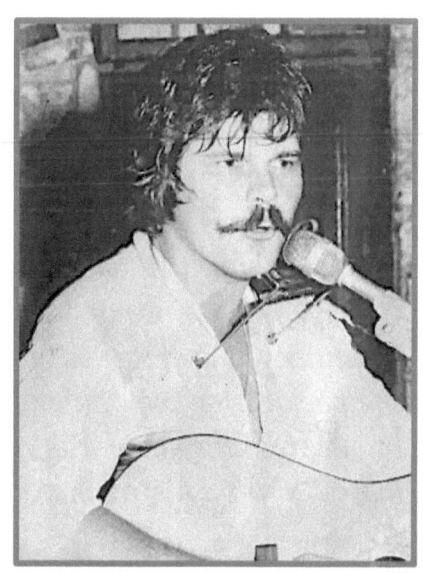

Walt Atkison

(Courtesy: Walt Atkison.)

Burdock was unlike other club owners. He became a very good friend, although he probably made many people feel that way. Everyone who played there said the same thing – he always went out of his way to pay you on time and make sure you got what you needed. I don't think I ever saw him pissed off. He had such a presence – he was always in a playful mood. Sometimes after a gig we would go to his house and party until the wee hours, but then he'd be right back at work.

No matter what the season, even having to travel the backcountry roads to get there, it was always a relief to get to The Cottage. There was something about the ambiance of the building and the room where we played. It was rustic, to be sure, but it also had a homey feel to it that other places couldn't match. It just felt good to be there. The locals always made it feel like someplace you'd want to go – you knew it was always going to be a good party!

I have to admit, though, that playing at The Cottage had its minor inconveniences. In the beginning, the stage was just the floor area at the back of the bar. Later they added a riser, but even so the stage was right in between the ladies' and men's rooms.

This sometimes made performing a little tricky, as there was a lot of traffic going back and forth, and when things backed up there was a terrible stench that would come from the bathrooms until someone went in with a bucket of ice and cleared things up. This was especially true in the heat of summer.

There was also an electric bowling machine that made loud 'bings' and 'beeps' that were a challenge if you were trying to play a ballad — we didn't play too many of those there! Nevertheless, we thought so much of the ambiance that in 1979 we recorded part of our album titled 'Walt Atkison & The Sun Mountain Fiddler' live at The Cottage.

(Courtesy: Walt Atkison.)

ଔ ଔ ଔ

From 1982-1998, Jacky and Baird Fisher also booked great bands. Then, until 2004, the music scene shifted slightly. Under Lou DiNardo's reign, when it was advertised as *'Lou's Cottage Hotel,'* bands and comedy acts would take the stage only about twice a month.

The groups that played on *The Cottage's* stage over the years ranged from old time bluegrass to acoustic to country to blues to reggae to rock 'n roll. Raunchy lyrics that comic *John Valby* crooned while pounding out tunes on his boogie-woogie piano rounded out the diverse music menu. (Valby's onstage antics often encouraged women at *The Cottage* to throw him their bras and panties.) There were also talent and comedy nights, fiddler contests, and open blues jams that advertised up to 30 artists. The only genre never, ever allowed at *The Cottage* was disco, for which many of us are eternally grateful.

Arm & Hammer String Band

A packed house was on hand last weekend to see and hear the Arm and Hammer String Band play some of their foot stompin', hand clappin' hillbilly music at the Cottage Hotel in Mendon.

Their music was exceptionally well-played and varied throughout the evening. But the lyrics were the best part of all. Only a country band from Vermont could sing: "Grandma, get off the stove, you're too old to ride the range."

All of the band members including Hillary Woodruff, the only girl, played several instruments including banjo, fiddle, guitar, mandolin, hammered dulcimer, ukelele and bass.

Ms. Woodruff was the most formally dressed member of the band with a long country gown and work boots. The other members, Sid Blum, Jack Eckhaus and Peter Sutherland, all sported beards and were dressed in jeans and shirts.

(Rochester Democrat and Chronicle, March 9, 1978.)

In 2005, after Hilary and David Stott bought *The Cottage,* and even before they acquired their liquor license in 2006, they were determined to continue the tradition of introducing up-and-coming local talent and launching new music careers. They also held *Open Mic* nights, with Ricky Wahlers as the M.C., and held regular *Bluegrass Happy Hours.*

Remember any of these bands?

Acoustic G	Beale Street Blues
Acoustica	Beat Beggars
Al White	Big Logic
& Cantry Smith	Bill Tracy
Alan Murphy	Bloodroots
Alex Dibiase	Bob Kosty
Alex Myth Trio	Bordertown
Alyssa Trahan	Bottle Train
Amanda Ashley	Bottleneck Blues
Amanda Lee Peers	Bottletrain
Amy Scheffer	Bradley Brothers
Annie Rhodes	Brian Ayers
Arm & Hammer	Brian Tomas
String Band	Brian Tomaszewski
Autumn Skies	Brian Williams
Ava Sauer	Bronco
B Free	Bryan Price
Bahama Mama	Buddy Sebastian
Barn Stormers	Buffalo Rose
Bat McGrath	Buzzo Sweat Band

Or these?

C&L Railroad
Cabo Frio
Cadillac Dawn
Canyon Ranger Leroy
Catherine Johnson
Chinchillas
Chip Mulligan
Chris Cady
Chris Matheos
Chris Moore
Christine Romano
Colin Jones
Connie Deming
Corey Bates Band
Cottage Pickers
Cottonwood
Country Rain
Craig Schwarz
Creeks Edge
Cricket
Dady Brothers
Dalla Greene
Dan Ripley
Darts
Dave McGrath
Dick Solberg (Sun Mtn. Fiddler)
Diluted
Dirty Blanket
Don Potter
Donni Brooke
Double Down
Double Trouble
Doug Moncrieff
Driftwood
Druids
Dusk
Earl Weems Revue
Ed Isely
Eggie

Elementals
Eli Carr
Elmer Cobb Band
Ende Brothers
Ethos
Evan Muellman
Evan Nordstrom
Fakers
Fatima
Fiasco Brothers
Firewheel
5 Second Rule
Fog
Folk Faces
Franklin Mint Band
Fresh Fish
Gary Rose
Gary Rosenthal
Glen Wyand
Gold Rush
Good Cracker
Good Timing
Good Trip Band
Gordon Munding
Gray Hounds
Greg Gascon
Greg Wachala
Groovy Roots
Hard Logic
Heather Taylor
Heatwave
Heatwave Bluegrass
Henri Brothers String Band
Hi Roller
Hinkley
Hogsback Ridge Band
Honey & Vinegar
Honey Badgers
Industrial Strength

Or these?

Inside Out
Isabella Barbagallo
Isaiah
Jack West
James Draudt
Jaspur
Jay J Downe
Jeff Acker
Jeff Clark
Jim Adams
Jim Bristol Band
Joan Burch
Joe Davy Brothers
Joe Head
   & John Houck
Joe Mama
Joey Belladonna
John Benedict
John Bolger
John Mooney
   Blues Band
John Valby
Johnny Bauer
Johnny Burgin
Jokin Steves
Juliette & Warren
Jumbo Shrimp
Justin Gurnsey
Justin Moyar
Justin Williams
Katie Wright
Kelly Schroeder
Ken Hardly
Kerry Canaan
Kevin DeHond
   & the Catman
Kevin Doherty
Key Dreamers
Kids in the Basement

Kip Packard
Kubicks Rube
Last Note
Laura Thurston
Lauren Ellen Band
Leah & the Upheaval
Left Lane
Lefty
Lexi Weege
Lickety Split
Liquid Wrench
Lisa Winter
Lonely Ones
Loren Blankfield
Lub Dub
Mac Ingles
Margit & the 62
   Reserves
Mark Bradley
Martin Whelan
Marty Roberts
Matt Seidel
Max Creek
Max Doud
Max Flansberg
McKain Miller Band
Memphis Hill
Men Behaving Badly
Meteors
Michael Stets
Midnight Blues Band
Mike Brown
Mike Edwards
Mike Egardy
Mike Joseph
Mike Nolan
Mike Pappart
Mike Speranza
Miller's Wheel
Mitty & the Followers

Or these?

Montrois	Painted Birds
Moon Hollow	Panda Handstand
Mossback Mule Band	Pardigm Shift
	Patrick Lynch
MTV Band (Moore,	Paul Lewis
Tyrell & Vaughan)	Paul McDonald
Nate Coffee	Paul Strowe
Neil Marvel	Paulsen, Baker
Goodtime Band	& Garvey
Nicholas Deluc	Pearlz
Nightfall	Pete Griffith
Nightflight	Peter Donato
Nightstalkers	PJ Elliott
Nuthin' Fancy	Plain Jane
Old Salt	Poke the Bear
Old Souls Band	Quinasia
Old World Warblers	Racquette River
On the House	Rounders
Open Cajun Jam	Rain & Leaves
Osborne-Nash	Random Accents

Red Hot Blues Band	Shades of Gray
Red Means Go	Shari Ratka
Red Scott Project	Silver Lining
Reef Airs	61 Ghosts
Reeves & Swiatek	Skeleton Keys
Rehabeneros	Skycoaster
Rescue 11	Skyway
Rhythm Devils	Skull
Rick Wahlers	Slipton Fell
Rock-it-Science	Sourmash
Rockhouse Riot	South Street
Rockin' Red	Mission Band
& Billy Joe	Southern Comfort
Rollin' Rust	Spencer Samolis
Roscoes Basement	Squid
Rugburn	St. James Band
Sam Kaiser	St. Regis Band
Sam Nistche	Stay the Plow
Sarah Michelle	Steve Anderson
Savannah King	Steve Bartolotta

Or maybe these?

Steve Geraci	Teddy Keaton
Steve West	Texas Son
Steven Sorenson	Theresa Wilcox
Stovall Brown Band	Thigh Masters
String of Pearls	3 Chord Monty
Strings	Thinkin' Big
Sunday Afternoon Free Band	3rd Degree
	ThreadBaron
Suntreader	Thunder Rain
Sunup	Timothy Clayton Brayley
Swamp Root Singers	
Swamp Root String Band	Todd Hobin Band
	Tom Chamberlain
Sweet Tones	Tom Gunderson
Swinging Richards	Tom Vincent Band
Tanglewood	Tommy Brunett Band
Taylor Kelly & the Phonies	Tradewind Band
	Travis Fitch
Teagan & Lou	Trevor Holly Band
Teagan & the Tweeds	Tuned Ink

And last, but not least, these?

Tyler Pearce	"Wee Willie" Smith
Uncorked	Wild Roots Swing Band
Uptown Groove	
Venton Clark Band	Wilkes Boothe
Vince & Book	Will Billys
Vintage	Wolfgang & Gretchen
Vinyl	Yesterday's News
Violet Mary	You Can't Dance
Walt Atkison	

There are five people (that we know of to date) who have written original songs about the *Cottage Hotel*: *Steve Anderson, Keith Baker, Johnny Bauer, Brian Venton, and Jeff Williams (a.k.a. Earl Weems).* It would be hard to imagine *The Cottage* without them or the other musicians who have been such a special part of *The Cottage* musical vibe.[124]

ಛಿ ಛಿ ಛಿ

Paul Strowe is one musician who has performed as a successful solo artist but has also jammed with many of the groups that played at *The Cottage* over the past 50 years. Some were bands of his own invention, such as *Good Cracker, The Sunday Afternoon Free Band,* and the *Fiasco Brothers.*

Deedee Dutcher remembers Paul playing at *The Cottage* in the late '70s when the ceiling over the back room suddenly fell in next to the stage, and saying to him at the time, "Wow, Paul! You really brought down the house this time!"

He's been a mentor to many up-and-coming artists and has been a major part of *The Cottage* music scene since the Buzzy Bronson days. From 1986, until a few years ago, he toured as part of the *Todd Hobin Band.*

Needless to say, he's seen a lot of things happen at *The Cottage.* There were the legendary bathrooms, which before they were moved to the front of the bar made for many amusing scenes. "I have to say, aside from the smell, it was fun to watch people stagger back and forth," he says.

---

[124] See: *The Cottage Hotel Songbook,* Azalea Art Press, 2023, for the lyrics and music to these original songs.

Paul Strowe
(Courtesy: Paul Strowe.)

Paul remembers Laurie Latham, who worked the door at *The Cottage*, fondly.

> *Everyone loved Laurie, who was honest as the day was long and always gave the musicians the money from the door that they worked so hard to earn. This was not always the case at other clubs.*
>
> *Laurie was the perfect door person. She wouldn't let anyone in without paying. We joked that if her mother showed up, she'd probably make her pay, too.*
>
> *Blues guitarist John Mooney, who was already quite famous at the time, came to hear us play. Laurie stopped him at the door and asked for the two dollars. "Do you know who*

> *I am?" John said. "Yeah," said Laurie. "Now cough up the two bucks or you can't come in!"*
>
> *Unfortunately, Laurie died in her twenties, but everyone loved her, especially the bands.*

Under Burdock's reign, Paul's group the *Fiasco Brothers* inaugurated the first *Mug Club* night and played there every Tuesday until Burdock's untimely death. As he tells us:

> *It was very prophetic and ironic that John decided to end his own life. One time at closing, Burdock confided in me, saying, "I had to get out of working for Dun & Bradstreet. The stress of a job like that will kill you . . . and I don't want to die young!"*

All in all, Paul echoes the sentiments that many of us have about *The Cottage*:

> *It's an authentic 'townie' bar, a place where everyone knows everyone, and everyone feels comfortable. Even if you're from out of town, you instantly feel like you're part of the place. (Plus, the food is really, really good!)*

଼ ଼ ଼

Another musician with special ties to The Cottage is Brian Venton. In 1977, when he was 17, Brian Venton began performing at *The Cottage* as the lead of the group *Autumn Skies*. That spring the band made a 45 record that attracted an agent, Pelican Productions, and for two years they played all over the state. But *The Cottage* was their first professional gig. Later on, they also played regularly at the *Mason Jar*, but *The Cottage* stage was their favorite.

Autumn Skies L-R Mark Smith, Brian Venton, Scott Brown (kneeling), and Randy Stuckless (standing)

(Courtesy: Brian Venton.)

From the early '80s, Brian created a succession of bands such as *NIK & The Nice Guys*, *The Boss Street Band*, and *Keys to the Caddy*. A chance meeting with Jeff Clark in 2018 led Brian to form the acoustic-rock *Venton Clark Band*, that now play at *The Cottage* once a month along with Steve Krauss (of Mendon) on drums and sometimes additional musicians. But the memories of those early days at *The Cottage* still burn bright.

"We were like moths to a flame," he says. "We'd play all night, party 'til dawn, then get up and do it all over again." And here's Brian's touching tribute to those good times:

On Cobblestone Fields[125]

It was a time, was a time
It was a time, oh what a time it was

Verse 1:

Late 70 something, as fortunes would tell
We all had a voice, we all found our song
Strummers and singers, played on played well
We ushered in angels, and flirted with hell

Of drovers and drummers, a silent dove sings
The river rolled on, the flow was so sweet
To celebrate life, on open wings
Aching with love, for better things

(Chorus:)

In the Cottage, on the corner, of Cobblestone Fields
It was a time, was a time
It was a time, oh what a time it was

Verse 2:

With love in the music, spirits run wild
The timing was perfect, a symphony score
Locals and newbies, a laugh and a smile
All in one head, at least for that while

After a show, at Burdock's old place
We danced under the stars, with freedom and grace
Before the sun peeked, with warmest goodbyes
We bid final farewell, to those warm smiling eyes

(Chorus:)

In the Cottage, on the corner, of Cobblestone Fields
It was a time, was a time
It was a time, oh what a time it was

---

[125] *On Cobblestone Fields* © Brian Venton, 2023.

❦ ❦ ❦

Jeff Clark, who has played at *The Cottage* since the mid-'70s (when he was in high school), also has vibrant memories of *The Cottage*.

> *The Cottage, always one of the go-to places for musicians, loved and encouraged local music. There was a communal atmosphere there with no competition between artists — we would invite each other up on stage and all have a good time.*
>
> *I was in a duo with Paul Strowe then called 'Good Cracker.' We would all play for the door, and sometimes I would come home with $400-500 in my pocket. Not bad for a 17-year-old!*

As it seems to be for most musicians, Jeff was propositioned many times by women who had had way too much to drink. Jeff's favorite line from one of the female patrons who had just invited him to dinner was, "Oh, by the way, I'm on birth control!"

Nothing like a bit of romance, eh Jeff?

After many years of being away, Jeff returned to Mendon. At *The Cottage*, he noted, the layout of the bar remained the same, with the exact same vibe of a place that was welcoming to everyone. But as Jeff attests, Dave and Hilary Stott have made it an even more community-minded endeavor.

Several years ago, Hilary started the Mendon Music Festival, and for several years in the parking lot of Mendon 64 she put together 8-10 local bands and a headliner for a day of music and camaraderie. After her costs, the profits from the event went directly to the local musicians — something that has led us to praise her as the "Godmother of Local Musicians." It's an example of how committed she was and is to Mendon hamlet and our community.

ଔ ଔ ଔ

One iconic band that has spanned generations of enthusiastic *Cottage* fans is *Paulsen, Baker & Garvey*.

John Paulsen, Keith Baker, & John Garvey
(Courtesy: Keith Baker.)

John Paulsen, Keith Baker, & John Garvey
(Courtesy: Keith Baker.)

For over 50 years, (until recently) they have played at *The Cottage* at least six times a year. Although John Garvey left the group seven years ago, John Paulsen and Keith Baker continue to perform, sometimes with special guests Tim Chaapel and Warren Paul.

"*The Cottage* is a classic," Keith Baker says. "Back in the day, everyone in Rochester knew about it, especially musicians. And it still has the ambiance and atmosphere that drew us to it in the first place."

Burdock was a big fan of *Paulsen, Baker & Garvey*. "He booked us at the *Mason Jar*, and we enjoyed both places, but we always felt more comfortable at *The Cottage*. John felt we belonged there. He was right. It was smaller, and homier, and better suited to our music."

They've seen a few things, too . . . like the time they walked in to set up early and found two huge Newfoundland dogs in front of the bar chewing on a cow's head. "You don't ask too many questions about a thing like that," Keith laughs.

Like other bands that played at *The Cottage*, they found that the location of the stage was often an occasion for humor.

> *We'd often joke to the audience that we planned to be near the ladies' room so we could watch them go by. Later on, when they tore the bathrooms out and relocated everything up front near the bar, some had a hard time remembering.*
>
> *One time, in the middle of a set, an obviously very drunk guy staggered past and began relieving himself right against the wall next to us, thinking he was in the men's room. That was quite an eventful night!*

On perhaps a much more inspiring note, Keith was so impacted by *The Cottage* that he wrote a tune titled *This Song*, with a chorus that perfectly describes the layout of the bar and the challenges of getting close to the band when *The Cottage* was packed with people—something anyone who has been there on a crowded night will relate to . . .

This Song[126]

Verse 1:

You heard the group was really good.
You'd like to see them, if you could
so you brought along a dozen friends or more.
When you arrived, the man said, "Wait!"
that you'd arrived a little late.
"There's only standing room, out on the floor."

(Chorus)

*Then, this song goes out to you,
in the back room, by the back door,
by the Foosball table, by the juke box, by the bar.
Yeah! This song goes out to those who don't know it,
'cause they can't hear me sing it, where they are.*

Verse 2:

You love someone who's in the band.
He's tall, good looking and well-tanned.
He smiles at you and sings your favorite song.
You hear him singing that song now.
You'd like to see him, if somehow
the crowd in front of you would move along.

(Chorus & Refrain):

*Well, it's nice to go out for some music.
and it's nice to sit down with a beer.
It's nice to share a song and, maybe, sing along
It's too bad when you can't even hear.*

---

[126] From *This Song* © Keith W. Baker, 1978, 2023. You can view the video sung by Keith Baker, John Garvey, and Tim Chaapel at:
https://www.youtube.com/watch?v=HTm0GXarkX8.

Verse 3:

They play the music, that you love,
still, you don't like to push and shove,
well, now they're at a concert hall, that's near.
The tickets cost you 80 bucks.
She buys a gown, you rent a tux,
but in the back row, you can hardly hear.

(Chorus)

John Paulsen, Keith Baker, & John Garvey
(Courtesy: Keith Baker.)

Another band known for performing an original *Cottage Hotel* tune is *Slipton Fell*. Beginning in August, 1978, while attending Pittsford-Mendon High School, members of *Slipton Fell*[127] played frequently at *The Cottage* when Burdock owned it. Later, also thanks to Burdock, they played regularly at the *Mason Jar*.

Slipton Fell at the *Cottage Hotel*
Steve Anderson, Mark DeAngelis, & Jeff Decker
(Courtesy: Steve Anderson.)

---

[127] *Slipton Fell* was formed by Steve Anderson (guitar, vocals), Chris Cady (guitar, vocals), Mark DeAngelis (drums) and Dave Knight (bass). They later added Jeff Decker. When Mark and Dave left the band, Joe West (drums) and Don Torpy (bass) joined, as did Kit Cady (keyboards) in 2012. Korie Pettee (keyboards, vocals), the newest member of the band, joined in 2022.

The group became well known for their original tunes, but also for their covers of the *Grateful Dead*, *Tom Petty & the Heartbreakers*, and *Little Feat* songs. Burdock personally championed the band's early career throughout Upstate New York and beyond.

Steve Anderson was so inspired by his experiences at *The Cottage*, that he wrote a ballad, *(You'll Never Feel Alone) at the Cottage Hotel,* as a testament to the good times we all had there; as well as *Powder Mill*, another song that features *The Cottage*.

Here are the lyrics to both:

(You'll Never Feel Alone) at the Cottage Hotel[128]

Verse 1:

I'm sittin' here at this bar,
drinking Tanqueray and tonics.
Glass filled full of stars, heart filled full of stones.
I've always been a dreamer, out there alone.
So I set down the glass, pick up my phone.

"Hey, it's me. I'm at the Cottage.
Yeah that's right. I know, big surprise.
So many roads we have travelled,
the children have all grown
But sittin' here at this bar, sure does feels like home."

---

[128] *(You'll Never Feel Alone) at the Cottage Hotel* © Steve Anderson, 2019. You can view the video for this tune at: https://www.youtube.com/watch?v=pffVf0fqb94 as well as the video for the song *Powder Mill* at:
https://www.youtube.com/watch?v=38p8KuD3HzY.

(Chorus)

So raise your glass.
A toast to our lost loved ones.
May they always walk among us.
Be our shining light.
Every person here tonight has a story to tell.
You'll never be alone at the Cottage Hotel.

Verse 2:

I see John behind the bar, he's laughin' with Craiger.
Laurie's at the door, in comes Space Invaders.
Jimmy's playing Foosball, Jeff's up on the stage.
And now everybody's dancin', but hey, it's gettin' late.

So one more drink, then I'll go.
I just wanted to let you know.
That I will always love you.
Please remember that.
May the winds of good fortune
be always at your back.

(Chorus)

Verse 3:

I'm still sittin' at this bar,
when you walk in door.
That smile upon your face, might be my saving grace.
Come now sit beside me, rest your weary bones.
We'll talk of trains and summer rain,
and places yet to roam.

It's closing time, it's time I go.
But I'll be back next time around.
Until we meet again, I wish you well.

The prettiest girls are at the Cottage Hotel.

(Chorus)

You'll never be alone at the Cottage Hotel.
You'll never be alone at the Cottage Hotel.
You'll never be alone at the Cottage Hotel.

Powder Mill[129]

Verse 1:

A church bell rings down in the village.
A smile, oft-remembered well.
Flowers bloom along the towpath,
As we drift on down along the old canal.
I see you standin' at Four Corners.
A certain sadness in your eyes.
Colonial Days parade, seems like yesterday.
Never had the chance to say goodbye.

(Chorus)

Walk with us into the summer.
Meet us down at Powder Mill.
We'll drink some beers, count the years.
We love you now, and always will.

Verse 2:

There's no more milk down at the Milk Store.
In the Basin, just passin' through?
Or maybe we all just dreamt the same dream—
Somewhere, beyond the moon?

(Chorus)

Verse 3:

Creek's run dry down by the Mill Wheel.
Skippin' school, but still passed the test.
Ever sweeter for the leaving, my friend.
Walk with your ghosts in Shady Rest.

(Chorus)

Verse 4:

Fish are jumpin' down at the hatchery.
The leaves have turned from green to gold.
Maybe we see the way things used to be.
Or maybe we're all just getting old.

---

[129] *Powder Mill* © Steve Anderson, 2019.

(Chorus)

Verse 5:

**Thought I saw you drinkin' whiskey.
At the ol' Hotel, after the fair.
But then the band begins to play,
and it all just fades away . . .
Let sweet soulful songs fill the air.**

(a cappella Chorus)

☙   ☙   ☙

Chris Cady, guitarist and vocalist for the band, credits Jeff Decker for giving *Slipton Fell* their first break. Decker, who had just joined the band, gave up one of his own regular solo Sunday gigs to make room for them to play at *The Cottage*.

As a child, Chris saw the *Cottage Hotel* sign every week on his way to church at St. Catherine's, and he wondered what the term "Legal Beverages Sold Here" meant, never suspecting how much time he'd spend at *The Cottage*—or how many legal beverages he'd eventually consume there!

Guitarist and lyricist Steve Anderson came to be a very close friend of Burdock's. He tells us this story about the early years of *Slipton Fell*:

> *In August of 1978, Slipton Fell was playing on the eve of my 18th birthday. Two other members of the band were also under 18, though we'd been playing there for well over a year already. Burdock knew this and didn't*

> care, but that night he got a tip they were going to be raided and said we couldn't play unless our parents were there.
>
> We all tore off in different directions to get our folks. Mine were playing tennis at the Mendon Tennis Club and I had to run onto the court waving my arms to get their attention. Thankfully for them, they only had to stay until midnight.

Chris Cady has this to add to that story:

> We learned later that it was the PTA of Pittsford-Mendon High School (where several of us were going to school), that out-of-the-blue decided to make a stink about us playing at The Cottage. But we never slowed down, and luckily after that first occasion we were never bothered by them again.
>
> A lot of us got into The Cottage when we were underage, as they wouldn't begin proofing anyone until they collected the cover charge at night. So by the time we played there for the first time, we'd already been coming to The Cottage for quite a while and I'd say most of the friends who came to see us were underage, too.

Chris also has wonderful memories of Burdock:

> Burdock was really good to us. The tradition of him passing around a bottle of peppermint schnapps between sets started with us at The Cottage and is celebrated in the song "Once Chance to Live it." We kind of introduced (or re-introduced) him to Grateful Dead tunes and we went to shows with him occasionally. He liked them so much that he brought a Dead-tribute band, Max Creek, to The Cottage that went on to have regional and even national success.

Chris remembers them playing the *Grateful Dead* song *U.S. Blues* and Burdock jumping up and down doing his famous dance—one that came to be known as "The Burdock Hop."

> John also had us play on Tuesday nights at the Mason Jar, which was a much larger venue than The Cottage. I'm not sure we would have played there it if wasn't for him.

> *Every time we played at The Cottage, it was an edgy, raucous affair. We would fill the place — and still do. Back then, we would step outside the front door at the end of the night and the place would just come apart. We were like rock stars in our own little world. Pretty heady stuff for teenagers!*
>
> *We'd go back in to play an encore and it would become an even crazier, mad affair. We were exhausted at the end of the night, but it was flat-out fun! All we wanted to do was to continue to the party . . . and often we did.*
>
> *It's a funny thing. We only played as a band from August of 1978 until New Year's Eve of 1981. It was just 3 1/2 years. Our first gig was at The Cottage and our last gig was at the Mason Jar (talk about bookends!) Since 1982, we've been playing class reunions and that tradition continues today.*

There came a time when the band, for various reasons, was ready to part ways. Chris Cady describes *Slipton Fell's* last official gig:

> *In 1981, following the band Lickety Split, we played our last New Year's Eve set, and after that the band dissolved. It seemed like the right time, as we had lost some of our key players and the momentum was gone. Both Jeff Decker and Mark DeAngelis are now deceased but we celebrate them each time we*

gather for reunion concerts – we've never gone more than two years without having one, beginning in 2006, when Hilary Stott reopened the Cottage.

Slipton Fell at the *Cottage Hotel*
Steve Anderson, Chris Cady, & Dave Knight
(Courtesy: Steve Anderson.)

Both Steve and Chris are also great admirers of Hilary Stott's dedication to local musicians. Says Chris:

Like Burdock, Hilary has been very good to us, always making special allowances to make things work. Before Covid, she had live bands six nights a week, including an open mic on Sundays. During Covid, she allowed us to play outside on the patio while people picked up their to-go orders. That kept us going.

When she started the Mendon Music Festival in 2021, that was a huge boost for local musicians who had been basically shut down during Covid. She's always had great creative ideas to promote us, leading us to give her the nickname "The Idea Factory."

Korie Pettee & Chris Cady
(Courtesy: Chris Cady.)

From 2017 on, Chris launched a solo career. He now plays 130 shows a year as a duo with good friend guitarist, vocalist, and keyboardist Korie Pettee — whom he met when he just happened to stop by Open Mic Night at . . . the *Cottage Hotel*!

ೂ ೂ ೂ

Beginning in the late '80s, Tom Price headed a popular band called *Gold Rush* that played at *The Cottage* over a ten-year span.

Tom Price, Joann Grieco, George Botticelli
(Photos courtesy: Tom Price.)

Gold Rush[130] was formed in 1986 by Tom Price, George Botticelli, and Rich Herb. The band covered

---

[130] A very versatile (and playful) band, they also appeared in costume at *The Cottage* on Halloween, calling themselves "Ghould Rush." (See their photo in costume on page 200.)

a wide range of music styles and genres including rock, soul, R&B, blues, and more. "We played live using instrumentation and recorded drum tracks that we created and used to give us a percussion background while playing our instruments and singing," says Tom.

They played as a trio for 11 years before Rich Herb left in 1997. Vocalist Joann Grieco joined the band, then singer/guitarist Peg Dolan. Joann Grieco rejoined the band through 2013 and Tom and George now perform with *Mr. Mustard*, a *Beatles* tribute band.

George Botticelli, Peg Dolan, Tom Price

Tom remembers one very memorable night when owner Lou DiNardo wanted to host an "Aloha Night" to celebrate the arrival of spring.

The band was pleased to be asked to perform. To add to the ambiance, we asked that people wear something tropical and then provided sunglasses and Hawaiian leis to those who attended! We and the crowd had a fabulous evening, and Lou was very happy with the turnout and the festive mood!

See anyone you know in these photographs?

Gold Rush Hawaiian Night at the Cottage Hotel

(Photos from the archives of Tom Price)

"We loved playing at The Cottage, says Tom. "Some of our best memories are there. It was the best!"

Johnny Bauer & Nikki Paris

Another musician with fond memories of *The Cottage* is Johnny Bauer, who has played there for over a decade. He now performs with his partner and bandmate Nicki Paris, whom he met and fell in love with at . . . you guessed it . . . *The Cottage Hotel*!

"I've met so many wonderful people at *The Cottage*," he says. "And I'm still friends with many of them after all these years."

Johnny's original song, *One Horse Town*, celebrates what it felt and still feels like to play at *The Cottage*.

One Horse Town[131]

Verse 1:

Some people came for me
While others just came to eat
I overheard her say, "I hope he's not too loud."
As the night goes on
And I'm strumming along
Looks like it's gonna be a pretty good crowd
Then the drinks start to flow
And the tips start to grow
All I can think is I hope she likes me

(Chorus)

Another beer another shot
Gonna give it all I've got
To play you your favorite songs
At the end of the night
When everyone is feeling alright
And the jukebox plays on and on
Until next week rolls around
I'll be back, back in this one horse town

Verse 2:

There's a girl at the bar
Watching me play guitar
I can tell that she'd love to dance
There's a guy named Jim
With a wide-eyed grin
Thinking that he might stand a chance
Then the beer starts to flow
And the tips start to grow
All I can think is I hope they like me

(Chorus)

---

[131] *One Horse Town* © Johnny Bauer, 2012.

Verse 3:

When the night draws to an end
I pick up my gear again
Hear the bartender yell "last call for alcohol!"
Have a toast with my friends
May these nights never end
With this I make my solemn vow

(Chorus)

ᘓ ᘓ ᘓ

Jeff Williams, founding member of *Earl Weems Revue*, is another talented creator of an original *Cottage Hotel* tune. Jeff first picked up a guitar at age twelve. Before long he had formed a band with two other Honeoye Falls musicians—blues guitarist John Mooney and drummer Jesse Presto.

By age 20, Jeff was playing places like the *Cottage Hotel* with drummer John Chaffer, guitarist Bill Jones, and Dave Helander on bass as the *Burned Out Blues Band*.

Jeff Williams
(Photo by: Chris Shaffer.)

Earl Weems Revue:
Mike Archer, Kerry Keating, Dave Helander,
John Chaffer, Earl Weems (Jeff Williams), Hap Harrison
(missing are Ed Kosenski & Pete Freeman)

Mooney played The Cottage before we did, and eventually we followed his lead and started playing there too. By the late '70s, the music scene was exploding. The Cottage was great. That was our stompin' grounds. We could count on the fact that on a Saturday night sooner or later everyone would show up and the place would be packed. We could take in over $300 just from charging $1 at the door. Pretty good bucks back then!

We kept adding band members and from 1976-1978 we performed as the Earl Weems Revue, which was named after my grandmother's pronunciation of our last name

Williams as "Weeyums." The 'Earl' part was a direct nod to Earl Scruggs, who at the time had a band with two of his sons — the Earl Scruggs Revue.

The Earl Weems Revue had myself on guitar and vocals, keyboardist Kerry Keating, Hap Harrison on pedal steel guitar, Mike Archer on guitar, Dave Helander on bass, John Chaffer on drums and Ed Kosenski on sax. Pete Freeman later joined on pedal steel guitar when Hap Harrison dropped out around 1977. The last edition of the Revue had seven players. It was definitely a Big Band sound!

We played a very eclectic mix of Blues, R&B, Western Swing, and Country Rock influenced by NRBQ (the New Rhythm and Blues Quartet), Bob Wills and the Texas Playboys, Asleep at the Wheel, and a variety of Chicago blues artists. It was great dance music — lots of people showed up to do swing dancing. Some of our live gigs were broadcast on WCMF.

For the last 32 years, Jeff has been a music teacher. In 2000, he built the "sunny face" guitar in the photo on page 250 that was based on the logo for the *Coolrays* out of San Diego. "It looks better than it plays," he admits. Since then, Jeff has recorded as *Jeffrey D & the J-Dubs,* and performs with the

Coolrays and the *Jackstraws* (Jeff Williams, Loren Smith, Jeff Bristol) in the San Diego area, where he now lives. Here's his original *Cottage Hotel* song:

Good Old Days[132]

Verse 1:

I think a lot about the good old days
when I was back in Honeoye Falls
About sticky summer days and cold winter nights,
but that's not what I like to recall.
I can't forget about the days with ZBB
and good rockin' with ol' Billy Jones
I used to spend a lot of nights down at Bates pond
with the people I could call my own

(Chorus:)

Those old days were good old days,
but these days are pretty good, too.
I may be a little bit older, a wee bit wiser,
but I can't choose between the two.
I don't know which I like better, but that's okay, too,
'cause those old days were good old days
but these are pretty good days, too.

Verse 2:

Well, you could hear a radio show,
live stereo with Rockin' Red or Roomful of Blues
Playin' in a bar on a fat guitar
that's liable to be hot enough to light any fuse.
If I went back today it wouldn't be the same,
but I got lots of friends who remember
That if you raise enough hell at the Cottage Hotel
you can keep the place warm in December.

---

[132] *Good Old Days*, © Jeffrey D. Williams, 2023.

Pretty good times! Pretty good times!

(Bridge:)

Well, thinkin' 'bout the days that used to be
is fun but you gotta move on
Gotta live for today and leave the past alone
you'll be wishin' your life away
Hey-yay, yeah!

(Guitar solo)

(Repeat chorus(es)

ZBB
(The Zero Blues Band)
Jeff Williams, John Weyl, John Mooney, Gus Buckman
(Courtesy: Geoffrey Navias.)

ಙ ಙ ಙ

Part 4
Wild Things

After combing her memory bank back to now forty years ago (no easy task for any of us these days), *Cottage* fan Anita Houston recalls: "There were just too many bands to remember! But I do recall Jeff Decker of *Slipton Fell* trying to keep his 12-string in tune on a cold night by sitting near the heater away from the draft from the front door."

She also recounts the time a woman pulled a knife on her for asking "her man" to dance."

> *I had no idea he was with her, and after all it was just a dance! Also, there was a Foosball table at the back of the bar then. When we weren't dancing, my friend (who had rather large breasts) and I would play Foosball — braless of course.*

"We won . . . a lot," Anita reports, with more than a glimmer of mischief in her voice.

And let's not forget the iconic jukebox at The *Cottage*. Dick Joint remembers that when he was 18 or 19 (almost 60 years ago) the jukebox played all, or almost all, country music . . . like *Hank Snow, Eddy Arnold, Patsy Cline,* and *Loretta Lynn*.

Rosemary (Heckman) Lewis, whose parents owned *The Cottage* for 22 years, hated country music back then, though she's since come to appreciate it.

> *I remember mostly '50s songs like "Rock Around the Clock" and one horrible earworm called "The Battle of New Orleans" that I can remember in its entirety even now and damn near drove me crazy! There were also some classic '40s tunes like "In the Mood" that my parents would jitterbug to — they had won dance contests during the war and were really good at it!*

In the late '60s, '70s, and early '80s, *The Cottage* jukebox played an eclectic mix of country, oldies, and rock 'n roll tunes.

Patty Gorham remembers the jukebox fondly, for it played some of her favorites: the *Rolling Stones*, the *Beatles*, and *Willie Nelson* and *Waylon Jennings* singing "Luckenbach, Texas (Back To The Basics Of Love)," the *Byrds'* version of "Mr. BoJangles," and that favorite of unhappy souls working a gig they can't stand: *Johnny Paycheck's* classic "Take This Job and Shove It."

As Patty recalls . . . [133]

---

[133] The original jukebox was replaced in 2003 with an internet jukebox.

> *For a quarter you could get three or four songs and since people kept popping quarters into the jukebox, music went on pretty much continuously during the day. It was fun to watch the record drop and the needle come down on the 45 rpm singles. Everything is digital now, of course, but I sure do miss that jukebox!*

One of the appeals of *The Cottage* has always been its tendency to be a little relaxed about a number of things. Back in the late '60s, Patty Gorham and her good friend, Cathy Calkins, then 15 or 16, would jump into Cathy's brand new baby blue *Mustang* convertible and drive from Canandaigua to *The Cottage* where the bartenders never blinked an eye.

> *The minimum drinking age was 18, but they always served us, even if we forgot our fake ID's. We loved coming to The Cottage because it was far enough away from our hometown that no one would recognize us. Plus, there were a lot of cute guys there from McQuaid High School who were around our same age. It was a place that we could let go of our inhibitions and just have a great time.*

Decked out in their tight jeans and tube tops, and with Cathy's ravishing blonde hair and Patty's long, sultry brunette locks, they must have made quite a duo pulling up to *The Cottage* in that baby blue *Mustang*.

We'd drink beer, mostly, but people also bought us shots of peppermint schnapps and tequila. We went there mostly during the day after school when things were relatively calm. At night things got a little crazier with people dancing on the tables. But not me! I was afraid I'd fall off! My parents were very strict, and I was grounded quite a number of times even though we did our best to sober up before heading back home.

That things could get a little wild on weekends at *The Cottage* might be an understatement. As Patty has remarked, dancing on the bar and tables was commonplace, and sometimes crowds flowed out into the streets.

Richard Crowther had one experience that sticks with him to this day:

This story goes back to sometime in the early summer of 1974. It was a Friday or Saturday night, probably around 8:00 p.m. and there was a line of people waiting to get into The Cottage. This was when they were using the entrance door on Route 64.

I don't remember what band was playing, but it was one that would attract a good crowd, possibly 'Old Salt.' At any rate, I was in line with my then girlfriend, Debbie Weiland, and a couple of other people. No doubt we had already started partying earlier in the evening so we were well on our way to having a great time.

Tommy Thompson, the manager, was standing around the entrance door when a fairly inebriated patron, whose name I won't use, wandered around the corner with a close-to-empty Heinekens bottle in his hand. In the blink of an eye, he was next to Tommy and raised the bottle and shattered it on his head.

The only time I had ever seen that happen was in the movies and those were of course fake bottles. Oddly, it didn't knock Tommy out, and the two of them then started fighting. The staff was out there in a heartbeat and pulled the two apart. Apparently they had been arguing earlier in the evening or that day.

(Rochester Democrat and Chronicle, August 24, 1975.)

> *This ended it and those of us waiting in line were let inside.*
>
> *Funny, but I don't remember why we were even waiting in line, but had we not been I would not have experienced this. I'll be honest — I don't remember much about the rest of the evening — which is not surprising. I'm sure we ended up having a great time drinking and dancing and who knows what else. It was a fun time back then!*

As Pittsford native Tad Van Zandt recalls, motorcycle gangs would occasionally show up at *The Cottage*. Usually they were not looking for trouble, but in one instance Tad was forced to jump into the fray.

> *I was at The Cottage in '77 getting trashed when six iron horsemen came through the door swinging three-foot doubled up chains! Everyone dove under tables anywhere they could and I went off to one side.*
>
> *They cleared the bar and since I'd had a previous encounter with them, I had attitude. I ran to my car, a Maverick with no muffler system, and chased them all the way to Pittsford. Then the shit hit the fan! I caught them!*

Tad doesn't tell us what happened next, but it couldn't have been pretty. He obviously lived to tell the tale, though.

According to the *Democrat and Chronicle*, fights at *The Cottage* were nothing new. Back on June 5, 1948, after seven minutes of deliberation, two men—one from Henrietta, the other from Fishers—were convicted of third-degree assault after a barroom brawl at 1:30 a.m. on May 16th at *The Cottage*. The trial "attracted a large crowd of townsfolk."

In 1951,[134] Lewis D. Woodward of Holcomb was arrested for carrying "a Japanese pistol" concealed under his coat. The man recklessly brandished the weapon in the *Cottage Hotel* bar, shouting, somewhat comically, *"I'll show you what I'm going to do. I'm going to plug someone."* The gun was wrested from his hands by two bystanders and the chamber found to be empty. It's not known if any charges were ever filed against him—at least there were no follow-up newspaper reports found.

Dick Joint recounts a time in the late '60s when he had been to a stag party in Rochester. Dressed (for some strange reason) in suits, Dick, the groom and his soon-to-be father-in-law, a friend who worked with Dick, stopped at *The Cottage* for a beer on their way home.

---

[134] From the March 6, 1951 issue of the *Canandaigua Daily Messenger*.

We were minding our own business when three or four guys from Rush came in and started a fight. I'd been a wrestler in high school and now I was a roofer, so I was built like a rock back then. In two seconds, I put one of them on the floor and together we tossed them out of the bar.

On their way out, they threw something and broke the front windows, then apparently went down the street to the Springwater Inn and caused a ruckus there. The next day, my spine was killing me. I didn't have any memory of it, but my friend said, "Don't you remember? One of those guys slammed you over the back with a wooden chair."

Accidents, of course, can also happen, and they can prove to be both dangerous and embarrassing. On January 6, 2014, when showing a pistol to a friend, a man having lunch at *The Cottage* accidentally shot himself in the hand. The bullet also grazed the ankle of his friend sitting next to him. Thankfully, their injuries were minor and no charges were filed (the gun owner had a permit), but it certainly added to the excitement of the lunch crowd that day, especially the mother whose baby was sleeping in its stroller at the next table.

One tale of local mischief that involves the *Cottage Hotel* is told by Fred Seager, a good friend of Robert F. ("Bob") Clifford:

Fred Seager & Pat Dwyer
with the refinished *Tallo's Towne Tavern* sign
photographed at *Thirsty's* in 2014
(Courtesy: Fred Seager.)

In July of 1971, on the last Saturday night before Tallo's Towne Tavern in Pittsford was sold to Gerry Clifford and officially became Thirsty's, as a joke someone made off with the Tallo's sign. Much like the "exchange" of mascots on college campuses, this was a time-honored tradition between Tallo's and the Cottage Hotel. Unfortunately, this particular prank caused the closing party at Tallo's to be cancelled.

There were a lot of disappointed people that night and the mystery was never solved until years later, when the sign showed up in the barn beside the Cottage Hotel. It had been stashed there by Phil Selke and Mike Clifford a.k.a. "Snowball" (no relation to the Pittsford Clifford family).

In August of 2003, my wife, Diane, and I came home and were surprised to see the sign leaning up against my garage. It remained at my home until 2014 when I refinished it and hung it back up at Thirsty's — but it had spent 34 mysterious years as a fugitive, silently hiding in the barn at The Cottage.

Jeremy Fisher, son of Baird Fisher and former Cottage owner Jacky (Muzdakis) Fisher, remembers seeing the Tallo's sign in The Cottage barn when he was growing up. He'd always wondered what it was doing there. Now he, and we, have the inside scoop!

ඏ ඏ ඏ

Weekends were naturally when most of the action happened at *The Cottage*, but weeknights were not exempt from a little insanity now and then. One veteran *Cottage Hotel* bartender laughs when he remembers a group of ladies getting very drunk the night before the dedication of the bridge that had just been rebuilt next to *The Cottage* over Irondequoit Creek.

The ladies all took off their bras and strung them together into a banner that they attached from one side of the bridge to the other. When the mucky-mucks from the state showed up the next day for the dedication, they were given quite an eye-popping surprise!

The bra story never made the papers, but it's still talked about in the hamlet. As P.T. Barnum once said, "There's no such thing as bad publicity." In the case of the *Cottage Hotel*, this might be particularly true, for from the beginning it has been considered by some to be more of a hardcore shot and beer-drinking tavern, what some might call a "dive bar" — but, as we've made clear earlier, that term being used only in the most positive sense.

**The Front Interior Exit
at The Cottage Hotel of Mendon**

*"You can check out any time you want,
but you can never leave."*[135]

---

[135] From the *Eagles'* song, "Hotel California."

With all the wild times that occurred, for many of us *The Cottage* was a home away from home—a place of friendship and unconditional acceptance that some had never experienced before, or since.

ഗ ഗ ഗ

That's how I like to think of those halcyon days—a time when we were still innocent and free, when we made love, not war, and when we gathered at the *Cottage Hotel* to listen to great music and just have a good time together. As far as we can tell those days are not over, not by a long stretch!

Chapter XIV

*And the Beat Goes On:
Cottage Kids Take the Stage!*

**In true *Cottage Hotel* spirit
Fiona Fisher celebrates turning one year old in 2019**
(Courtesy: Keegan and Jeremy Fisher.)

A beautiful manifestation of the power of love that *The Cottage* symbolizes lives on in the generations of *Cottage Babies, Cottage Kids,* and *Cottage Grandbabies* who are an inseparable part of *Cottage Hotel* history.

According to local legend, some *Cottage Babies* may have actually been conceived right here on the premises. No matter where their parents may have been at that exact moment, the second their progeny cross the *Cottage Hotel* doorstep they are considered honorary *regulars*.

☙ ☙ ☙

The Cottage has always been a family affair, especially if your parents owned the place.

When they bought *The Cottage*, in 1950, Al and Mary Heckman had two young children, Tommy and Rosemary, to raise.

Rosemary (Heckman) Lewis lived at *The Cottage* from the time she was four until she was in her early twenties when her parents sold the bar in 1972 to Bob Clifford. She remembers growing up there as if it were yesterday.

> *The Cottage had sixteen rooms. There were eight bedrooms and a living room on the top floor that looked out over the balcony and the Mendon Hotel across the street. Downstairs were the tap room, two dining rooms, two kitchens, and several storage rooms.*
>
> *The spooky basement had a dirt floor with two cisterns to capture the rainwater from the roof, the oil furnace, a pump for the well, and a bottle chute.*

On the next page is Rosemary, top row center, in first grade at Honeoye Falls Central School in 1953. Her best friend, Holly Feldman, is in the top row, second from left.

It was great living there! My father worked the day shift and my mother worked nights until well after closing at two in the morning, so my brother and I, unlike other kids our age, felt like we had a lot of freedom growing up, despite the fact that everyone else in the hamlet kept an eagle eye on us. (In reality, we really couldn't get away with anything!)

Of course we weren't like most of the other children in the hamlet. We saw and heard a lot of things that most kids would not — sometimes by listening at the heat registers in the floor above (where you could hear almost every word!), and by peeking through the crack in the floor near the back stairs.

From an early age my brother and I had a lot of responsibility, which also set us apart from other kids. We helped my mother and the cooks in the kitchen. We cleaned up the bar on Sundays, scaled the haddock on newspapers out in the yard for the fish frys, sliced cabbage for the coleslaw, and peeled and hand made all the French fries with a Guillotine-like machine.

It was my job to do all the dishes. There was a chute behind the bar that led to the basement, and my brother was in charge of sorting all the beer bottles for recycling. That was a whole lot of work, too.

Mendon was a working class town. Some of the parents wouldn't allow their kids to play with us because we lived above a bar but The Cottage was really a family situation. A lot of the same people who came there almost every day also celebrated holidays with us. We knew everyone and they all looked out for us.

Like other hamlet kids, we had dogs and rabbits for pets. I took piano lessons on the piano in the bar. We played on the balcony until my mother had it torn down and in the backyard where Ike and Hazel Stanley had a large cage next door with a pet squirrel. It was surrounded by lilac bushes of all colors. In spring, when the breeze blew, the scent of the lilacs (not the squirrel) was just like heaven!

> *Although I sometimes wished my parents worked normal jobs, we were just normal regular kids.*
>
> *In winter we sledded on the hill behind the cobblestone house across from The Mendon Academy, had snowball fights, and ice skated and played hockey on the creek. We looked forward to eating sundaes and banana splits made with the homemade ice cream from Habecker's next door. Banana Splits cost $1 and had three slices of banana, six scoops of ice cream, whipped cream, and 'jimmies.' If you could eat two, you'd get the third one free! One person actually did!*

ଔ ଔ ଔ

Jeremy Fisher, now 39 years old, also has fond memories of growing up at *The Cottage*. He was eight years old when his father, Baird Fisher, and his stepmother, Jacky, moved Jeremy and his younger sister, Megan, into a house just a few doors north of *The Cottage* on Pittsford-Mendon Road. Their sister, Lindsey, was born nine years later.

> *We did the usual things that most kids in the hamlet did — we played in Irondequoit Creek, endlessly explored the gravel pit, walked on the trestle bridge, built forts, and rode our bikes. (If you wanted to find someone, you just looked for their bike.)*

My good friend Billy Lang and I were always on the lookout for more excitement. One time a truck from National Grid, the power company in the Southern tier, happened to park in front of The Cottage and we talked them into giving us rides up and down in the lift. That was pretty cool!

We had our share of mischief, too. One time a group of us stole a golf cart from the country club down the road and we spent the day doing donuts in the intersection. I think we finally rolled it. This was a small place where everybody knew everyone's business — how we got away with it, I'll never know — but this was way before being able to capture things on cell phones or video. It was just good times with friends.

I had my own responsibilities at the bar. It was my job to clean it. In the '90s, I would often find rolled-up $50 and $100 bills that people probably used to snort cocaine. Sometimes my friends would come by and we'd drink a little beer (I was never old enough to legally drink while my parents owned it) and play video games or darts. There was also a golf machine and an electronic poker game that we liked to play. Twenty-five years later, I run into people I knew then, and we're still friends.

I often helped my dad in any renovations he was doing. He built the removable rails on the stage and remodeled the bathrooms and kitchen. He also took out the drop ceiling and exposed all those beautiful vintage beams. I fixed the back roof with him and together we replaced the sagging beer-soaked wooden floor with a concrete one.

Even though my parents worked a lot, they included us in everything they could. We were well taken care of and had everything we needed. We knew everyone who came into the bar and they knew us. Joe Formicola, who worked at The Cottage from time to time and partnered with my dad in his framing company, was like an uncle to me. He gave me $50 for my high school graduation. That he remembered to do this even when he was dying of cancer was very meaningful to me.

My friend Billy's parents, Pete and Kathleen Lang, were like a second family. Pete, who tended bar at The Cottage on Tuesdays was quite a popular, funny guy! He's deceased, but as his wife still laments, "There used to be a lot of memorable people at The Cottage. There are just no <u>characters</u> anymore."

Characters like John Shelby . . . back then there weren't credit cards. People would run up "tabs" and then pay them off when they *could. When John's tab got too high my dad would ask him for some money. John would shell out maybe $5, then keep on charging. My dad would kick him out the back door and then John would turn around and walk right back in the front! When he lost his driver's license, John drove his lawn mower to the bar. That's what I call "a character."*

Everyone, of course, had their place, their own stools at the bar. You knew exactly where they would sit and what they would drink. After Craig ("Craiger") Williams died, people would buy a bottle of Bud and put it in the spot where he used to sit. They do that to this day. It was a family atmosphere then and even more so now that Hilary and David are there. They've done a good job of turning it from a good bar that happened to serve food to more of a good restaurant that serves good drinks.

Those were different times, of course. Back then, you knew everyone's story and they knew yours. Back then if you got pulled over for driving under the influence, the cops would follow you to make sure you got home safely. I think my sisters and I were there during the best of times at The Cottage. It will never be recreated, that's for sure.

ಓ ಓ ಓ

Two recent amazing *Cottage Grandbabies* are Fiona Fisher and Mary Kate Fisher, both of whom visited *The Cottage* while *in utero*, and were at *The Cottage* literally weeks after each was born.

These two sisters possess a very special lineage — their father is the aforementioned Jeremy Fisher. As their mother, Keegan Fisher, tells us:

> *In October of 2018, our daughter, Fiona, who is now 4 1/2, was just a few weeks old when she first visited The Cottage. She slept on the stage through 90% of the meal. We continued that tradition with Mary Kate, who was born in March of 2023, and also visited The Cottage when she was two weeks old.*
>
> *At the end of our dinners, Hilary Stott held them each time. All the waitresses were so excited, as they had watched my belly grow with both babies and have watched Fiona grow up. Now they get to see Mary Kate do the same. Hilary has already said that Fiona can have her first job washing dishes at The Cottage when she comes of age.*

On the next page is the most recent Fisher addition — adorable little Mary Kate, making her debut fast asleep on *The Cottage* stage.

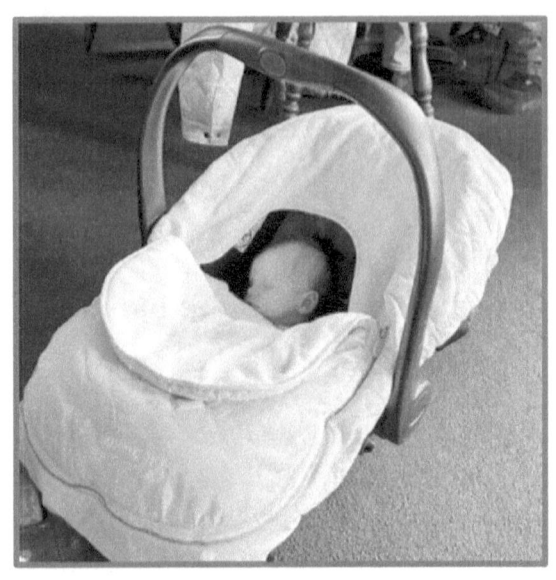

**Mary Kate Fisher
on the *Cottage Hotel* stage
and with her mother, Keegan Fisher
& father, Jeremy Fisher
March 24, 2023**
(Courtesy: Keegan & Jeremy Fisher.)

And here is the lovely Fiona Fisher as an infant in the arms of her father and her mother during her own debut at *The Cottage* in 2018.

Jeremy Fisher & Fiona Fisher   Keegan Fisher & Fiona Fisher
(Courtesy: Keegan and Jeremy Fisher.)

As far as Keegan and Jeremy are concerned, the love that Hilary and David Stott have showered upon their family and the entire community is a magical thing — one that keeps the spirit of Mendon hamlet vibrant and alive.

ଔ   ଔ   ଔ

Hilary and David have raised three children together and now have seven grandchildren who are all growing up basking in the lovely ambient glow of the *Bevador*.

At the time of this writing, Hilary's eldest daughter, Madison "Maddie" (Babigian) Trickey and her husband Kyle Trickey, have four beautiful children: Zoey (14), Zane (5), River (2), and Ari (almost 1). Maddie and Kyle are a dynamic creative duo: Kyle did the recent women's room renovation and Maddie painstakingly repainted the vintage *Cottage* sign before it was replaced in 2023 with a new one designed and constructed by Alan Sartain.

Like many *Cottage Kids*, from the age of 13 Maddie began working at *The Cottage* by bussing tables, then as a server when she got to be around sixteen.

The Trickey Family
Maddie, River, Zane, Kyle holding Ari, & Zoey
(Courtesy: Maddie Trickey.)

As an adult, she tended bar, witnessing *The Cottage*'s all-out party atmosphere at that time. She also got to see its transformation to a more family-friendly place.

The bar lifestyle turned out to be a less-than-healthy one for Maddie. It took time, but she attributes her turn-around and now eight years of sobriety to Jesus and to the love she has for her wonderful husband, children, and family.

Harout Babigian was around 10 when Hilary and David Stott bought *The Cottage* and he and his sister moved from Fairport to the hamlet. His parents worked a lot at first to get the business started. "We ate a lot of pizza around that time," he laughs.

Harout also worked at *The Cottage* off and on throughout his life. He began as a cook and tended bar from time to time, where his high energy is still missed. Harout experienced a lot of the wild times at *The Cottage*—you can hear another one of his stories in Chapter 11. As Harout says:

> *The Cottage is a country tavern. We would all hang out and we all partied a little too hard. People would buy you drinks and when you were ripping the shots sometimes you wouldn't realize how drunk you were.*
>
> *We were a very tight crew, though. We were super cool with each other. The politics were*

defined by the employees. If you joined the staff and didn't jive right away, then there'd be drama. You couldn't be like maple syrup on a cold day. You had to fit in. Like so many bars and restaurants, people came and went.

But the regulars at the bar were always interesting . . . there were characters like 6' 5" tall Charlie Hastings, who wore overalls and probably the same hat forever. He was a great guy. Then there were other folks (one I won't name), who would be fun for about a second, but then would say something horrible and start causing trouble and we'd have to throw him out.

What I liked most was that there were people from all different walks of life. There was the golf crowd, the Republican crowd, the farmers, the professors, the construction workers — just about every element of society. They could all come together and it felt completely natural.

But I have to say — although band nights were really fun, I wasn't into country rock. To me, the music kind of sucked!

From the age of 17, while she was still in high school, Molly (Phillips) Babigian began working for *The Cottage,* later helping Hilary to launch *Mendon 64.*

I'd known Hilary and the Stott family for a long time. When I was working at the pizza place in town, I'd send notes and draw pictures on the pizza boxes for Amanda, who was little at the time. Hilary would always ask me when I'd come to work for her at The Cottage, and finally I did!

There, she began dating Hilary's son, Harout. They worked together off and on through the years, and it was *The Cottage* that allowed them, as a couple and later as young parents, the flexibility to make and save money to create a solid future for themselves.

The Babigian Family
Ahren, Emrys, Molly, Harout, & Melkon
(Courtesy: Molly Babigian.)

The rest, of course, is history. Together Molly and Harout have three wonderful boys: Melkon (age 10), Ahren (age 8), and Emrys (now 1). As Melkon says," The thing I like best about *The Cottage* are the arcade machines. They also make good *Shirley Temples*. And, oh yeah, great steaks!" His brother, Ahren chimes in, "I like *everything* about *The Cottage*. I think it's really cool that *Grammy* and *Bumpa* own it. The kids at my school do, too!"

Last but not least in the family lineup is Hilary and David's daughter, Amanda, now 19 years old. Amanda was just a few years old when her parents bought *The Cottage* and her memories of growing up there are very vivid.

> *I remember that in summer there was a room upstairs where they stored liquor that had wallpaper from back in the 1950s. When I was little, I turned it into a playroom where I used to drink root beer and eat my saltine crackers, the kind that come wrapped in plastic for your soup.*
>
> *During the school year, when it was time for my mom to pick me up, Meko, my Golden Retriever, would already be sitting by the door to remind her. I'd go up to my playroom with him and my mom would order me a burger for a snack. When I turned 10, I decorated one of the offices upstairs and kept*

my toys there. I would go there to do my homework with Meko by my side.

I started working the floor a few days a week around age 11, taking drink and food orders. If I was working, Meko would sometimes get lonely. You'd hear the door upstairs slam open and then he'd come bounding down the stairs looking for me.

Each time I worked, my mom would give me $20 and people would give me good tips because I was so little and cute. Of course this was all under the table. I also had my own candy machine that I had bought for $50. I'd fill it up and then keep the money. It was quite profitable!

Other things I did to make money were to open the bar, fill the sinks with ice, make the morning coffee, and do little odd jobs like grabbing things from the basement or the upstairs. My dad would also pay me to clean and take the money out of the video machines. I would put the quarters into coin sleeves then take them to the bank for him, and in exchange I got to keep 5% of the money.

My friends loved coming to The Cottage. We'd play the electronic dart game and sometimes my dad would let us keep a stuffed animal from the crane machine that is still there. My best friend, Carly Banker, and I would get to play together almost every day. Her mother worked for my mom.

We did normal kid stuff. Sometimes we'd go to the creek and put our toes in the cold water or sneak into the barn to look around — there were a ton of bats in there that they filmed one time for a tv show! It was all great fun!

When I turned 14, I began dating my boyfriend, Austin Hamilton, and we've been together ever since. We weren't allowed to be alone together at The Cottage, so we'd cuddle in the public break room, which was the only place we were allowed to go.

There is a lot of personal family memorabilia inside The Cottage. There is a large fork (about the size of my head) that is on the wall opposite the bar in the dining room. It came from my headpiece when I was in a production of 'The Little Mermaid.' My dad is a collector of license plates, and you can see these here and there throughout the interior. Our family made a point of collecting stickers from our travels and the front inside door is full of them.

Austin and I were the ones who stapled all the record album covers to the ceiling of The Cottage. We also took the old original drink tokens and glued them to the wall above the game room to spell out the word 'Cottage.'

Austin Hamilton and Amanda Stott
(Courtesy: Amanda Stott.)

Since my dad's office was also at The Cottage, I was there quite a lot, but mostly during the day. I knew all the employees really well. It sometimes made me sad when they left or got fired. I didn't understand the reality of all that. It was confusing although I was already very aware of the trouble alcohol and drugs could cause.

I saw this in my own family, and also by observing what went on at the bar. There was a crack in the ceiling over the kitchen where we could listen to what the cooks were saying. That was an education in itself!

My mom was very open about her recovery from alcoholism. She spent a lot of time teaching me about the dangers of addiction. Both parents taught me how to drink responsibly and that went a long way for me in avoiding going down that road.

☙ ☙ ☙

Those who have grown up at *The Cottage* share some special qualities. Because they work alongside their parents from a young age, they develop a strong sense of independence early on. They see the inner workings of the adult world on a daily basis, and in witnessing many sides of humanity up close (both the pretty and the not-so-pretty), their awareness of others seems more highly sensitized than others.

Even if you aren't immediate family, many hamlet kids become part of the clan when they are given their first jobs at *The Cottage*. Those experiences have helped launch them as responsible adults. All of Steve and Jennifer Miller's children, Ben, Sam, and Kathryn ("Katie"), have worked there at one time or another. Like most, they started by washing dishes, then bussing tables, then serving.

For Sam, seeing the banter in the kitchen and interacting customers has gone a long way in helping him acclimate to a more social world. Katie, now 19, in time-honored tradition, now tends bar.

We should all be so lucky to be *Cottage Kids*! Living in a small, tight-knit community gives them a sense of belonging and inter-connectedness that many of us yearn for in today's divided world. *Cottage Kids* know exactly who they are and where they come from — their appreciation of their own history and that of *The Cottage Hotel* is truly inspiring.

Chapter XV

*Moonlight in Mendon:
Tales of Love & Romance
at the Cottage Hotel*

[136]

Twelve years ago musician Johnny Bauer met his love partner and now bandmate, Nicki Paris, while playing a gig at *The Cottage*.

> *I looked out and saw this girl with the most beautiful smile I'd ever seen. She was with someone else, but I couldn't keep my eyes off her while I was playing. Later we found out we both worked at the University of Rochester, but we never*

---

[136] Art by Kent Rockwell, 1918. Courtesy: Smithsonian American Art Museum.

> *would have connected without that night at the Cottage Hotel. She now plays bass guitar in the band and we've played hundreds of gigs together.*

That's just one instance of what I call "Cottage Magic."

Innocent flirtations, spontaneous trysts, a classic rendezvous or two—no matter what time of day, you can bet your bottom dollar that love at *The Cottage Hotel* is and always has been in the air.

Deedee Dutcher met her first husband, Rick Coleman, in 1976 when she was managing *The Cottage*. They were an energetic, good-looking couple that many admired.

Says Deedee:

> *I hired Rick because he was the only person who could keep up with me drinking! (Also, he was quite handsome and a nice guy to boot.) While tending bar, Rick became friends with Cottage regulars Baird Fisher, a future Cottage owner, and Joe Formicola, and teamed up to work with them in Baird's construction business—yet another match made in heaven.*

For both the very young (meaning 20 and younger) and the still-on-the-pretty-side of 80 crowd, *The Cottage* was always a great place to meet or take a casual date. There was live music to dance to, inexpensive drinks, and people of all ages and walks of life gathered to make life interesting.

Music-inspired love affairs sometimes extended beyond *The Cottage's* walls. One patron, happily married, and who prefers to remain anonymous, tells this story:

> *My girlfriend at the time would make a quick stop at The Cottage around 7:00 p.m. to have a beer, then walk over to the Presbyterian Church, where we had found a way to access the church steeple.*
>
> *Greatest view of Mendon ever! My girlfriend and I would get it on until after dark, then go back to The Cottage to listen to the live music. We did this four days a week, which tells you how much I dug The Cottage music scene (and my girlfriend) back then.*

Even if you aren't a spring chicken, *The Cottage* was, and still is, a go-to destination. Where else can you have lunch and a beer and not break the bank? Where else will the handsome *Cottage* bartenders and charming barmaids (as they called them back in the *olden days*) flirt with you shamelessly and listen to your stories of days gone by?

For the most part, *The Cottage* was a safe place to party and bring your friends. Even in the 1950s, women could feel free to walk into *The Cottage* on their own without an escort—and often did.

Some *Cottage*-goers had interactions that were deeply passionate, but short-lived. The excitement of live music and dancing, combined with copious amounts of alcohol, often played a part in how people paired up.

So was the tug of loneliness and the universal human need for touch. There were certainly those moments for some at last call when the person sitting next to them started looking pretty darn attractive. Inopportune decisions might, and undoubtedly did, ensue.

It's a testament to the owners and bartenders who created such a friendly, open atmosphere at *The Cottage* that two souls might zero in on each other across the crowded barroom, come together, and just *click*.

Some found the one they still consider to be the absolute love of their life at *The Cottage*, whether or not it lasted. Others got luckier still and found true romance that resulted in marriage or long-term partnerships.

03 03 03

As teenagers, Amanda Stott and Austin Hamilton did just that. They both worked at *The Cottage* together in high school, and it didn't take long before they fell deeply in love.

The same thing happened with Molly Phillips and Harout Babigian. As Molly tells us:

> *There was a time when we broke up for a while, but even so we still worked together. We've been through a lot of phases of our life together at The Cottage ever since.*
>
> *We moved to Colorado at one point, but we moved home not long after to be closer to our family and support. Thank goodness for The Cottage! I was able to work during my first pregnancy and earn some money before and after the baby came. We married when we turned 21, and now we have a beautiful family of three boys.*
>
> *The Cottage has always been there for us. We sometimes had to patch things together, but we always made it through. That's what The Cottage is all about!*

ଓଃ   ଓଃ   ଓଃ

Writing partners and local historians Deb (Gonyea) Smith and her husband, Tim, found love both early on and later in life.

In 8th grade I was a Lima Indian and Tim was a Honeoye Falls Hornet. The merger of the two school districts took place between 8th and 9th grade for us, so we were the first class to spend all four years of high school as Honeoye Falls-Lima Cougars.

We met on the first day of high school, dated for all four years, then went to separate colleges. We wound up not seeing each other again for literally 40 years, until Tim's mom passed away. I heard it about it through the grapevine in Virginia Beach where I was living at the time.

I wrote Tim and he wrote back, and one thing led to another. I came back home and because we both have Native American blood, we were married in 2015 by Tim's former student, R. J. Maute, along with the tribal leader at the Native American Historical Site of Ganondagan. We're now living happily ever after in beautiful downtown Mendon!

And that, as they say, is not all! When they heard of Deb and Tim's romantic reconnection, Chris and Betsy Carosa, publishers of the *Mendon-Honeoye Falls-Lima Sentinel*, were so intrigued that they asked them to write an article about it for the paper.

Suddenly we were off and running with no slowing down in sight! There are times when we are sharing ideas that we just crack each other up, and other times when we've brought each other to tears. It's a wonderfully collaborative process.

Deb & Tim Smith
(Courtesy: The Smiths)

From May to October, the Smiths set up shop outdoors with their computers at the hamlet's four corners, where they live right next door to the *Sentinel*. As Tim and Deb say:

As the local literary liaisons between people and the paper, we couldn't be working from a better Sentinel lookout location. It's the

> *perfect ambiance to be creative and interact with the community at the same time. We've had so many conversations with folks parking and heading to or coming back from the Cottage Hotel!*

It's truly a rare thing to find both your soul mate and creative partner all rolled into one. With the *Cottage Hotel* keeping careful watch over them, you can be sure that Deb and Tim will be blessed with a long and happy union!

CR CR CR

There are two special *Cottage*-goers, Geri Noll Hughes and Kent Hughes, who, along with a little subtle matchmaking, fell under the *Cottage Hotel's* magical spell . . .

"It was all Hilary Stott's doing," says Geri Hughes. "She had become one of my dearest friends and knew I had gone through a tough time with my divorce." As Geri explains:

> *She introduced Kent and I at the bar one afternoon in 2007 by asking us to come up with ideas for a singles' event — a pretty clever way of breaking the ice between two people she suspected would have a lot in common.*

Kent and I got to chatting and immediately found out we both loved to ski and we both loved to travel, among many other things. That very day, Kent asked me out to dinner and on December 5th we went on our first "almost" date.

I say, 'almost' because we were to go to an organic restaurant in Lima, but when we got there it was closed. We ended up eating at The Whistlestop in Victor and had a great time, even so. He picked up the check, pecked me on the cheek, and then . . . I never heard another word from him! I tried calling him to thank him, but never heard back.

I was busy with life. Christmas came and went and then on January 22nd I attended a meeting of the Nordic Ski Patrol at St. Catherine's Church, as I was on their board.

Afterwards, the members all went to The Cottage and were sitting and talking and having a beer when suddenly there was Kent. Kent came over to our table and began talking with the rest of the men. They all seemed to know him quite well. It was then that I realized that he was not an axe murderer!

One by one, they all left until it was just the two of us. We talked until it was time to go home, then walked outside onto the stair outside The Cottage.

Kent & Geri Hughes
Bonaire Island, 2010
(Courtesy: Kent Hughes.)

There is nothing like the full moon in the hamlet. That night it illuminated the soft flakes of snow that were just beginning to drift from the sky, gently caressing our faces. As Kent leaned over to kiss me, it was if the entire sky was offering us its blessing.

From then on we were inseparable, and we continued to find correspondences to our lives and our hearts and minds. We both had gone through difficult divorces. We both had two children around the same ages (all who coincidentally worked at The Cottage from time to time). So many things . . . it's almost impossible to list them!

We were married a few years later on October 7, 2017 in an off-the-charts wedding in Cummings Nature Center in the middle of a clearing in the pines. And now, every time we cross country ski over a bridge, we kiss as a memory of that first time outside The Cottage Hotel, when fate, the full moon, and the falling snow brought us together.

As Kent attests: "We bonded in a way that doesn't always happen. Fifteen years have now passed. I have been happier with Geri than I ever could have imagined. And it all came about because of the Cottage Hotel!"

**All roads lead
to *The Cottage Hotel of Mendon***

※ ※ ※

Love, in all its many manifestations, is the true and lasting legacy of the *Cottage Hotel*.

If you don't have a tear in your eye by now, or at least a catch in your throat, heaven help you. And if you're not a believer in the enchantment that has always been a part of *The Cottage*, I challenge you to find another place that for over two hundred years has brought so much joy, happiness, and friendship to so many.

May we all find that positive spirit in whatever we do — safe in the knowledge that we will never, ever feel alone whenever we cross over the threshold of the special world that is the *Cottage Hotel of Mendon*.

In 2023, the vintage *Cottage Hotel* sign had finally deteriorated beyond repair and a new sign was designed by Alan Sartain.

As Alan tells us:

> I ordered a 42" X 71" red cedar sign blank from a California company. Die Max of Rochester, Inc. then painted and lathed both sides of the blank to form a relief of the logo. Thirty coats of polyurethane were put on both sides of the sign, and finally Die Max built the sign frame from stainless steel and powder-coated it black to match the original vintage sign.

The original sign is on display at *The Cottage Hotel of Mendon*.

APPENDICES

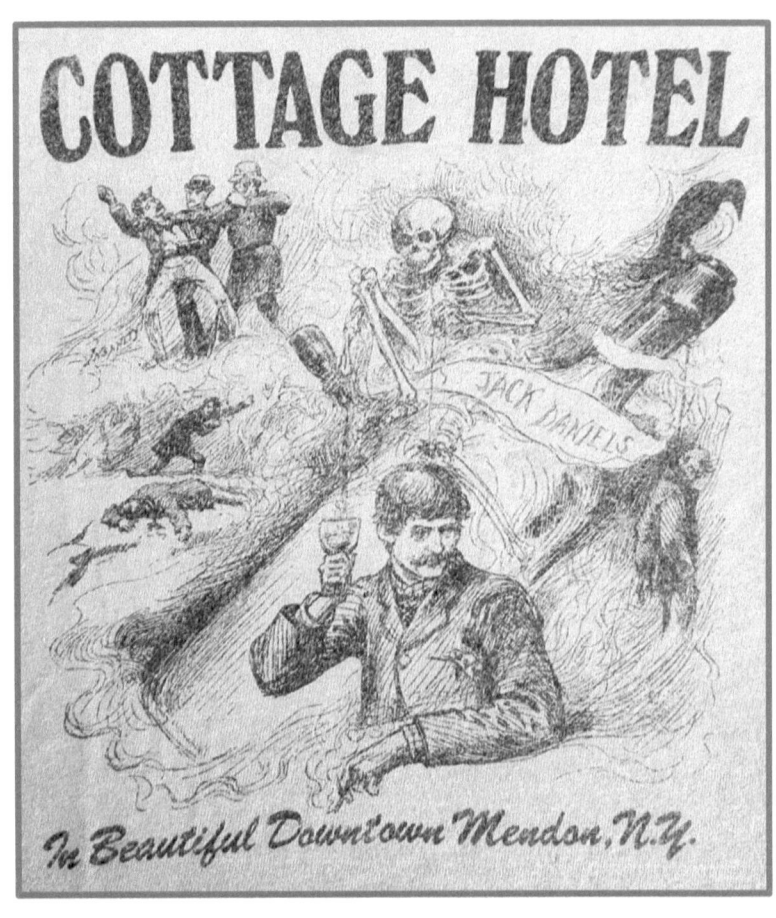

(Courtesy: Brian Lyons.)

Appendix I

Cottage Hotel Owners & Lessees *(in italics)* from 1822-2023

A Brief History:

There have been 15 owners of the Cottage Hotel since 1822.

In 1817, George S. Stone & Co. are noted in East Mendon (Mendon hamlet) as "in production of liquors and their retail." In 1818, the land beneath the Cottage Hotel on Lot 30 is purchased by George S. Stone and his older brother, Jeremy S. Stone.

Building of the Cottage Hotel may have begun as early as 1819, although no firm date of its construction has been confirmed. The Cottage officially opens its doors as a licensed stagecoach inn in 1822. It is possible, but not documented, that it operated as a tavern before that time.

The owners of The Cottage of the longest duration were Thomas ("Yankee Tom") Finucane for 51 years; George S. Stone and his brother, Jeremy S. Stone (the builders of the Cottage Hotel) for 32 years; and Albert Thomas ("Al) and Mary Heckman for 22 years.

Robert F. ("Bob") Clifford purchased The Cottage in 1972. It then had a series of lessees. In 1981, Ann Chaintreuil (sister of John Urquhart ("Burdock") Ross) inherited the lease and she and her husband, Renier Chaintreuil, became owners in 1984. It was then sold in 2005 to the current proprietors, Hilary and David Stott.

What follows is a summary of the chain of ownership of The Cottage Hotel, an annotated listing of the taverns in Mendon hamlet, and a timeline of dates, people, and world events that you may find of interest.

1817
George S. Stone & Co. of East Mendon (Mendon hamlet) is "in production of liquors and their retail."

1818
George S. Stone and his older brother Jeremy S. Stone purchase Lot 30 in Mendon hamlet from John W. Cady and Maria C. Cady for $1,000, as recorded in Monroe County on October 31, 1818.

Construction on the foundation of the *Cottage Hotel* begins at an undetermined date after 1819. It is not known whether it operates as a tavern or whether guests stay at *The Cottage* until it legally opens as a stagecoach inn in 1822.

1822-1854 (32 years)
George S. Stone and Jeremy S. Stone.

1854-1855 (1 year)
Susan Stone
from her husband George S. Stone's estate.

1855-1866 (11 years)
Chauncy D. Tuttle and Matilda Tuttle
from George S. Stone estate.
Jediah (or Jedidiah) P. Fowler
for a $2,000 mortgage from Chauncy and Matilda Tuttle.

1866-1868 (2 years)
George W. Peer and Emma J. Peer purchase
the "hotel property" in Lot 30
from Chauncy D. Tuttle and Matilda Tuttle.

1868-1871 (3 years)
Ely (or Eli) Phelps and Harriet Phelps
from George W. Peer and Emma J. Peer.

1871-1886 (15 years)
John Smith and Mary Smith
from Ely (or Eli) Phelps and Harriet Phelps.

1886-1937 (51 years)
Thomas ("Yankee Tom") Finucane
from Mary Smith (widow of John Smith).

1937-1945 (8 years)
Nathan D. Fletcher and Harriet M. Fletcher
from May Finucane Bridges
as part of Mary Finucane's estate.

1945-1946 (1 year)
Ferdinand V. Masso and Frannie Frehmeyer
from Nahum D. Fletcher and Harriet M. Fletcher.

1946-1948 (2 years)
Paul Streb
from Ferdinand V. Masso and Fannie Frehmeyer.

1948-1950 (2 years)
August Van Castiles and Martha Van Castiles
from Paul Streb.

1950-1972 (22 years)
Albert Thomas ("Al) Heckman
and Mary Elizabeth Heckman
from August Van Castiles and Martha Van Castiles.

1972-1984 (12 years)
Robert F. ("Bob") Clifford
from Albert Thomas ("Al") Heckman
and Mary Elizabeth Heckman for $75,000.

1972-1975 (2 years)
Paul S. Gordon ("Buzzy") Bronson
for no down payment
and a triple net lease of $467.

1975-1981 (6 years)
John Urquhart ("Burdock") Ross
for $20,000 (for improvements)
and a triple net lease of $2,177.50.

1981-1984 (3 years as lessees)
Ann and Renier Chaintreuil
from the estate of John Urquhart ("Burdock") Ross.

1982-1998 (16 years)
Jacqueline ("Jacky") Fisher
from Ann and Renier Chaintreuil
with no down payment
and a triple net lease of $2,177.50.

1984-2005 (19 years as owners)
Ann and Renier Chaintreuil
from Robert F. ("Bob") Clifford for $90,000.

1998-2004 (6 years)
Louis C. ("Lou") DiNardo.
from Jacqueline ("Jacky") Fisher
for $30,000 and an undisclosed triple net lease.

Note: Upon Louis C. ("Lou") DiNardo's death in 2004, his partner Nancy Marinelli manages The Cottage Hotel until its sale in 2005.

2005-present (18 years as of 2023)
Hilary and David Stott
from Ann and Renier Chaintreuil for $230,000
with a 15-year $135,000 mortgage held by the Chaintreuils.

Appendix II

An Annotated History of the Stagecoach Inns & Taverns of Mendon Hamlet

Cottage Hotel

1817
George S. Stone & Co. is licensed in the local production of liquors and their retail. These proprietors become known as "dram sellers."

1818
John W. Cady and Maria C. Cady of Johnstown, Montgomery County, New York sell 4.5 acres in Lot #30 of Mendon hamlet to George S. Stone and his older brother, Jeremy Stone, for $1,000. The deed is recorded in Monroe County on October 31, 1818.

1822
The *Cottage Hotel* opens its doors to the public.

Horses for the hotel will be kept in a barn located behind the house next door until a new barn is built by Thomas ("Yankee Tom") Finucane in 1896.

1834
Jeremy S. Stone, co-owner of the *Cottage Hotel* with George S. Stone, dies in November.

1854
George S. Stone dies on October 18 at the age of 61. His wife, Susan Stone, assumes ownership of the *Cottage Hotel*.

1855

Chauncy D. Tuttle and his wife Matilda Tuttle purchase the *Cottage Hotel* from the estate of George S. Stone. On February 22nd of that year, Jediah (Jedidiah) P. Fowler takes out a mortgage from Chauncy D. Tuttle for $2,000 for one acre of land "being the Tavern Stand premises" and Jediah (Jedidiah) P. Fowler is listed as innkeeper.

1858

The property of the *Cottage Hotel* is shown as *J. P. Fowler's Hotel*.

1866

George W. Peer purchases the *Cottage Hotel*, plus an adjoining 2-acre lot, from Chauncy D. Tuttle and his wife, Matilda Tuttle, on September 22, 1866.

1868

Ely Phelps and Harriet Phelps purchase the *Cottage Hotel* from George W. Peer and Emma J. Peer on May 1, 1868.

1871

John Smith and Mary Smith purchase the *Cottage Hotel* from Ely Phelps and Harriet Phelps on November 11, 1871.

1876

No new liquor licenses in Mendon are granted due to fears of "the evils of intoxication." *History of Monroe County*, (Everts, Ensign & Everts, New York, 1788-1877), 835.

1886

Thomas ("Yankee Tom") Finucane purchases the *Cottage Hotel* from Mary Smith (widow of John Smith) on December 1, 1871.

1894
The *Cottage Hotel* name is recorded by Thomas ("Yankee Tom") Finucane, and he receives a liquor license that year as does Jacob Schlaefer, owner of the *Mendon Hotel* across the street.

1896
A 30' x 40' barn is built by Thomas ("Yankee Tom") Finucane just north of the *Cottage Hotel* for a total of $407.91. Construction begins on April 22, 1896, and is completed on May 15, 1986. The barn still exists and is renovated in 2020 by Hilary and David Stott.

1935
Thomas ("Yankee Tom") Finucane dies on March 31 at the age of 79. Ownership passes to his wife, Mary Finucane, (1856-1944).

1937
Nahum D. Fletcher and Harriet M. Fletcher purchase the *Cottage Hotel* from May Finucane Bridges on December 2, 1937, as part of the Mary Finucane estate.

1945
Ferdinand V. Masso and Fannie Frehmeyer purchase the *Cottage Hotel* from Nahum D. Fletcher and Harriet M. Fletcher on October 4, 1945.

1946
Paul Streb purchases the *Cottage Hotel* from Ferdinand V. Masso and Fannie Frehmeyer on July 8, 1946. His father, Paul Streb, Sr., may have been co-owner. The grand opening is announced in the Rochester *Democrat and Chronicle* on November 3, 1946.

1948
August Van Castiles and his wife, Martha Van Castiles, purchase the *Cottage Hotel* from Paul Streb.

In the News: The Rochester Democrat and Chronicle reports that on May 16, after 7 minutes of deliberation, two men (one from Henrietta, one from Fishers) are convicted of third-degree assault after a barroom brawl at the Cottage Hotel.

1950
Albert Thomas ("Al") Heckman and his wife Mary Elizabeth Heckman purchase the *Cottage Hotel* from August Van Castiles and his wife Martha Van Castiles on June 29, 1950. Al and Mary manage *The Cottage* together and live with their two children, Tommy Heckman and Rosemary Heckman, and family friends Earl and Dell Woodard, on the top floor.

In the News: the Canandaigua Daily Messenger reports that Lewis D. Woodward of Holcomb is arrested for carrying "a Japanese pistol" and brandishing it the Cottage Hotel. Two bystanders divest him of his gun and the chambers are found to be empty.

1955
In the News: The Honeoye Falls Times reports that on October 7, a fire starts at the Cottage Hotel but is quickly put out by the Mendon Fire Department. Victor firemen come to their aid.

1972
Robert F. ("Bob") Clifford purchases the *Cottage Hotel* from Albert Thomas ("Al") Heckman and his wife, Mary Heckman, on January 27, 1972 for $75,000.

Paul S. Gordon ("Buzzy") Bronson acquires the *Cottage Hotel* from Robert F. ("Bob") Clifford on a triple net lease of $467/month, with no money down. He renovates and runs the *Cottage Hotel* until 1975, when he sells it to John Urquhart ("Burdock") Ross.

1972-75
Connie Alissa, John Bronson, Mark Dennis ("Coach"), Deidre ("DeeDee") Dutcher, Doug Foxall, Don Jeffries, Joe Polosi, Peter Silos, Erick Thompson, and Gus Yates are all managers/bartenders at *The Cottage*.

1974
Deidre ("Deedee") Dutcher manages *The Cottage* for nine months for Paul S. ("Buzzy") Bronson until it is purchased by John Urquhart ("Burdock") Ross in 1975.

1975
John Urquhart ("Burdock") Ross leases the *Cottage Hotel* for $20,000 and a triple net lease of $2,177.50 from Paul S. Gordon ("Buzzy") Bronson and manages the business.

1977
Anthony "Tony" Demeo is listed as manager of the *Cottage Hotel*.

1981
On October 19, 1981, John Urquhart ("Burdock") Ross dies. The lease of the *Cottage Hotel* legally passes to his estate, administered by his younger sister, Ann Chaintreuil.

1982
Beginning in 1982, Jacqueline ("Jacky") (Muzdakis) Fisher owns and manages the *Cottage Hotel* on a lease of $2,177.50 from the estate of John Urquhart ("Burdock") Ross. At age 24, she is the youngest person to obtain a liquor license in New York State.

1984
Ann and Renier Chaintreuil purchase the *Cottage Hotel* building and business from Robert F. ("Bob") Clifford for $90,000. It is leased to various managers until 2005, when it is sold to Hilary and David Stott.

1985

Jacqueline ("Jacky") Muzdakis marries Baird Fisher in 1985, and together they run the *Cottage Hotel* until 1998, until it is sold to Louis C. ("Lou") DiNardo.

Cottage patron Joe Formicola helps manage *The Cottage* with Jacky and Baird Fisher until Joe's death at age 48 from cancer on October 15, 1996.

1991

Robert F. ("Bob") Clifford, former owner of the *Cottage Hotel*, dies on January 4.

1992

Paul Streb, former owner of the *Cottage Hotel*, dies on November 4, 1992. Drink tokens are later found in an attic belonging to Paul Streb's aunt. Examples of the tokens can be seen at *The Cottage Hotel of Mendon* spelling out the word '*Cottage*' above the entrance to the game room. They were installed by Amanda Stott and Austin Hamilton.

1998

Jacqueline ("Jacky") (Muzdakis) Fisher and Baird Fisher sell the *Cottage Hotel* lease to Louis C. ("Lou") DiNardo for $30,000 and an undisclosed triple net lease. Lou and his partner, Nancy Marinelli, manage the *Cottage Hotel* together until Lou's death in 2004.

In the News: The Mendon-Honeoye Falls-Lima Sentinel reports that a catastrophic storm causes extensive flooding in the hamlet when Irondequoit Creek crests sometime after midnight on January 14, 1998. Waters flood the basement of the Cottage Hotel and a small fire is caused by the furnace motor burning out.

2004

Louis C. ("Lou") DiNardo dies of cancer on March 4th. After Lou's death, Nancy Marinelli oversees management of the *Cottage Hotel* until its sale in 2005.

2005
In April, Hilary and David Stott purchase the *Cottage Hotel* from Ann and Renier Chaintreuil for $230,000 with a 15-year $135,000 mortgage held by the Chaintreuils. It is renamed *The Cottage Hotel of Mendon*. The business is legally owned by Hilary Stott, and the property by David Stott.

A Sno-Cone Machine is installed at the *Cottage Hotel* and remains until 2010.

2006
A beam from the barn next door to the *Cottage Hotel* is installed as a foot rail at the bar.

2009
Nancy Marinelli, partner of Louis C. ("Lou") DiNardo (former owner of the *Cottage Hotel*), dies on December 17th.

2011-2012
The pool table at the *Cottage Hotel* is removed and the game room completed in 2012. The first kitchen renovation and expansion is made. The kitchen will be expanded two more times during the upcoming years.

2014
In the News: The Rochester Democrat and Chronicle reports that John Cassata shoots himself in the hand and injures friend Charles Raab, when Cassata's licensed firearm goes off accidentally during lunch hour at the Cottage Hotel. No charges are filed.

2016
Hilary and David Stott renovate the iconic *Bevador* beer cooler, at a cost of $6,000. The work is done by Pat Falin at *Mantique & Oddities Etc.* in Bloomfield, New York in May of that year.

2018
A DEC-approved water treatment system is installed at *The Cottage*, costing $120,000 and requiring monthly maintenance fees of approximately $3,000.

2020
Hilary and David Stott renovate the barn next to the *Cottage Hotel*.

2023
A new sign for the *Cottage Hotel of Mendon* is designed and constructed by Alan Sartaine. The original vintage sign is on display at *The Cottage*.

Mendon Hotel

1812
A log cabin tavern, later known as the *Mendon Hotel*, is built by John Brown on the northwest corner of Mendon hamlet's four corners.

1814
John Brown is shown as being a tavern keeper in East Mendon (Mendon hamlet). "Dram sellers" at the time paid $5 for a liquor license.

1815
Ezra Sheldon, Jr. is listed as owner of the *Mendon Hotel*.

1825
While touring the United States, on June 7th, Gilbert du Motier, the Marquis de Lafayette, arrives in Mendon hamlet via carriage and is celebrated with a grand reception at the *Mendon Hotel*.

1890
Jacob Schlaefer, his wife Mary, and family, own and operate the *Mendon Hotel* for 19 years. A third story floating floor ballroom is built of black walnut wood and later moved to the dining room.

Ben Peer relocates in Florida and sells the *Mendon Hotel* to Robert Dunchie and John E. Tomlinson. John E. Tomlinson becomes solo owner of the *Mendon Hotel*.

1897
Edward Strong listed as the owner of the *Mendon Hotel*.

1909
Charles Wangman is listed as the owner of the *Mendon Hotel*.

1942
Ernest Ehrenberg is listed as the owner of the *Mendon Hotel*.

1945
Harold Folts leases the *Mendon Hotel* from Ernest Ehrenberg. Folts is the grandfather of Pat Freeman, the current owner of *Ye Olde Mendon Tavern*, formerly the *Springwater Inn*.

1946
Edward Butts and his wife, Winifred Butts, and Frederick Mahrt and his wife, Gertrude Mahrt, purchase the *Mendon Hotel*. Their families, including the Mahrt's son, Russell ("Russ") Mahrt, and his first cousins Judy Butts, Jim Butts, and Jackie Butts, live in the rooms above the hotel.

1957
The *Mendon Hotel* is sold to the Gulf Oil Company. The furnishings are put up for auction.

On July 25, 1957, the *Mendon Hotel* is used as a realistic firefighting demonstration by the Mendon Fire Department and nine other fire crews from Brighton, Bushnell's Basin, East Rochester, Egypt, Fairport, Fishers, Penfield, Pittsford, and Victor.

1980
The property becomes the *K & K Food Mart* and gas station.

2002
Crosby's Gas Station and Mini-Mart is constructed on the land where the *Mendon Hotel* once stood.

Ye Olde Mendon Tavern
(formerly the Springwater Inn)

1890
Originally an apple and peach drying house, a building with a tavern on the first floor, and an apartment on the second floor is built and is listed at 3771 Rush-Mendon Road.

1915
Ye Olde Mendon Tavern is rebuilt.

1945
Harold Folts purchases the building that becomes the *Springwater Inn*. Harold Folts also leases the *Mendon Hotel* from Ernest Ehrenberg that same year.

1948
Robert Folts, purchases the building, listed as the *Springwater Inn*.

1956
Harold Folts (1904-1956) passes away upstairs at the *Springwater Inn* at age 51. His spirit is said to haunt the premises ever since. His daughter, Pat Freeman, assumes ownership of *Ye Olde Mendon Tavern*, formerly known as the *Springwater Inn*.

1963
Gordon Beck is listed as proprietor of the *Springwater Inn*.

1971
The property listed as the *Springwater Inn* is noted to have been built in 1915.

2023
On June 2nd, Robert J. ("Bob") Freeman, husband of Pat Freeman, dies at age 75. The address of the *Springwater Inn*, now called *Ye Olde Mendon Tavern*, is listed as 3868 Rush-Mendon Road.

Appendix III

A Compendium of Important Dates, People, & World Events Affecting the Hamlet of Mendon, New York

This timeline has been gleaned from a variety of sources noted in the Resource section of this book.

1577
The Seneca village of Totiakton, the earliest known settlement in the Town of Mendon, is documented by British explorer Wentworth Greenhalgh.

1620
The *Mayflower* lands at Cape Cod, Massachusetts, on November 21st.

1668
An early Jesuit mission is established on Plains Road by Father James Fremlin, who lives with the Seneca Indians at Totiakton.

1677
Totiakton is home to approximately 1,000 people. The town at the bend of Honeoye Creek, extends over 30 acres, and has large fields under cultivation.

1687
The Governor of New France, General Marquise de Denonville, in an effort to control the fur trade, invades Totiakton (along with 3,000 French and Canadian soldiers, and Huron allies) and destroys Totiakton and all its crops. The Seneca flee south and west. They never rebuild the city.

1775
The American Revolutionary War begins.

1777
High taxes, one aftermath of the American Revolutionary War, push New England farmers to relocate westward.

Gilbert du Motier, the Marquis de Lafayette, volunteers for the continental army, becoming a major general under George Washington. "He will lead American forces to several victories, including the Battle of Yorktown."

1779
In retaliation for a massacre of colonists by The Loyalists and the Iroquois, The Sullivan Expedition (4,000 troops sent by George Washington and led by Major John Sullivan and Brigadier General James Clinton) decimates 40 Seneca Indian villages and appropriates the region. Many of those forced to flee die by freezing and starvation.

1780
Colonists' farms and crops are destroyed by Iroquois warriors and Loyalists in an act of vengeance.

1783
Fighting in the American Revolutionary War ends, two years after the British surrender.

1788
Oliver Phelps and Nathaniel Gorham speculatively purchase 2,250,000 acres of land in Western New York from the Iroquois in exchange for $5,000 and yearly annuity of $500.

1789
In January, Ontario County is formed, including the Town of Mendon (later formed on May 26, 1812.) Mendon is known as Township 11, Range 5. East Mendon (Mendon hamlet) is settled by Samuel Miller.

1791
In spring, the first settlers come to Mendon via waterways and covered wagon and set about building cabins and log barns. Pioneer Zebulon Norton establishes "Norton's Mills" which will later be known "West Mendon" or Honeoye Falls.

1792
A general store and post office are located in the hamlet across from where the *Mendon Hotel* would later be built in 1812.

1793
Covered wagons, pulled by oxen, bring 13 families to East Mendon, also known as Mendon Village and Mendon hamlet.

1797
Mendon-Ionia Road (Route 64) is surveyed. It is originally a Seneca Indian trail from Canandaigua to Rochester, and later the route of a stagecoach line from Canandaigua to Buffalo begun by Sam Hildreth in 1817 that comes through Mendon hamlet.

1798
The Mendon Feed Mill is established on land owned by Jonas Allen.

1800
Twenty-five families now live in Mendon hamlet (now known as East Mendon or Mendon Village). On October 17th, a road is opened from Mendon hamlet westward.

1802
The first sawmill is built on Irondequoit Creek in Mendon hamlet by Jonas Allen. A carding mill is built by A. H. Rand. Both will burn down in 1816.

1809
The first meetings of the First Baptist Church are held at the residence of Cornelius Treat.

1810
The first stagecoaches begin to pass through Mendon.

1811
North of the hamlet, the Old Mendon Cemetery on the east side of Pittsford-Mendon Road is established.

1812
On May 26, 1812, The Town of Mendon, originally in Ontario County, is officially formed and annexed to the southern border of Monroe County.

A log cabin tavern, the *Mendon Hotel*, is built by John Brown on the northwest corner of Mendon hamlet's four corners.

A carding mill is built on Irondequoit Creek by A.H. Rand.

Victor-Mendon Road (Route 251) is first surveyed.

1813
The first Mendon town meeting is held on the first Tuesday in April. Jonas Allen is the first town supervisor. Ninety dollars are voted for "contingent expenses" and $100 designated for the poor.

The first post office is established in Mendon hamlet (or Mendon Village as it is sometimes known). Timothy Barnard is the first postmaster at his residence a mile northwest of the hamlet.

1814-15
Ezra Sheldon, Jr. is listed as the first operator of the *Mendon Hotel*. Licenses are required for inn or tavern keepers for a fee of $5.00.

1815
The Presbyterian Church is established on January 5th.

1816
The first sawmill and the carding mill built in Mendon hamlet both burn down. The earliest burial is made at Mendon Cemetery (originally known as Baptist Hill Cemetery) on the east side of Mendon-Ionia Road.

1817
The village of Rochesterville is surveyed. It will be renamed Rochester in 1823.

A stagecoach line begun by Sam Hildreth goes from Canandaigua to Buffalo, the first organized line to run through Mendon hamlet.

Seven licensed distilleries and taverns are in operation in Mendon, including a license given to George S. Stone & Co. (future owner of the *Cottage Hotel*), for the local production of liquors and their retail.

1818
John W. Cady and Maria C. Cady of Johnstown, Montgomery County, sell 4.5 acres in Lot #30 to George S. Stone and Jeremy Stone for $1,000. Recorded in Monroe County on October 31, 1818.

1819
Construction on the *Cottage Hotel* as a post-and-beam stagecoach tavern may have begun on the northeast corner of Mendon hamlet across the street from the *Mendon Hotel*. It may have been a tavern prior to becoming a licensed stagecoach inn in 1822. Horses will be kept in a barn located behind the house next door until a new barn is constructed in 1896 on the east side of the *Cottage Hotel* by Thomas ("Yankee Tom") Finucane.

Mendon Hotel owners are Ben Peer, Robert Dunchie, and John E. Tomlinson until it is sold in 1890 to Jacob and Mary Schlaefer and family in 1890.

1821
The Town of Mendon is annexed to Monroe County from Ontario County. The population consists of 185 families.

1822
The *Cottage Hotel* opens its doors to the public. The hamlet of Norton's Mills will be changed to that of "West Mendon."

1823
Joseph Smith, Jr. unearths "The Golden Plates" buried at Hill Cumorah in Palmyra, New York, 17 miles south of Mendon hamlet.

1825
The Erie Canal is completed and officially opens on October 26, 1825. More than 217,000 tons of goods are transported in the first year.

While on a tour of the United States, on June 7th, Gilbert du Motier (General Marquis de Lafayette) arrives by carriage and is welcomed at a grand reception at the *Mendon Hotel*.

The First Baptist Church of Mendon is built with a 1/2 acre cemetery adjacent to the church. Its bell can be heard throughout the hamlet until the church is torn down in the 1920s.

The Mendon Presbyterian Church's cornerstone is laid on July 13th. The first meeting is held in the completed church a year later.

1826
The first gristmill (on the opposite side from the sawmill) is built by Milton Sheldon and Daniel Allen on the north side

of Irondequoit Creek. It is later owned by Hugh Sherry (1830), and Nathan Stone (1878), and finally Fred Ernst.

Milton Sheldon (a physician) owns the general store in the hamlet. He later becomes a Monroe County representative in the New York legislature.

1828
Brigham Young, age 27, a carpenter and skilled metallurgist, moves to Mendon with his wife, Mariam Works Young, and their daughter. He operates a chair factory on his father John's farm (later owned by Samuel Hutchinson) at the corner of Mendon-Ionia and Cheese Factory roads. His chairs sell for $.50 each. He is destined to become the second president of the Church of Latter-day Saints, the Mormon Church.

A scarlet fever epidemic hits Mendon.

The Society of Friends (Quakers) have their first assembly in a log house owned by H. T. Lord. They thrive in the Mendon Center area until 1915.

1830
On October 24, 1830, the population of the entire Town of Mendon, including Mendon hamlet, is 1,922 residents.

Joseph Smith completes his translation of "The Golden Plates" and writes *The Book of Mormon*. On March 26, 1830, he begins selling *The Book of Mormon* in Palmyra's Grandin Building Bookstore, where the translation took place. On April 6, 1830, the Mormon Church is organized by Joseph Smith, along with founding committee members, Hyrum Smith, Oliver Cowdery, Peter Whitmor(e) and Samuel H. Smith. On October 24, 1830, Brigham Young sees a copy of *The Book of Mormon* for the first time.

1832
Brigham Young becomes an elder in the Mormon church. His wife, Miriam Works Young, the first of 56 wives, acquires tuberculosis and succumbs on September 8th. She is cared for by the Heber C. Kimball family and is buried in Tomlinson's Corners Cemetery.

Cholera victims begin arriving in Rochester via The Erie Canal. A cholera epidemic sweeps through Mendon hamlet claiming 14 lives.

On August 25th, The Society of Friends (Quakers) purchase one acre of land in Mendon Center just south of Rush-Mendon Road for the site of their first meeting house. A small cemetery is the only remaining evidence of the Friend's presence.

1833
The daily newspaper, *The Balance*, is first published, later becoming known as *The Daily Democrat* and over a hundred years later, in 1928, as the Rochester *Democrat and Chronicle*.

After reportedly being attacked and stoned by area residents, Brigham Young, Heber C. Kimball, and their families, leave the area to join Joseph Smith and the Saints in Kirtland, Ohio.

1834
Rochester's city charter is granted.

Jeremy S. Stone, older brother and co-owner of the *Cottage Hotel* with George S. Stone, dies in November.

1835-36
The Mendon Academy, a two-room cobblestone school-house, is built on the west side of Mendon-Ionia Road. It operates as a private school before becoming Mendon District #2 (of 17 districts) and incorporated in 1836. Tuition

is $3 a quarter, $4 for instruction in "higher English," and $5 for Latin, Greek, and French. It closes in 1950 and the building is sold to the Mendon Fire Department.

1838
The name of Mendon hamlet is shortened from "East Mendon" to "Mendon."

1839
There are 93 students at The Mendon Academy.

The original Congregational Church (built in 1816) is moved to Mendon hamlet after the Presbyterians break from the Congregational Society. It is in use until 1899, when a new brick church is built, and the building is purchased by the Mendon Grange.

1840
The large public library in the hamlet is in full free use.

1844
While awaiting trial for treason in Illinois, Joseph Smith and his brother, Hyrum Smith, are shot and killed by a mob in Illinois.

1847
Brigham Young becomes the second president of the Mormon Church.

1852
Ernest Shackleton arrives in Mendon and opens a blacksmith and wagon shop on the east side of Irondequoit Creek, known as "Shack's." It is later moved north of the hamlet's four corners. His son, Frank, later takes over the business.

1854
George S. Stone dies on October 18 at the age of 61. His wife, Susan Stone, assumes ownership of the *Cottage Hotel*.

1855
Chauncy D. Tuttle and his wife Matilda purchase the *Cottage Hotel* from the estate of George S. Stone. Jediah (Jedidiah) P. Fowler takes out a mortgage from Chauncy D. Tuttle for $2,000 and is listed as innkeeper.

The harness shop in Mendon hamlet is owned by M. Amborn; the shoe store by M. F. Ives; and the clothing store by A. Downing.

1858
The building of the *Cottage Hotel* is shown as *J. P. Fowler's Hotel*.

1860
The Town of Mendon now contains three hamlets: Mendon, Sibleyville, and Rochester Junction. The only village is that of the Village of Honeoye Falls. The town encompasses 23,000 acres of farmland.

The Pony Express begins its express mail route from Missouri to San Francisco on April 3rd. It will be in operation for only 18 months before going bankrupt on October 26th the following year.

1861
The American Civil War begins on April 12th.

1865
The American Civil War ends on April 9th.

1866

George W. Peer purchases a one-acre lot containing the *Cottage Hotel* from Chauncy D. Tuttle and his wife on September 22, 1866, plus another adjoining two-acre lot.

1868

Ely (or Eli) and Harriet Phelps purchase the *Cottage Hotel* from George W. Peer and Emma J. Peer on May 1st.

1869

Members of The Good Templars lodge members number 75.

1871

John and Mary Smith purchase the *Cottage Hotel* from Ely (or Eli) Phelps and Harriet Phelps on November 11th.

1874

The Mendon Hamlet Grange is organized on February 7th, meeting in various locations until the purchase of what was originally the Presbyterian Church in 1919.

1876

Hemlock and Canadice Lakes supply drinking water to Mendon.

No new liquor licenses in Mendon are granted. "In the spring of 1876 the people, aroused by the evils of intoxication, combined without regard to party and both nominated and elected anti-license excise commissioners. These officers have stood firm in their trust and since the organization of this board no licenses have been granted in town." *History of Monroe County*, (New York; Everts, Ensign & Everts; 1788-1877), 835.

1878

Rudolph Teschner begins the manufacture of ocarinas in the kiln on his farm at 267 Parrish Road. He will make an average of 15-20,000 ocarinas a year. Before his death in 1920, a last order for 5,000 ocarinas sells to a firm in Chicago.

1879
A Greek Revival barbershop, operated for 55 years, is built at 3897 Rush-Mendon Road, and operated by Addison Hodge. Later it is purchased by Mr. and Mrs. Furlong and operates as a hardware partnership by Hicks & Furlong. It later becomes Broomfield Hardware, Inc., a place where, according to Jane Broomfield, "until 1979 sold baling twine on credit, collecting the tab after the grain harvest." Next door is a meat market operated by Fred Richards.

Across the street from the barbershop is a harness shop owned by Adam Baer and later his son, Fred J. Baer, until his retirement in 1935. Next door to the harness shop is a shoe and cobbler shop operated by Barney Murphy.

1885
By this date the hamlet of Mendon has a steam flouring mill, a steam sawmill, a coal and lumber business, a farm produce business, an apple and peach drying house, two general stores, two hotels (the *Cottage Hotel* and the *Mendon Hotel*), Shackleton's blacksmith shop, and 200 inhabitants.

1886
Thomas ("Yankee Tom") Finucane purchases the *Cottage Hotel* from Mary Smith (widow of John Smith) on December 1, 1886.

1890
Jacob Schlaefer and family own and run the *Mendon Hotel* for the next 19 years. In an article in the *Honeoye Falls Times* on July 25, 1957, Lillian Schlaefer, their daughter, recalls that: *"The building had around 10 bedrooms, wide halls, lengthy staircases, and the lower floor was given over to a large lobby, public living room and dining room, and the private living room of the proprietor's family, and a bar on one side."* A third story

spring floor ballroom is constructed that same year of black walnut wood and later moved to the dining room.

1892
A Lehigh Valley Railroad depot is constructed in Mendon hamlet. Clive Harmon is the first station master, followed by Darwin W. Turner, from 1900-1938. Signals are hand operated and special round trips to Rochester via Rochester Junction are 78 cents. Later, passengers will board trains in nearby Fishers hamlet.

The *Mendon Hotel* passes through several owners: Ben Peer sells the *Mendon Hotel* to relocate in Florida to Robert Dunchie and John E. Tomlinson, who then becomes sole owner.

1894
The *Cottage Hotel* name is recorded by Thomas ("Yankee Tom") Finucane. Liquor licenses in Mendon hamlet are granted to Thomas Finucane and Jacob Schlaefer.

1895
A dry goods store and a general store are side-by-side across from the *Mendon Hotel*.

George Selden of Rochester is granted the patent for the gasoline automobile engine and its use in a 4-wheeled car in 1895. By the early 1900s, Henry Ford and other auto company executives challenge Selden's patent, eventually ending the patent in 1911.

1896
On April 22, 1896, Thomas ("Yankee Tom") Finucane begins building a barn for stagecoach horses to the north of the *Cottage Hotel*. The barn is completed in May for a total of $407.91. The building costs were: $99.45 for labor, $257.50 for lumber, $34.96 for digging and building the foundation wall, and $16.00 for nails. The barn still exists in renovated form.

The *Black Diamond Express,* "a palace on wheels," is conceived on May 18th by Charles S. Lee, General Passenger Agent of the Lehigh Valley Railroad. Twin luxury passenger trains running the 447 miles from New York to Buffalo in ten hours or less, each becomes renowned as "the handsomest train in the world." *The Black Diamond Express* becomes cherished by honeymooners making their way to Niagara Falls, also earning it the nickname "The Honeymoon Express." The *Black Diamond* is discontinued a week shy its 63rd birthday on May 11, 1959.

The *Raines* law is passed on April 1st, banning the sale of liquor on Sunday. The law has a good-sized loophole: alcohol can be sold with complimentary meals in hotels with more than ten rooms. Within months, hundreds of "Raines hotels" are in operation, many said to also serve as brothels.

1897
Edward Strong is listed as Manager of the *Mendon Hotel.*

1900
The first scheduled Mass is held in Mendon on May 25 by John J. Donnelly from Victor.

1902
St. Catherine of Sienna Catholic Church is built next to the Mendon Academy and is dedicated by Bishop McQuaid. Services are held earlier in 1900 before the church is built.

Ernest Ehrenberg is listed as the owner of the *Mendon Hotel.*

1903
Mendon resident David O'Connor builds the Bean Milling Company next to the railroad tracks on Route 251 just west of Route 64.

1904
St. Mark's Lutheran Church is built using mostly native hemlock lumber. Ground is broken for the Lutheran Church on Victor-Mendon Road (Route 251). Services are first held in both English and German.

1908
The first "Model T" is built for sale on October 1, 1908, at a price of about $850.

1909
The Schlaefer family cease operating the *Mendon Hotel*. Charles Wangman is listed as Manager of the *Mendon Hotel*.

1912
Dunn Oil Company, Inc. is begun by Fred Dunn as a produce and lumber business. The heating oil business will be added in 1934.

1914
The Mendon Fire Department is established.

1914-1918
World War I begins and ends.

1917
On December 18, the 18th Amendment, prohibiting the sale or creation of any beverage with alcohol above 0.05%, is passed in both chambers of Congress.

The first firefighting equipment, a hand pumper that requires 16 men to operate, is purchased by the Mendon Fire Department.

1919
On October 28th, the National Prohibition Act, or *Volstead Act*, is passed to enforce legislation of the 18th Amendment.

The 18th Amendment is ratified on January 16th. The 19th Amendment, giving women the right to vote, is passed on June 4th.

1920

The 19th Amendment is ratified on August 18th.
The Mendon Baptist Church is torn down. Road paving begins, but most Mendon hamlet roads are composed of dirt until 1930.

The Mendon Fire Department purchases a retrofitted Ford *Model T* pick-up truck. It will not be replaced until 1932, when a new Chevrolet fire truck costing $750 is bought.

1921

On April 5th, the *Mullan-Gage State Liquor Enforcement Law* goes into effect. It is an attempt of the State of New York to enforce Prohibition, making violations of the *Volstead Act* also violations of state law, requiring both state and local police to enforce federal law.

1922

A hand-operated fire truck pumper is purchased by the Mendon Fire Department. Previous included ladders and round-bottomed buckets, which could not be set down during bucket brigades.

In the news: The Rochester Democrat and Chronicle reports that on May 18th Sheriff Henry S. Morse initiates a raid in Fairport, New York, of selected hotels, cafes, storefronts, and a private home. Most raids target working class immigrant drinking establishments on North Main Street.

The first radio is introduced in the White House by President Warren G. Harding. Automobiles, "moving pictures" and jazz are popular.

1923

The Baptist Church in Mendon is dismantled for its lumber. The Mullan-Gage State Liquor Enforcement Law is repealed.

1928

Mendon Ponds Park, previously known as *The Mendon Kames*, is inaugurated, thanks to the efforts of Professor Herman LeRoy Fairchild.

1929

The American Stock Market crashes on October 24th, signaling the beginning of the Great Depression.

1931

In the News: on December 30th, the Rochester Democrat and Chronicle reports that "dry agents" raid the Mendon Hotel, seizing two half-barrels of beer from owner Ernst (Ernest) Ehrenberg.

1932

The Mendon Fire Department acquires its first pumper truck. A new fire truck will not be purchased until 1950.

1933

The 18th Amendment is repealed by the passage of the 21st Amendment, which is ratified on December 5th.

1935

Thomas ("Yankee Tom") Finucane, owner of the *Cottage Hotel*, dies on March 31, age 79.

1937

Nahum D. Fletcher and Harriet M. Fletcher purchase the *Cottage Hotel* from May Finucane Bridges on December 2, 1937 as part of the Mary Finucane estate.

1939

Hitler invades Poland on September 1st and World War II begins.

1940

A water system is established in Mendon, but never expanded. To this day, homes in the hamlet rely on septic systems.

1941

The Japanese attack Pearl Harbor on December 7th.

1945

On May 8, 1945, Germany surrenders.

The first atomic bomb is dropped on Hiroshima in Japan. Three days later, a second atomic bomb is dropped on Nagasaki.

The Japanese surrender on August 15th and World War II ends on September 2nd.

Ferdinand V. Masso and Fannie Frehmeyer purchase the *Cottage Hotel* from Nahum D. and Harriet M. Fletcher on October 4, 1945.

Ernest Ehrenberg leases the *Mendon Hotel*.

Harold Folts leases the *Mendon Hotel* from Ernest Ehrenberg. Folts is the grandfather of Pat Freeman, current owner of *Ye Olde Mendon Tavern*, formerly the *Springwater Inn* in Mendon hamlet.

1946

Paul Streb purchases the *Cottage Hotel* from Ferdinand V. Masso and Fannie Frehmeyer on July 8, 1946. The grand opening is announced on November 3, 1946.

Edward Butts and Winifred Butts and Frederick Mahrt and Gertrude Mahrt are final owners of the *Mendon Hotel* before it is purchased by Gulf Oil Company in 1957.

The Cold War begins on March 12th.

1948
On May 16, after 7 minutes of deliberation, two men (one from Henrietta, one from Fishers) are convicted of third-degree assault after a barroom brawl at the *Cottage Hotel*.

1950
Albert ("Al") Heckman and Mary Elizabeth Heckman purchase the *Cottage Hotel* from August and Martha Van Castiles on June 29, 1950. Al and Mary manage the *Cottage Hotel* together and live on the top floor, along with their two children, Tommy and Rosemary, and family friends Dell and Earl Woodard.

The Korean War begins on June 25th.

The Mendon Academy closes and is sold to the Mendon Fire Department.

Lewis D. Woodward of Holcomb is arrested for carrying "a Japanese pistol" and brandishing it at the *Cottage Hotel*. Two bystanders divest him of his gun and the chambers found to be empty.

1952
The Lehigh Valley Railroad depot in Mendon hamlet is torn down.

1953
The Korean War ends on July 27th.

1954

The New York Thruway is built on the northern border of Mendon, becoming Interstate I-90 in 1957 when the Interstate Highway System is created.

1955

The Vietnam War begins on November 1st.

On October 7, a fire starts at the *Cottage Hotel* but is quickly put out by the Mendon Fire Department. Victor firemen come to their aid.

1956

Harold Folts, owner of the *Springwater Inn* (now *Ye Olde Mendon Tavern*) dies on site at age 51. His spirit is said to haunt the tavern to this day.

1957

The *Mendon Hotel* is sold to the Gulf Oil Company. The furnishings are put up for auction.

On July 25, 1957, the *Mendon Hotel* is used as a realistic firefighting demonstration by the Mendon Fire Department and nine other fire crews from Brighton, Bushnell's Basin, East Rochester, Egypt, Fairport, Fishers, Penfield, Pittsford, and Victor.

1959

On May 11th, the Lehigh Valley Railroad luxury trains named the "Black Diamond Express" makes their final run, some 63 years after they were conceived.

1960

Cooking and heating gas comes to Mendon hamlet for the first time on August 11th when gas mains are dug beneath the four corners by Rochester Gas & Electric. Forty-seven customers sign up for the initial phase of the three-year, $209,000 expansion project, to be completed on September 1,

1960. The gas mains are installed 3′ 6″ deep and 30″ beneath the creek bed.

1961
Passenger service ends on the Lehigh Valley Railroad. There is freight service only until 1976.

1972
Robert F. ("Bob") Clifford purchases the *Cottage Hotel* from Albert ("Al") Heckman and Mary Elizabeth Heckman on January 27, 1972 for $75,000.

Paul S. Gordon ("Buzzy") Bronson leases the *Cottage Hotel* from Robert F. Clifford for $467 a month on a triple net lease and begins developing it as a music venue.

1973
Doug Foxall is listed as Manager of the *Cottage Hotel*.

1975
John Urquhart ("Burdock") Ross leases the *Cottage Hotel* from Paul S. Gordon ("Buzzy") Bronson for $20,000, as reimbursement for improvements, and a triple net lease of $2,177.50 per month, and manages the business.

The Vietnam War ends on April 30, 1975.

1976
On March 31st, the Lehigh Railroad tracks begin to be pulled up and replaced by the *Rails to Trails* system of hiking, biking and equine trails established by *The Mendon Foundation*, a nonprofit land trust.

1977
Anthony "Tony" Demeo is listed in the Rochester *Democrat and Chronicle* as Manager of the *Cottage Hotel*.

1978
The Grange Hall is sold to the Mendon Playhouse.

1981
On October 19th, John Urquhart ("Burdock") Ross dies. The ownership of the lease of the *Cottage Hotel* passes to his estate, administered by his younger sister, Ann (Ross) Chaintreuil, and continues the triple net lease of $2,177.50 per month.

1982
Jacqueline ("Jacky") (Muzdakis) Fisher owns and manages the *Cottage Hotel* on a simple lease of $2,177.50 from Ann Chaintreuil, executor of John Urquhart ("Burdock") Ross's estate. At age 24, she is the youngest person to obtain a liquor license in New York State.

1984
Ann Chaintreuil and Renier Chaintreuil purchase the *Cottage Hotel* property and business from Robert F. ("Bob") Clifford for $90,000.

1987
Howard "Ike" Stanley (January 30, 1909-February 7, 1987), owner of the two-pump service station and general store north of the *Cottage Hotel*, dies on February 7th, age 78.

1991
Robert F. ("Bob") Clifford, former owner of the *Cottage Hotel*, dies on January 4, 1991, at age 82.

The Cold War ends on December 26th.

1992
The Mendon Historic Preservation Commission is appointed by the Town Board.

1998
Louis C. ("Lou") DiNardo and his partner, Nancy Marinelli, run the *Cottage Hotel* until Lou's death in 2004. It is known in print advertisements as *Lou's Cottage Hotel*.

A catastrophic storm causes extensive flooding in the hamlet when Irondequoit Creek crests sometime after midnight on January 14, 1998. Waters flood the basement of the Cottage Hotel and a small fire is caused by the furnace motor burning out.

2004
Louis C. ("Lou") DiNardo, owner of the *Cottage Hotel*, dies of cancer on March 4th. His partner, Nancy Marinelli continues its management until its sale in 2005.

2005
The *Cottage Hotel* is purchased by Hilary and David Stott for $230,000 in April from Ann (Ross) Chaintreuil and Renier Chaintreuil, sister and brother-in-law of John Urquhart ("Burdock") Ross. A 15-year $135,000 mortgage is held by the Chaintreuils. The Stotts devote themselves to preserving the *Cottage Hotel's* 200-year history.

A Sno-Cone Machine is installed at the *Cottage Hotel* and remains until 2010.

2006
The foot rail from a beam from the renovation of the barn next door to the *Cottage Hotel* is installed at the bar. Upon further repairs, Hilary and David Stott reopen the Cottage Hotel after obtaining a liquor license.

2009
Nancy Marinelli, partner of Louis C. ("Lou") DiNardo, former owner of the *Cottage Hotel*, dies on December 17th.

2011-2012
The pool table at the *Cottage Hotel* is removed and the game room completed in 2012. The first kitchen renovation and expansion are made. The kitchen will be expanded two more times during the upcoming years.

2014
John Cassata shoots himself in the hand and injures friend Charles Raab, when Cassata's licensed firearm goes off accidentally during lunch hour at the Cottage Hotel. No charges are filed.

2016
The *Bevador* beer cooler in the *Cottage Hotel* bar is renovated by Hilary and David Stott at a cost of $6,000. The work is done by Pat Falin at Mantique & Oddities Etc. in Bloomfield, New York, in May of that year.

2020
The barn adjacent to the *Cottage Hotel*, built in 1896 by Thomas ("Yankee Tom") Finucane, is renovated by Hilary and David Stott. Old circus posters are discovered in the barn.

The *Cottage Hotel's* original bar top is switched out and replaced by one crafted by Mendon local Steve Tubbs. One section, with an embedded dime, is on display at *The Cottage*.

2023
On June 2nd, Robert J. ("Bob") Freeman (husband of Pat Freeman, owner of *Ye Olde Mendon Tavern*), dies at age 75. The *Cottage* Hotel sign is replaced with one designed and constructed by Alan Sartain. The original sign is on display at *The Cottage*.

Mendon hamlet still relies on septic systems for wastewater management. The *Cottage Hotel of Mendon* is still one of the most beloved down home watering holes in all the land!

Resources

Music Track by Jeff Williams
Good Old Days
https:soundcloud.com/jeffrey-d-1/good-old-days.

Music Videos by Steve Anderson & Slipton Fell
One Chance to Live it
https://www.youtube.com/watch?v=OyZe3p7zHlQ features John Urquhart ("Burdock") Ross on camera.

(You'll Never Feel Alone) at the Cottage Hotel
https://www.youtube.com/watch?v=pffVf0fqb94.

Powder Mill
https://www.youtube.com/watch?v=38p8KuD3HzY.

Music Video by Keith Baker
This Song
sung by John Paulsen, Keith Baker, & Tim Chappell
https://www.youtube.com/watch?v=HTm0GXarkX8.

Music Video by Johnny Bauer
One Horse Town
https://youtu.be/EIQnD8cGGCU.

Music Video by Brian Venton
https://www.facebook.com/ventonclarkband/videos/5500729750004401.

Videos
The Black Diamond Express
https://www.youtube.com/watch?=jVvabY7Y7fw.

South Park, Season 7, Episode #12:
https://www.youtube.com/watch?v=W4NemVO4JL0.
https://southpark.cc.com/video-clips/enc33g/south-park-joseph-smith-part-1.
https://southpark.cc.com/video-clips/k6ostk/south-park-joseph-smith-part-2.
https://southpark.cc.com/video-clips/xfp519/south-park-joseph-smith-part-3.

Online Resources:

Autobiography of Heber Chase Kimball, circa 1842-1858
https://catalog.churchofjesuschrist.org, MS 627.

A Brief History of Cobblestone Architecture
"Cayuga County Cobblestones,"
Richard F. Palmer
https://www.cayugagenealogy.org/misc/Cayuga_Cobbles.pdf.

BYU Studies
"Joseph Smith's 1826 Trial: The Legal Setting"
Gordon A. Madsen
https://byustudies.byu.edu/PDFLibrary/30.2MadsenJosephSmiths-12a5c181-05a1-4e48-b7a4-2d039c4c16f0.pdf.

Cayuga County Cobblestone
https://www.cayugagenealogy.org/misc/Cayuga_Cobbles.pdf.

Cobblestone Masonry
Carl F. Schmidt
https://www.cobblestonemuseum.org/CobblestoneStructuresCatalog/Cob%20Mas%20jpg/Page%201.htm.

The Code of Handsome Lake, Arthur C. Parker, 1913
https://www.sacred-texts.com/nam/iro/parker/index.htm.

Crooked Lake Review
https://www.crookedlakereview.com.

Democrat and Chronicle (Rochester)
https://nyhistoricnewspapers.org.

Dialogue Journal
"Scrying for the Lord: Magic, Mysticism, and the Origins of the Book of Mormon"
Clay L. Chandler
https://www.dialoguejournal.com/wp/content/uploads/sbi/issues/V36N04.

GenWeb Monroe County New York
https://www.mcnygenealogy.com.

The Henry Ford
https://www.thehenryford.org

History of Monroe County | History of the Towns and Villages | Mendon
http://genealogytrails.com.

Historic Aerials
http://historicaerials.com.

Honeoye Falls Times
https://nyshistoricnewspapers.org.

Lehigh Valley Railroad
http://www.lvrr.com.

Mendon-Honeoye Falls-Lima Sentinel
https://mhflsentinel.com.

Newspapers.com
https://www.newspapers.com.

Ocarina app.
https://apps.apple.com/us/app/ocarina/id293053479.

RocWiki: The People's Guide to Rochester
https://rocwiki.org.

Stagecoach Days, "Getting There by Stages"
Richard F. Palmer
https://stagecoachdays.blogspot.com, September 2011.

Statements in Stone
Paul S. Gordon ("Buzzy") Bronson
https://www.statementsinstone.com/specialwords.

Tariff Hearings Before the Committee on Ways and Means
Volume 2. United States Congress House Committee on Ways and Means, Paragraph 326 1/2, #751, p. 1875.
https://babel.hathitrust.org/cgi/pt?id=mdp.39015016761101&view=1up&seq=751&q1=Rudolph%20Teschner.

Transportation in America's Postal System
Rickie Longfellow, *Back in Time*, June 27, 2017
https://www.fhwa.dot.gov/infrastructure/back0304.cfm.

Traveling to the Thousand Islands by Stagecoach
Richard F. Palmer, Thousand Islands Life, Volume 18, Issue 8, August 2023.
https://thousandislandslife.com/traveling-to-the-thousand-islands-by-stagecoach.

United States Postal Service: An American History
https://about.usps.com/publications/pub100.pdf.

Organizations:

Cobblestone Museum
https://www.cobblestonemuseum.org.

East Bloomfield Historical Society
https://www.ebhs1838.org.

Honeoye Falls-Town of Mendon Historical Society and Museum
https://hfmhistorical.org.

Landmark Society of Western New York
https://landmarksociety.org.

Lehigh Valley Railroad Historical Society
http://www.lvrrhs.org.

The Mendon Foundation
https://mendonfoundation.org

Town of Mendon
https://townofmendon.org.

Victor Historical Society | Historic Valentown Museum
www.historicvalentownmuseum.org

West Bloomfield Historical Society
https://wbhsny.org.

Publications:

An Insufficient Canon: Popul Wuj, Book of Mormon, and Other Neophyte Scriptures
Thomas Murphy
Mormon Association Meeting 2002.

Around Mendon and Honeoye Falls
Diane C. Ham and Roberta Luce-Majewski
Arcadia Publishing, 2004.

Brigham Young as a Mendon Craftsman: A Study in Historical Archeology
J. Sheldon Fisher
Cornell University Press
New York History, Vol. 61, no. 4 (October 1980), 447.

Brigham Young, Carpenter and Cabinet Maker
John G. Sheret
Crooked Lake Review, Fall 2006-Winter 2007.

Cobblestone Masonry
Carl Frederick Schmidt
University of Michigan, 2007.

The Cottage Hotel Songbook
Karen Mireau
with songs by Steve Anderson, Keith Baker, Johnny Bauer, Brian Venton, and Jeff Williams.
Azalea Art Press, Sonoma, California, 2023.

The Farm Journal Illustrated Rural Directory
of Monroe County, New York
Wilmer Atkinson Company, Philadelphia, 1918-1923.

From Forests to Farming in Mendon, New York
Diane C. Ham, 2001.

From the Stage Coach to the Pulpit: Being an Auto-Biographical Sketch with Incidents and Anecdotes of Elder H. K. Stimson
Elder H. K. Stimson
R. A. Campbell, St. Louis, 1874. Page 70.

Gazetteer and Business Directory of Monroe County, New York for 1869-70
Hamilton Child
Erastus Darrow, Rochester, New York, 1869.

Geologic Story of the Genesee Valley
and Western New York
Herman Leroy Fairchild / Henderson-Mosher Inc.
Rochester Book Bindery, Rochester, New York, 1928.

"Haulin' in the Mail:
A Slice of Nostalgia in Mendon, New York"
Paul S. Worboys
Mendon-Honeoye Falls-Lima Sentinel,
August-September, 2012, revised August, 2023.

History of Monroe County
Everts, Ensign & Everts
New York, 1788-1877.

The History of Spiritualism, Vol. I and II
Arthur Conan Doyle
Cassell & Company, Ltd., Great Britain, 1926.

History of the Town of Mendon 1813-2000
and Village of Honeoye Falls 1838-2000
Diane C. Ham, Anne Bullock
Edited by Julia P. Dickinson
Honeoye Falls-Town of Mendon Historical Society, 2000.

Honeoye Falls, N.Y.: Its Beginning . . . . .
David K. Maloney
O'Brien Bros. Printing Co., Inc.,
Honeoye Falls, New York, 1963.

Honeoye Falls and Town of Mendon History Tour:
A Visit to Points of Interest in the Town of Mendon
and Village of Honeoye Falls
Anne Bullock and Diane C. Ham
Photocopied Booklet, 1988.

In the Mendon Cemetery from 1825 to 1890
Daniel Allen
J.W. Watkins, Mendon, NY, 1890. Introduction.

Mendon — The Early Years | Stagecoach Hotels
John G. Sheret
Crooked Lake Review
Winter 2006.

Mendon's Cobblestone Landmarks
Diane C. Ham
Mendon Foundation Newsletter, Vol. 8, No. 2, Fall 2000.

Murder and Mayhem in Mendon and Honeoye Falls
Diane C. Ham and Lynne Menz
History Press, Charleston, South Carolina, 2013.

New Genesee Farmer and Gardener's Journal,
"Cobblestone Buildings," Vol. 2, No. 5, 1841.
D. T. Greatfield. Rochester, New York,
Bateham & Crosman, 66-67.

On the Lehigh Valley:
The Great Double Track Scenic Highway
The Passenger Department | Lehigh Valley Railroad
A.A. Heard, Charles S. Lee, Henry H. Kingston, 1901.

On the Origin of the Names of Places
in Monroe County, New York
Franklin Hanford
Scottsville, New York, 1911.

The Pioneers of Mendon:
Early History of the Town and Its Settlers
Compiled for the Times by Mrs. Anah B. Yates.

Rochester and Monroe County: A History and Guide
Genesee Book Club of Rochester
Scrantoms | City of Rochester, New York, 1937.

Skyler Smith's Tour of Mendon: The Cottage Hotel, Part II,
Deb and Tim Smith
Mendon-Honeoye Falls-Lima Sentinel, April 26, 2018, 2.

Skyler Smith's Tour of Mendon: The Mendon Hotel
Deb and Tim Smith
Mendon-Honeoye Falls-Lima Sentinel, January 31, 2019.

Stagecoach Towns
Arch Merrill
Louis Heindl & Sons, Rochester, New York, 1947.

The Struggle for Monroe County |
Read before the Rochester Historical Society
Howard L. Osgood, May 23, 1992.

Town of Mendon, New York | *Honeoye Falls* |
150th Anniversary Celebration | *Town of Mendon* |
August 14th through 18th | *1963* | *Souvenir Program
and History 1813* | *Sesquicentennial, 1963*
O'Brien Brother Printing, Honeoye Falls, New York, 1963.

Symphony Iroquoian
Carleton Burke, Rochester Museum of Arts and Sciences,
Rochester, New York, 1937.

Tell Me Again | *That the Dead* | *Do Dream*
Poems about Mendon hamlet and John Urquhart
("Burdock") Ross
Karen Mireau
Azalea Art Press, 2022.

Trails Westward to Mendon:
By Covered Wagon, Stagecoach, and Tavern c. 1821
Diane C. Ham, 2022.

Uncle Dale's Readings in Early Mormon History
The Gem | of Literature and Science
Rochester, NY, Vol. II, No. 2, Sunday, May 15, 1830.

*Upstate Cauldron: Eccentric Spiritual Movements
in Early New York State*
Jocelyn Godwin
State University of New York Press | Excelsior Editions
Albany, New York, 2015.

"When Circuses Came to Honeoye Falls"
Paul S. Worboys
Reprinted from the *Mendon-Honeoye Falls-Lima Sentinel*
Thursday, August 22, 1991.

Acknowledgments

*My deepest gratitude to all those
who have gifted me with their creative time
and energy, and who have supported me
so fully in researching and writing
all the amazing stories about Mendon hamlet
and the Cottage Hotel.*

Cottage Hotel Owners:

Paul S. Gordon "Buzzy" Bronson
My many conversations with Buzzy
about Mendon hamlet history and his tenure developing
the *Cottage Hotel* into a popular music venue were more
than enlightening—they provided first-hand details that
brought the history of *The Cottage* into sharp focus.

Ann (Ross) Chaintreuil
& Renier ("Rennie") Chaintreuil
Ann, the sister of John Urquhart ("Burdock") Ross,
and her husband, Rennie, have been an essential part
of this book from the very beginning. Their open-hearted
support and generosity in providing private photos and
information were beyond gracious—without their help,
this book would be greatly diminished.

Jacqueline "Jacky" (Muzdakis) Fisher
& Baird B. Fisher
Jacky's personal recollections of managing
and owning the *Cottage Hotel* during the '80s
with her husband, Baird Fisher, added much to my
understanding of *The Cottage's* illustrious
(and sometimes notorious) history.

Hilary & David Stott

It was Hilary's idea that prompted me in 2022 to begin writing the history of *The Cottage Hotel*. The Stott's enthusiasm and hands-on help in connecting me to others and providing me with their own special memories were essential to birthing this book.

Historians:

Chris & Betsy Carosa

This dynamic duo, who are the publishers of the *Mendon-Honeoye Falls-Lima Sentinel*, have been a rich source of information, assistance, and ongoing support. They are tireless advocates of Mendon hamlet history and a true asset to the community.

Diane C. Ham
Mendon Town Historian

I am especially grateful to Diane, Mendon's historian since 1979, for her many generous contributions to this book. Her research and writings were the backbone of early chapters, and her insight, depth of knowledge, and willingness to share resources prevented many a potential *faux pas*. My thanks also to Diane's husband, Rodney ("Rod") Ham, for his support and assistance.

Lynne Menz, Honeoye Falls Historian
Bill Lane, Mendon-Honeoye Falls Museum interim Curator

These accomplished educators and custodians of our local local history lent their expertise at every turn. They were instrumental in tracking down facts, archival photos, and quickly answering my sometimes obscure questions, no matter how big or how small.

Richard F. Palmer

Richard's highly crafted and well-researched works provided a wealth of facts about life in early Upstate New York and greatly contributed to my understanding of that time period. His writings are exemplary, as you might expect from a former newspaper editor, reporter, and passionate historian.

Paul S. Worboys (a.ka. P. J. Erbley)

Paul's extensive knowledge of Mendon and Honeoye Falls and his ability to engage others in learning about the history of the area in an entertaining way is legendary. I am indebted to Paul's expert guidance in helping me edit and research this book as well as its companion volume of poetry. My gratitude to him is truly beyond measure.

Contributors:

Harout Babigian & Molly Babigian & Melkon, Ahren & Emrys

Harout's anecdotes of growing up at the *Cottage Hotel* and working there as a cook and bartender gave me a humorous inside look at *Cottage* life. His wife Molly's views of working at *The Cottage* added even more insight into its day-to-day workings. Their comments by their sons Melkon and Ahren about *The Cottage* are simply priceless! I am so thankful for all their contributions to the book.

John Bronson

John played a special dual role at *The Cottage* as a bartender, and also as brother to former owner Paul S. Gordon "Buzzy" Bronson. His intimate stories of the many incidents of mischief that went on at *The Cottage* during the '70s were truly entertaining.

Sarah Jane Clifford & Tim Clifford

I am indebted to my dearly loved friends of 50 years whose vibrant memories of the *Cottage Hotel* helped me recall and confirm my own recollections of the special nature of this place. It was Sarah who encouraged me to apply for a job at *The Cottage* when she left for college. A pivotal moment, indeed!

Richard Crowther

Richard's candid story of partying at the *Cottage Hotel* and witnessing some of the shenanigans that occurred there is a priceless recollection that may spark memories for others of their own wild times at *The Cottage*.

John Drogan

John's anecdotes about *The Cottage* and his memories of working with Burdock were a balm to my soul. Thank you, John!

Deidre "Deedee" Dutcher

The Cottage wouldn't have been the same without "The Dutchess" at the helm in the mid-70s. Her amusing reveries of that time period made me laugh so hard it literally brought tears to my eyes.

Jim Edmon

I have admired artist Jim Edmon for over 50 years, both as a friend and as a fan of his highly-creative designs and his brilliant multi-media pieces. I feel so fortunate that he agreed to create the covers for this book!

Jeremy Fisher
& Keegan Fisher

Jeremy's unreserved stories of growing up
with parents Baird and Jacky Fisher at *The Cottage* gave me
fresh (and funny) insights into day-to-day life there.
I am so thankful to his wife, Keegan, for her
immense help in gathering family facts and photos.

Doug Foxall

As a manager and bartender at *The Cottage*
in the '70s and early '80s, Doug's vivid memories
and details of those days added an unexpected
flavorful dose of spice to this book.

David Friedlander

The current owner of the farm on Parrish Road
where Rudolph Teschner built his ocarina factory in the
1800s, provided essential facts and photos that led
to a deeper, clearer understanding of its origin.

Patty Gorham

Many may relate to Patty's candid stories
of hanging out with underage friends at *The Cottage*
in the 1960s and beyond. I am in awe of her openness
and refreshing honesty.

Bill Haywood

My thanks to Bill for connecting me to those who
were such a huge part of *Cottage* life during the '70s,
and especially for his good memories of tending bar,
playing softball, and traveling with Burdock.

Hendo

Hendo's recollections of Burdock (his friend, mentor,
and housemate) brought back tender memories. I am so
grateful to Hendo for being so forthcoming and for taking
the time to relay these very special moments to me.

Anita Houston
There are some who can evoke so clearly and in just a few words what life was like in the late '70s, and Anita's memories are spot on. Her well-told tales of listening to bands and partying at *The Cottage* are greatly amusing. Thank you, Anita!

Geri Hughes & Kent Hughes
The beautiful love story of Geri and Kent is a remarkable testament to the magic that has always been a part of the legend of the *Cottage Hotel*. I am so happy that they chose to share their story with us.

Dick Joint
A longtime Mendon hamlet resident and dedicated 60-year member of the Mendon Fire Department, Dick's frank conversations revealed valuable insights about *Cottage* history.

Rosemary (Heckman) Lewis
Rosemary's remarkable first-person recollections of growing up above the *Cottage Hotel* during her parents' 22-year tenure as owners provided amazing details about *The Cottage* and life during that time.

Brian Lyons
Brian's photos of his extensive *Cottage Hotel* t-shirt collection made a wonderful addition to our sense of *Cottage* history and sensibility. Merci beaucoup, Brian!

Donna MacKenzie
The *Mendon-Honeoye Falls-Lima Sentinel's* very talented writer, editor, and designer was especially helpful to me. I truly appreciate her contribution.

Russell ("Russ") Mahrt
Russ's vibrant recollections of his boyhood living above the *Mendon Hotel* provided essential first-hand details about what life was like in the hamlet, especially for children of tavern owners during the 1950s.

Steve, Jennifer, Ben, Sam, & Katie Miller
My heartfelt thanks to the Miller family for their stories about *The Cottage* and the hamlet, which made me wish I had grown up there, too!

Pete Moss
Pete's tall tales about life in the hamlet kept me laughing, writing, and carefully searching for the truth.

Kimberly ("Kim") Ormiston
Kim's renderings of the interior of the *Cottage Hotel* seen in this book and on the covers of *The Cottage Hotel Songbook* were originally t-shirt designs. They reflect the magical nature of *The Cottage* so beautifully! I am so grateful she allowed me to feature her illustrations.

Fred Seager & Diane Seager
Fred and Diane Seager were immensely helpful in tracking down stories and photos, particularly those about former owner Robert F. ("Bob") Clifford. My hat is off to them for so enthusiastically sharing their time and resources!

Deb (Gonyea) Smith & Tim Smith
How lucky are we that Deb and Tim found each other again after 40 years! This dynamic literary duo (and love birds) has been a treasure trove of local lore ever since they

rode into town and began writing their weekly column: *Sentinel Lifestyles: Life with the (Word) Smiths* for the *Mendon-Honeoye Falls-Lima Sentinel*. Their investigative work to reveal the inside stories of our environs and their enthusiasm for life is a true inspiration to me. I am especially grateful for their editorial contributions.

Amanda Stott
& Austin Hamilton

Amanda's fond memories give us an insider's view of growing up at the *Cottage Hotel*. She and her partner, Austin, contributed much to the interior decor of *The Cottage* over the years, and it's good fun to go there now and to see the results of their artwork.

Madison ("Maddie") (Babigian) Trickey
& Kyle Trickey

I am so grateful for Maddie's recollections of growing up and working at *The Cottage*, which gave me a deeper understanding of what it was like to be a young adult during that time period.

Tad Van Zandt

My thanks to my good friend Tad, whom I've known since I was twelve. I have always admired his intrepid and adventurous spirit—and his ability to tell a first-rate tale.

Philip J. Welch

Phil went out of his way to send me articles and ideas for the book. His expert help in finding key people and facts about the hamlet was a boon to my research.

Hannah Whitney

The beautiful line drawing of *The Cottage* by the very talented Hannah Whitney adds a lovely grace note to this book. I am so thankful for her contribution.

Julie Williams

My thanks must also go to Julie for making the connection to Hannah Whitney and letting me know about her drawing of the *Cottage Hotel*. It's always an amazement to me to see how exactly the right resources show up when you most need them!

Musicians:

Steve Anderson

As the lead guitarist and a composer for *Slipton Fell*, Steve's candid photos and memories of playing at the the *Cottage Hotel*, and of his special friend Burdock added much to the integrity of this book.

Walt Atkison

As one of the musicians who regularly played at *The Cottage*, Walt's special stories of what it was like to be part of that scene in the '70s and '80s were fun and fascinating to hear.

Keith Baker

As a member of the iconic trio *Paulsen, Baker and Garvey*, Keith and the band were favorites of John Urquhart ("Burdock") Ross. His memories of that time added much to my understanding of the musicians' special point of view.

Johnny Bauer

Johnny Bauer's humorous recollections of his experiences at *The Cottage* as a solo performer during the past decade lent yet another valuable dimension to this story.

Chris Cady

As a founding member of *Slipton Fell*, Chris's happy memories of entertaining us at *The Cottage* gave me yet another perspective of the sometimes wild times that came with being a young musician. Chris was also instrumental (no pun intended) in connecting me to other *Cottage Hotel* musicians.

Jeff Clark
Jeff's amusing anecdotes as part of *Good Cracker* with Paul Strowe made me wish we could all travel back in time once again and hear them play.

Tom Price
As a member of *Gold Rush*, who often played at *The Cottage* in the '70s and '80s, the memories and photos Tom shared made that time period come alive.

Paul Strowe
As a mentor to many other musicians, Paul has always been a special part of *The Cottage* and the Rochester music scene. His heartfelt stories and excellent words of advice are more than greatly appreciated by me.

Brian Venton
Brian's candid conversations with me added much to my understanding of Burdock's relationship to the musicians at *The Cottage*. Thank you, Brian!

Brian Williams
As part of the *Swamp Root String Band*, one of the original groups that played at *The Cottage* in the '70s, Brian's recollections of *The Cottage Hotel* are a wonderful reminder of those good times.

Jeff Williams
Jeff (alias Earl Weems) took great care and time to assist me with writing the section on the Earl Weems Revue and also contributed anecdotes and photos about the Mendon music scene that were most valuable.

The Town of Mendon:

Jim Callerame
Jim's sharp memories added another layer of knowledge of how local people perceived the Lehigh Valley Railroad and its fascinating history.

Andy Caschetta
Andy's knowledge of the highways and byways of the hamlet truly benefitted my understanding of the area.

Bruce Fullerton
Bruce's guidance in locating people as well as adding his own insights about the hamlet were truly valuable.

Corey Gates
Corey is an amazing connector to people and information in the hamlet. I'm grateful for his generous help.

John Moffitt
John is a delight to talk with, and as someone who is an expert on Mendon facts, he was a very helpful resource.

And to those of you who have encouraged and continue to support my writing life in so many wonderful ways . . .

Patti Edmon
Best of friends for over 50 years, abstract artist Patti Edmon has read and critiqued every word I've written since the age of twelve. There will never be any way for me to properly thank her for her love, support, and all-essential honesty.

Marjory Harris
As a dear friend and an astute beta reader, I can always count on Marjory to provide intelligent and insightful guidance. I am so thankful for her contribution!

Jane Hirsch & Jeff Splitgerber
Jane and Jeff deserve a medal for enduring my seemingly endless renditions of *Cottage Hotel* arcana and ocarina stories. Their superb friendship and ongoing support are something I will always treasure.

Brenda Zimmermann Kessler
Brenda's always-positive nature and her ongoing editorial and moral support have been essential to the process of writing this book. Her experiences of the paranormal were instrumental in encouraging me to seek out similar stories.

Eric S. Kozlowski
My brother Eric's steadfast faith in my ability to get to the finish line kept me going and I am deeply grateful for that, as well as for his many creative ideas along the way.

Cynthia Leslie-Bole
For over 20 years, Cynthia has been my trusted go-to editor, literary guide, and spiritual advisor. She is a highly-talented wordsmith and poet in her own right. Her friendship and guidance mean the world to me.

Jennie Rose
Jennie is, and always will be, a valued confidant and friend without whose love and guidance I would surely be lost. Her expertise in trauma therapy, helped me find a deep tap root, giving me the strength and courage to write this book with greater clarity.

Shoey Sindel

I must thank my excellent friend of 17+ years —
the very artful portrait photographer Shoey Sindel,
who gave me the *hutzpah* to have a professional photo
made for this book. I am so grateful for her positive
creative spirit and enthusiasm for life!

Carol Van Zandt

My dear friend Carol, an accomplished painter, potter,
fabric designer, gourmet cook, and quilt artist, has inspired
me ever since our trippy wanna-be-hippy days back in the
'70s. I thank the universe every day for friends like her.

And last, but never least . . .

Raymond Jaye Rimmer

My wonderful husband, Ray, whose insight
and unwavering patience with the many hours
devoted to this book gave me the freedom
to research and write it with unlimited joy. It was a true
gift to have him by my side cheering me on
and I will always be forever grateful!

Index

18th Amendment—78, 332-334. *See Prohibition.*
19th Amendment—33, 333. *See Suffrage.*
21st Amendment—83. *See Prohibition.*

A

Abbott Downing Concord Coach—5, 6
Abolition—84
abolitionist—33
acid | LSD—206
Acknowledgments—351
addiction—153, 208, 286
Adventists—36, 191
alcohol—Contents, 8, 40, 74-75, 78-79, 123, 154, 163, 169, 193, 205, 208, 249, 285-286, 291, 331-332
alcoholic—123
alcoholism—193, 286
Alcorn, Mike—115
Alexander, Marguerite Olive—64-65
Alissa, Connie—165, 310
Allen, Daniel—323
Allen, Daniel (author)—348
Allen, Ethan—77
Allen, George W.—43
Allen, Jonas—320-321
Amborn, M.—327
American Civil War—327
American Moses—49
American Revolutionary War—318-319
American Stock Market crash—334
Anderson, Steve—135, 139, 177, 179, 185, 189, 206, 223, 235, 236-240, 243, 342, 347, 359
Angel Moroni—39
Anthony, Susan B.—33
anti-slavery—34
Apostles—42, 49
Arcadia Publishing—346
Archer, Mike—251-252
Architecture 83—129, 140
Atkison, Walt—114, 211-214, 359
Autumn Skies—226-227
Azalea Art Press—Copyright Page, 135, 347, 350, 374, 376

B

Babigian, Ahren—281-282, 353
Babigian, Emrys—281-282, 353
Babigian, Harout—162, 170-171, 279, 281-282, 283, 292, 353
Babigian, Madison ("Maddie")—171, 278-279, 358. *See: Trickey, Madison ("Maddie").*
Babigian, Melkon—281-282, 353
Babigian, Molly (Phillips)—162, 201, 280-282, 292, 353
Baer, Adam—329
Baer, Fred J.—329
Baker, Keith—138-139, 223, 230-234, 342, 347, 359
band(s)—107, 130, 132-133, 138, 161, 166, 168-169, 179, 199, 204, 207-210, 212-214, 217-228, 230-233, 235-236, 239-247, 250-252, 254-225, 258, 280, 288-289, 356, 359-360. *See: individual band name listings on pages 219-223.*
Banker, Carly—283
Baptist | Baptist Church—36, 43, 48, 76, 321-323, 333-334
Baptist Hill Cemetery, 322
barmaids—290
barn(s)—9, 21, 26-30, 68, 88, 92, 130, 155, 262-265, 284, 307, 309, 313-314, 320, 322, 330, 340-341
Barnard, Timothy—7, 321
bartender(s)—71, 104, 123-124, 126, 136, 146, 148, 159-162, 164-165, 169-174, 177, 180, 186-187, 196, 249, 257, 264, 290-291, 311, 353, 355
bartending, tending the bar—105, 144, 159-160, 162, 169-171, 175, 194
basement—22-23, 25, 31, 127, 194, 200, 268, 270, 283, 191, 312, 340. *See: cellar.*
Bateman & Crosman—19, 338
bathrooms—203, 206, 217, 225, 232, 273
Bauer, Johnny—14-15, 139, 223, 248-250, 288, 342, 347, 359
Baum, Frank L.—193
Beatles—246, 256
beatniks—210
Beeney, Bill—89
beer—Contents, 72, 79, 82, 105, 109-111, 113, 118, 126, 131, 133, 146, 149, 155, 158, 160, 166, 173 (stein), 175, 178-180, 184, 186-187, 189, 233, 238, 248-249, 258, 261, 265, 270, 272-273, 282, 290, 296, 313, 334, 341
Berlin, Irving—74
beloved—Contents, 105, 109, 341
Bevador—Contents, 86, 109-118, 130, 155, 186, 277, 313, 341
beverage(s)—78, 110-111, 239, 332
Black Diamond Express—53, 57-61, 64-65, 70, 72, 331, 337, 342
Bloomfield—36, 116, 313, 341,
Bloomfield, East, 89, (Inn) 134, 345
Bloomfield, West—89, 116, 134, 346
bluegrass—132, 136, 218-219
Bluegrass Happy Hour(s)—219
blues—213, 218, 225, 241, 246, 250, 252, 253-254
boogie-woogie—218
Book of Mormon—39, 45-46, 48-49, 51, 324, 344, 346
bootleggers—95
booze—81
Boughton Hill Road Cemetery—42
Borrman (friend of Russell ("Russ") Mahrt)—68
Boss Street Band—227
Botticelli, George—200, 245-246
bottle chute—268, 270
bowling machine—130, 159, 164, 166-168, 217
bra story—265
Bristol, Jeff—253
Bronson, Paul S. Gordon ("Buzzy")—31, 113, 128-137, 141, 150, 159-160, 164-167, 210-211, 213-214, 224, 306, 310-311, 338, 345, 35, 353
Bronson, John—126, 160, 165, 310, 353
Broomfield, Jane—329
brothel(s)—195, 331

Brown, John — 8, 315, 321
Brown, Scott — 227
Buckman, Gus — 254
Buffalo, New York — 16, 57, 61, 110, 320, 322, 331,
Bud(weiser) — 274
Bullock, Anne — 38, 348
Burdock — Dedication, In Memoriam, Contents, 114, 133, 135-141, 143, 146, 167, 173, 178-180, 182-183, 186-187, 198, 206-209, 214-216, 226-228, 231, 235-236, 239-241, 244, 303, 306, 310-311, 338-339, 341, 350-351, 354-355, 359-360
Burke, Carleton — 350
burger(s) — 107, 131-32, 150, 167, 196, 249, 282
    See: Cottage Burger.
Burned Out Blues Band — 250
Burned-Over — 32, 35-36, 38, 190
Burnt-Out — Contents, 32
Burnt-Over — Contents, 35, 52
Butts, Edward and Winifred — 68, 316, 336
Butts, Jackie — 68, 316
Butts, Jim — 68, 316
Butts, Judy — 68, 316
Byrds — 256

C
Cady, Chris — 235, 239-245, 359
Cady, John W. and Maria C. — 17-18, 304, 307, 322
Cady, Kit — 235
Caged Alpha Monkey — Contents, 129
Cagney — 71
Calkins, Cathy — 257
Callerame, Jim — 361
Canadice Lake, 328, 373
canals — 1
Canandaigua — 1, 9, 16, 132, 178, 257, 261, 310, 320, 322
Canandaigua Daily Messenger — 1, 261, 310
Carosa, Betsy — 293, 352
Carosa, Chris — 149-150, 293, 352
Caschetta, Andy — 361
Cassata, John — 313, 341
Cassell & Company, Ltd. — 348
Catholic — 36, 331
CB Brewers | Brewcrafters — 115
cellar — Contents, 23, 25, 31, 191. See: basement.
cemetery — 11-12, 42, 64, 321-323, 325, 348. See
    Mendon Cemetery, Old Mendon Cemetery,
    Tomlinson's Corners Cemetery.
Chaapel, Tim — 231, 233
Chaffer, John — 250-252
Chaintreuil, Ann — 140-142, 144, 146, 153, 303, 306, 311, 313, 339-340, 351
Chaintreuil, John — 140
Chaintreuil, Alexander John — 140
Chaintreuil-Jensen-Stark — 140
Chaintreuil, Renier ("Rennie") — 140, 142, 303, 306, 311, 313, 339-340, 351
Chandler, Clay L. — 45, 180, 344
Chappell, Tim — 233, 342
Charles, Fourier — 36
Cheers | television series — 139, 176
cherrywood — 130, 159
child | childhood — Contents, 75-76, 86, 92, 154, 193, 239
Child, Hamilton — 336

children — 21, 29, 40, 64, 121-122, 142, 146, 202, 236, 268-269, 277-279, 286, 297, 310, 336, 357.
    See Kids.
cholera epidemic — 11, 325
Christmas — 75, 77, 296
church(es) — 12, 35-36, 40-43, 48-49, 52, 55, 191, 238-239, 290, 296, 321-326, 328, 331-334, 343
Church of Jesus Christ of Latter-day Saints — 40-42, 190, 343
cisterns — 127, 260
Clark, Jeff — 229-230, 360
clay — 19, 86-91, 99
Clay, Langdon — 25
Clifford family — 126, 264
Clifford, Gerry — 125, 129, 132, 134, 263
Clifford, Mike — 263
Clifford, Robert B. — 125
Clifford, Robert F. ("Bob") — 113, 125-129, 131, 141-142, 262, 268, 303, 305-306, 310-312, 338-339, 357
Clifford, Sarah Jane — 171, 354
Clifford, Tim, 354
Clifford, Tom — 125
cobblestone(s) — 20-21, 23, 228, 271, 325, 343, 345, 347-349
Cobblestone Museum — 343, 345
cocaine — 136-137, 207, 272,
cocktail(s) — 83, 133, 189
Coleman, Rick — 289
community — 11, 14, 36, 38, 72, 76, 137, 175, 181, 227, 229-230, 277, 287, 295, 352
Community of Christ — 45
Congregational Church | Congregational Society — 326
Congress — 78, 80-81, 94, 332, 345
consists — 25, 59
Continental Congress — 3
Cool Rays — 252
Cooper, James Fenimore — 193
Cornell University Press — 346
Corning, New York — 96
Cottage Burger — 107, 131-132, 150, 167, 196, 282
Cottage Hotel | The Cottage — Copyright page, Dedication page, In Memoriam, Contents, Preface, 2, 4, 8-9, 14-19, 22-31, 33-34, 37-38, 41, 46, 52, 54-55, 67, 69, 71-72, 78, 82, 84-86, 99-108, 111, 114, 116, 119-121, 125, 128-129, 133, 139-140, 145-148, 151, 153, 157-159, 161-162, 164-165, 169, 173-174, 176, 178, 183, 187, 189-191, 194-196, 200, 202, 204-205, 207, 209, 213-214, 218, 227-228, 230, 235-237, 239, 243, 245, 247, 250, 253, 261-268, 276, 278, 287-288, 295, 298-299, 303-304, 306-314, 322-325, 327-330, 334-342, 347, 349, 351-354, 356-360, 362
Cottage Hotel of Mendon — Dedication page, 9, 100, 114, 159, 174, 190, 195, 200, 298, 299,
Cottage Hotel Songbook — 139, 224, 347, 357
Cottage-goer(s) — 291, 295
counterfeiting — 44
Covid — 50, 156, 169, 244
Coyle, Chandler — 182
crack cocaine — 136-137, 207
craftsman | men — 9, 20, 44, 159, 346
Craiger (Craig Williams) — 187, 198, 237, 274
Crooked Lake Review — 43, 343, 346, 348,
Crosby, Bing — 96
Crowther, Richard — 258, 354

crystallomancy—44, 46
Cummings Nature Center—298
Curie, Marie and Pierre—193
customer(s)—4, 17-18, 46, 55, 101, 126-127, 131-132, 146-147, 149, 160, 162, 170, 172, 286, 337

D

dancing—23, 252, 255, 258, 260, 291
dartboard | dartgame | darts—103, 272, 283
Dave (ATV group)—71
Davenport, Reuben Briggs—194
De Wolfe, Martin—Copyright page, 119
Dead Heads—163-164
DeAngelis, Mark—235, 242-243
death—62, 90-92, 96, 137, 139-142, 145, 151, 194, 209, 214, 226, 306, 312, 329, 340
Decker, Jeff—235, 239, 242, 255
Demeo, Anthony ("Tony")—311, 338
Dennis, Mark ("Coach")—165, 310
depot(s)—Contents, 12-13, 53-54, 58, 63, 65-66, 330, 336
Dickinson, Julia P.—38, 348
DiNardo, Louis C. ("Lou")—106, 147-148, 153, 171, 218, 246, 306, 312-313, 340
DiNardo-Marinellis—106
Dingley Act of 1897—95
disco—136, 218
dive—Contents, 100-108, 265
divination—44-45
Doggett, Tommy—165
Dolan, Peg—200, 246
Donati, Guiseppe—87
Donnelly, John J.—331
Douglass, Frederick—33-34, 193
Downing, A.—327
Doyle, Arthur Conan—193, 348
dram sellers—307, 315
drink tokens—284, 312
drink(s)—2, 15, 44, 75-77, 79, 101, 104, 127, 133, 159-160, 164, 169, 180, 184, 186-187, 204, 229, 237-238, 248, 258, 272, 274, 279, 282-284, 286, 289-290, 312
drinker—76
drinking—7, 40, 75, 123, 153, 179, 181, 207-208, 236, 239, 257, 260, 265, 333
drinking water—328
Drogan, John—354
drovers—9, 17, 228
drugs—Contents, 141, 163, 202, 205-208, 285
drumlin—19, 45
drums—228, 235, 252
dry agents—82, 334
drystone—21
Dunchie, Robert—315, 323, 330
Dunn, Dennis ("Denny")—68
Dunn, Fred—332
Dunn, Tommy—101, 172, 188
Dutcher, Deidre "Deedee" (The Dutchess)—165, 167-168, 208, 224, 289, 310-311, 354
Dwyer, Pat—263

E

Eagles—265
Earl Weems | Earl Weems Revue—132, 250-252, 360
East Bloomfield, New York—89
East Bloomfield Historical Society—345

East Rochester, New York—316, 337
Edmon, Jim—Copyright page, 354
Edmon, Patti—361
Ehrenberg, Ernest—82-83, 316-317, 331, 334-335, employees—122, 147, 207, 280, 285
Erastus Darrow (publishing company)—347
Erbley, P. J.—85, 94-95, 353. *See: Paul S. Worboys.*
Eric Kozlowski—180, 262
Erie Canal—11-13, 20, 35, 75, 323, 325
Ernst, Fred—324
eskers—19
Euchre Card Nights—133
evangelist(s)—11, 33, 35, 43
Everts, Ensign & Everts (publishers)—74, 308, 328, 348

F

Fairchild, Herman Leroy (professor)—334, 347
Fairport, New York—81, 279, 316, 333, 337
faith(s)—35, 43, 48
Falin, Pat—116, 313, 341
farmer(s)—Contents, 14, 19, 21, 40, 86, 166, 175, 181, 183, 280, 319, 349
Federal Census Map, 1830—32
Feldman, Jeff—68
Feldman, Nick—68
Feldman, Holly—69, 268
Fiasco Brothers—224, 226
fiddler—132, 215, 217-218
Fiehn, Heinrich—95
Finger Lakes—13, 132, 178, 215, 373
Finney, Charles Grandison—35
Finucane, Thomas ("Yankee Tom")—2, 9, 26-27, 54, 303, 305, 307-309, 322, 329-330, 334, 341
fire (catch fire, on fire, wildfire)—31, 35, 62, 180, 190, 192, 310, 312, 337, 340
firefighting—14, 316, 332
Fire Marshall—134
fish frys—102, 132, 150, 270
Fisher, Baird—106, 144, 146, 171, 183, 217, 264, 271, 312, 351, 355
Fisher, Fiona—267, 275, 277
Fisher, J. Sheldon—44, 92, 346
Fisher, Jacqueline "Jacky" (Muzdakis)—106, 144-146, 171, 180, 183, 217, 264, 271, 306, 311-312, 339, 351, 355
Fisher, Jeremy—146, 264, 267, 271, 275-276, 277, 355
Fisher, Keegan—267, 275-277, 355
Fisher, Lindsey—146, 271
Fisher, Mary Kate—275-276
Fisher, Megan—146, 271
Fishers, New York—34, 92, 261, 310, 316, 330, 336-337
Fitroy 'Brother' James—168
Fletcher, Nahum D. and Harriet M.—305, 309, 334-335
flood(s)—23, 312, 340
Folts, Harold—316-317, 335, 337
Foosball—233, 237, 255
Ford, Henry—330
Formicola, Joe—273, 289, 312
Forsyth, Frank—89
foundation(s)—Contents, 18, 20-24, 33, 304, 330
four corners—8, 55, 67, 238, 294, 315, 321, 326, 337
four-horse stagecoaches—16
Fourier, Charles—36

Fourierist—36
Fowler, J. P. | Jediah (Jedidiah)—304, 308, 327
Fox Hollow—129
Fox, Ann ("Leah")—191-194
Fox, Catherine ("Kate")—191-194
Fox, Margaretta ("Maggie")—191-194
Foxall, Doug—165, 310, 338, 355
Freckles—186
Freeman, Robert J. ("Bob")—317, 341
Freeman, Pat—201, 316-317, 335, 341
Freeman, Pete—251-252
Freemasons—37
Fremlin, Father James—318
Friedlander, David—88, 90-91
friendship—266, 299, 362
Frehmeyer, Fannie—305, 309, 335
Fullerton, Bruce—361
Furlong, Mr. and Mrs.—329. *See: Hicks & Furlong.*

G

G. W. Dillingham Company (publisher)—194
Gall, Franz Joseph—36
Garfield—183
Garling, Frederick Martin ("Fred" | "Freddie")—81, 86, 90-92, 99, 175
Garvey, John—138, 230-234, 359
gasoline wagons—13
Gates, Corey—361
Genesee Book Club—349
Genesee Country—32
Genesee lager—Contents
Genesee Valley—347
Genny—112
ghost(s)—Contents, 190, 200-201, 238
Ghould Rush—200, 245
glacial—45
glaciers—Contents, 19-20, 107
Godwin, Jocelyn—350
gold—45, 59, 99, 238,
Gold Rush—200, 245-247, 360
Golden Plates—39, 46, 52, 323-324
Good Cracker—229
Good Old Days—253
Goofy Bob—210
Gorham, Patty—256-257, 355
Gottfried, Jessica—188
grandbabies, Cottage—267, 275
grandchildren—202, 277, 364
grandkids—156
grandfather—68, 92, 316, 335
Grandin Building Bookstore—324
Grange | Grange Hall—12, 326, 328, 339
Grateful Dead—180, 186-187, 207, 236, 241
great-grandmother—181, 191
Greatfield, D. T.—19, 349
Grieco, Joann—245-246
guitar | guitarist—139, 179, 211, 213-214, 225, 235, 239, 245, 246, 249-250, 252-254, 289, 359
Gulf Oil Company—13, 316, 336-337

H

Habecker, Steve—68
Habeckers—127, 271
Haggett, Gordon—128
Halloween—112, 200, 245
Ham, Diane C.—12, 18, 25, 27-28, 30, 36, 38, 113, 121, 346-350, 352

hamburger historian—150
Hamilton, Austin—284-285, 292, 312, 358
hamlet(s)—*See Mendon Hamlet, Norton's Mills, Sibleyville, Rochester Junction.*
hand-hewn—23, 25
Hanford, Franklin—349
Handsome Lake—38-39, 343
Harmon, Clive—54, 330
Harrington, Michelle—116
Harris, Marjory—362
Harrison, Hap—251-252
Hastings, Charlie—280
haunted—Contents, 190, 194
Haywood, Bill, 178, 355
Heckman, Albert ("Al")—112, 121-125, 127, 209, 268, 303, 305, 310, 336, 338
Heckman, Mary Elizabeth—29, 112, 121-125, 127, 209, 268, 303, 310, 336, 338
Heckman, Rosemary—*See: Lewis, Rosemary (Heckman).*
Heckman, Tommy—121, 209, 268, 310, 336
Heindl, Louis & Sons (publishers)—1, 11, 349
Heineken(s)—Contents, 114, 259
Helander, Dave—250-252
Hemlock, New York—178
Hemlock Lake—328
Hendo—139, 162, 172, 183, 355
Henrietta, New York—Contents, 71, 136, 178-179, 261, 310, 336
Henry Ford.org—5-6
Herb, Rich—245-246
Hicks & Furlong—329
Hicksite Quaker—34
hijinks—202
Hildreth, Sam—9, 16, 320, 322
Hill Cumorah—39, 46, 49, 51, 323
Hirsch, Jane—362
historian(s)—10, 18, 25, 27-28, 30, 36, 55, 92, 97, 113, 121, 150, 292, 352-353
historic—134
history—Title page, In Memoriam, Contents, 6, 31, 36, 38, 40, 44, 47, 70, 74, 83, 97, 106, 108-109, 120, 124, 155-156, 192-193, 267, 282, 287, 303, 307-308, 328, 340, 343-346, 348-353, 356, 361
History Press (publisher)—349
hockey, air—166
hockey, ice—180, 271
Hodge, Addison—329
Holcomb, New York—261, 310, 336
Honeoye Creek—89
Honeoye Falls, New York—38, 81, 124, 250, 253, 320, 327, 346, 348-350, 352-353
Honeoye Falls-Town of Mendon Historical Society—37-38, 63, 85, 96, 348
Honeoye Falls-Town of Mendon Historical Society Museum—41, 85, 85, 88-89, 93, 97, 99, 345
Honeoye Falls Central School | Cougars | Hornets—124, 268, 293
Honeoye Falls Times—28, 96, 299, 310, 330, 344
horse(s)—2-3, 9, 14-17, 21, 26, 54, 107, 111, 155, 248, 307, 322, 330, 342
hostlers—2, 17
Houston, Anita—255, 356
Howard, Osgood L. (author)—350
Hughes, Geri and Kent—295, 297-298, 356
Hutchinson, Samuel H.—324

Hyde, Orson—49
Hydesville, New York—191-192

I
inn—Title page, Copyright page, Contents, 2, 4, 8, 13-14, 17-18, 26, 38, 55, 79, 108, 119, 125-126, 128, 134, 262, 303-304, 307, 316-317, 321-322, 335, 337
innkeeper—2, 8, 308, 327
international—94, 96, 168, 192
Ionia, New York—92
iPhone—98
iron horse—1
iron horsemen—260
Irondequoit Creek—38, 69, 264, 271, 312, 320-321, 324, 326, 340
Ives, M.F.—327

J
Jabout—68
Jackstraws—253
James, William (author)—193
Jeffrey D & the J Dubs—252
Jeffries, Don—165, 310
Jewett Company of Buffalo, New York—110
jitterbug—256
John Mooney | John Mooney Blues Band—132, 212-214, 225, 250-251, 254
Joint, Dick—124, 138, 208, 255, 261, 356
Jones, Bill—250

K
kames—19, 334
Keating, Kerry—251-252
Keenan, Florence T.—88, 92
kegging up—76
kegs—115, 131
Kessler, Brenda Zimmerman—196-199, 362
kettles | kettle lakes | ponds—19
keyboard(s) | keyboardist—235, 245, 252
Keys to the Caddy—227
kids—Contents, 68, 132, 141, 143, 154, 180, 210, 267, 269-271, 278, 282, 286-287. *See: child | children.*
Kimball, Heber Chase—39-42, 48-49, 325, 343
Kimball, Helen—48
Kirtland, Ohio—49, 325
Kneale, Bob—68
Knight, Dave—235, 243
Kodak—187
Kosenski, Ed—251-252
Kozlowski, Eric—180, 362
Krauss, Steve—227

L
LDS church—48-49, 52
Labatt | Labatt Blue—Contents, 113-114, 186
Lafayette, General Marquise du | Gilbert du Motier—315, 319, 323
Lake Ontario—20
Lake, Richard—68
Lamour, Dorothy—96
Landmark Society of Western New York—346
Lane, William ("Bill")—96-97, 352
Lang, Billy—272-73
Lang, Kathleen and Pete—273
Langpap—129, 211
Latham, Laurie—225-226, 237

Latter-day Saints, Church of Jesus Christ of—40-42, 191, 324
LaVilla, Lou—168
law—Contents, 17, 78-82, 149, 178, 181, 207, 331, 333-334
Legend of Zelda—98
Lehigh Valley Railroad Depot—12-13, 53, 58, 63, 330, 336
Lehigh Valley Railroad (LVRR)—Contents, 12, 53-54, 56, 68, 70-71, 330-331, 336-338, 344, 346, 349, 361
Lehigh Valley Railroad Historical Society—53, 57-58, 346
Lehigh Valley Trail—13, 71-72
Leslie-Bole, Cynthia—362
Lewis, Rosemary (Heckman)—Copyright page, 14, 69, 119, 121-124, 210, 256, 268, 310, 336, 356
license(s), licensed—8, 26, 38, 74, 80, 83, 120, 145-146, 219, 274, 303, 307-309, 311, 313, 315, 321, 322, 328, 330, 339, 340-341
license plates—105, 284
Lima, Town of—75, 293, 296
limestone—18-19
liquid bread—79
liquor(s)—74, 78-80, 83, 122, 145-146, 158, 219, 282, 303-304, 307-309, 311, 315, 322, 328, 330-331, 333-334, 339-340
Little Feat—236
Little League—102
Livingston County—21
Lloyd, Orpha—88
locomotive—62, 64
Longfellow, Rickie—3, 345
longhouses—39
Lord, H. T.—324
Loretta Lynn—255
Loudon, Bennett J.—150
love(d)—Dedication, In Memoriam, Contents, 36, 122-124, 126, 143, 150, 153, 156, 166, 168, 175-176, 186, 204, 210, 225-226, 228-229, 233-234, 237-238, 247, 249, 256-257, 266-267, 277, 279, 283, 288-292, 296, 299, 354, 356-358, 361-362
lovers—83, 215
LSD—206
Luckenbach Texas (Back To The Basics Of Love)—256
Lutheran | Lutheran Church—36, 332
LVRR—53, 344. *See Lehigh Valley Railroad.*
Lynn, John P.—43
Lyons, Brian—183-185, 302, 356

M
MacKenzie, Donna—356
Macon, Chaintreuil & Associates—140
Madsen, George A.—46
Magic Mushrooms—206
Mahrt, Frederick and Gertrude—68, 316, 336
Mahrt, Russell ("Russ")—13, 68-69, 316, 357
Malin, Ermina—25
Mammano, Pat J.—128
manager(s)—Contents, 116, 119-120, 133, 141, 150-151, 162, 164, 167-168, 259, 311, 331, 332, 338, 355
Mantique and Oddities Etc.—116, 313, 341
Maple Leaf train | New York-Toronto—70
Maplewood Inn—125-126, 128

marijuana — 205, 207
Marinelli, Nancy — 106, 148-151, 306, 312-313, 340
mason(s) — 20-21
mason jar(s) — Contents, 72, 105, 150, 177-181, 188-189
Mason Jar, the — 133, 136-137, 162, 178-180, 223, 227, 231, 235, 241-242
Mason Jar Mondays — 188
Masso, Ferdinand V. — 305, 309, 335
Maute, R. J. — 293
Max Creek — 241
McKinley Tariff Act of 1890 — 94
McQuaid High School (cute guys!) — 257
mediums — 191-193
Meko the Golden Retriever — 282-283
Mendon 64 — 156, 230, 272, 280
Mendon, Town of — 7, 11, 14, 17, 38, 63, 85, 120, 134, 319, 321, 323-324, 327-328, 339, 344-346, 348, 350, 352, 361. *See: Mendon hamlet* and *Honeoye Falls-Town of Mendon Historical Society.*
Mendon Academy | Mendon District #2 — 124, 271, 325-326, 331, 336
Mendon Cemetery — 11-12, 64, 311, 321-323, 325, 348. *See: Old Mendon Cemetery and Tomlinson's Corners Cemetery.*
Mendon Fire Department | Mendon Fire — 90, 138, 208, 310, 316, 326, 332-334, 336-337, 356
Mendon Foundation — 13, 71-73, 338, 346, 348
Mendon hamlet — Title page, Contents, Preface, 1-2, 4, 7-14, 16-18, 20-21, 23, 26, 29, 32-36, 38-42, 48, 52-58, 64-65, 67-68, 70-86, 99, 107, 121, 124, 126, 132, 138, 152, 163, 178, 189-190, 201, 230, 264-265, 271, 277, 303-304, 307, 312, 315, 318-330, 333-337, 341, 350-352, 356-361
Mendon Historic Preservation Commission — 339
Mendon-Honeoye Falls-Lima Sentinel | MHFL — 56, 65, 85, 149, 164, 293, 312, 344, 347, 349-350, 352, 356, 358
Mendon Kames, The — 334. *See Mendon Ponds Park.*
Mendon Music Festival — 156, 230, 244
Mendon Plat Map, 1924 — 54
Mendon Playhouse — 339
Mendon Ponds Park — 19, 34, 334,
Mendon Post Office — 4, 7, 9, 64, 320-321
Mendon-Ionia Road — 42, 320, 322, 324-325
Mendonites — 48
Menz, Lynne — 349, 352
Merrill, Arch — 1, 10-11, 349
mescaline — 206
Mesmer, Franz — 36
Mesmerism, Mesmerists — 36, 191
methamphetamines — 206
Methodist — 36, 48
Midney, Tom — 14, 118
mill | milling — 38, 89, 320-323, 329-330
millpond — 42
Miller, Ben — 286, 357
Miller, Kathryn ("Katie") or Lucy — 169, 286, 357
Miller, Sam — 286, 357
Miller, Samuel — 319, 357
Miller, Steve and Jennifer — 155, 286, 357
Millerites — 36, 191
Minchin, III, James — 214
mind-altering — 206

Mireau, Karen — Title page, Copyright page, Contents, Preface, 30, 74, 100, 347, 350, 363-366
Moffitt, John — 361
Mooney, John — 132, 212-214, 225, 250-251, 254
Monroe County — 7, 17, 20, 74, 163, 304, 307, 321-324, 328, 344, 347-350
Montgomery County — 17-18, 95, 307, 322
moonshiners — 81
Mormon(s), (ism) church, doctrine, religion — 39-40, 42, 44-49, 51, 324-326, 344, 346, 350
Moroni, the Angel — 39
Moss, Pete — 357
Mucker-Pucker Ware — 39
Mullan-Gage State Liquor Enforcement Law — 78, 333-334
Murphy, Barney — 329
Murphy, Thomas W. — 39, 346
music | musical — Contents, 14-15, 50-51, 86, 94, 96-99, 111, 130, 132-133, 136, 146, 156, 166, 196, 200, 204-219, 224-225, 228-234, 244, 246, 251-252, 255-257, 266, 280, 290-291, 338, 342, 351, 360
music video(s) — 15, 98, 233, 342
musician(s) — 96, 102, 114, 133, 136, 138-139, 156, 204-208, 212-213, 215, 218-225, 228-231, 243-244, 248, 250. *See: individual musician listings on pages 218-223.*
Mustang convertible — 257
Mutch, Don — 115
Muzdakis, Jacqueline ("Jacky") 106, 144-146, 171, 180, 183, 217, 264, 271, 306, 311-312, 339, 351, 355. *See: Fisher, Jaqueline ("Jacky").*
mystics | mysticism — 35, 37, 45-46, 191, 344

N
Naples, New York — 132
national — 78, 83, 100, 110, 168, 241, 33278,
National Broadcasting Company (NBC) — 176
National Prohibition Act — 78, 83, 332-333. *See: Volstead Act.*
Native American — 33, 293
Neophyte Scriptures — 39
New York Thruway — 337
Niagara Falls — 9, 57, 331
Nick Tahou — 131
NIK & The Nice Guys — 227
Nintendo 64 — 98
Noble Experiment, The — 84
North Dakota Snowshoe — 167
Norton's Mills | West Mendon — 320, 323. *See: Honeoye Falls.*
nostalgia — 14, 56, 65, 72, 347

O
O'Brien, Thomas — 88
O'Connor, David — 331
ocarina(s) — Contents, 85-99, 328-329, 344, 355, 362
occult — 37, 192
Old Mendon Cemetery — 321, 323
Old Salt — 258
On Cobblestone Fields — 228
One Chance to Live It — 241
One Horse Town — 15, 248-250, 342
Oneida Community — 36
Ontario | Ontario County — 17, 20, 163, 319, 321, 323

Ormiston, Kimberly ("Kim") — 158, 176, 180, 184-185, 186-188, 201, 357

P
packet boats — 11, 13
Palmer, Richard F. — 4, 10, 13, 15, 59, 62, 343, 345, 353
Palmyra, New York — 39, 44, 49, 323-324
Pandamensional Solutions, Inc. — 150
pandemic — 50, 156
paranormal — 196, 201, 362
Paris, Nicki — 248
Parker, Arthur C. — 38
Parrish, Rena and Ward — 92-93
Partridge Hill — 129, 140
party — 136-137, 148, 162, 204-205, 207, 211, 216, 228, 242, 250, 261, 263, 279, 291, 328
partying — 141, 163, 168, 259, 354, 356
patron(s) — Contents, 111, 147, 149, 171, 196, 229, 259, 290, 301, 312
Patsy Cline — 255
Paul, Warren — 231
Paulsen, Baker & Garvey — 138, 230-234, 342,
Paulsen, John — 138, 230-234, 331, 348, 359
peepstones — 45. *See: seer stones*.
Peer, Ben — 315, 323, 330
Peer, George W. and Emma J. — 304, 308, 328
Pelican Productions — 227
Penfield Pourhouse — 156
percussion — 243
Perfectionists — 191
Pettee, Korie — 235, 244-245
Phelps, Ely (Eli) and Harriet — 304-305, 308, 328
Phelps, Oliver — 319
Phrenologist | Phrenology — 36, 191
pictograms — 39, 47
pinball — 130, 161, 166, 172
Pintsch, Carl Friedrich Julius | Pintsch gas — 60
Pittsford, New York — 35, 125, 130, 133, 161, 167 260, 263-264, 271, 316, 337
Pittsford-Mendon High School — 235, 240
Pittsford-Mendon Road — 25, 29, 66, 132, 146, 271, 321
Polosi, Joe — 165
Pony Express — 327
pool | pool table — 149, 159, 166, 172-173, 199, 204, 313, 341
Porter, Jimmy — 68
post office — 2-4, 7, 9, 40, 64, 320-321. *See: Mendon Post Office*.
post roads — 3
postmaster — 3, 7, 321
post-and-beam | beams — 25, 27, 273, 322
Powder Mill — 236, 238-239
Powder Mill Park — 238
Pratt, Orson — 49
pre-Columbian — 86
Presbyterian Church — 12, 290, 322-323, 328,
Presbyterians — 326
Presto, Jesse — 250
Price, Tom — 200, 245-247, 360
Prohibition — Contents, 74, 78, 81, 83-84, 101, 332-333
prophet(s) — 35, 38-39, 42
prophetic — 226
proprietors — 4, 17, 303, 307, 317, 329
psilocybin — 206
psychedelic(s) — 206

Psychic Highway — Contents, 35
Pullman Car Company | Pullman Palace — 59

Q
Quaaludes — 206
Quaker(s) — 33-34 36, 39, 191, 324-325
Quaker Meeting House Road — 33
Queen Victoria — 193
Quimby, Reverend Henry — 34

R
Raab, Charles — 313, 341
Radio Flyer — 64
raid(s), raided — 81, 240, 333-334
railcars — 69
railhead — 55
railroad(s) — 8, 11-13, 53, 56-59, 64-65, 68, 70-71, 330-331, 336-337, 344, 346, 349, 361. *See Lehigh Valley Railroad* and *Underground Railroad*.
railroad depot — Contents, 12-13, 53, 58, 65, 330, 336
Railroad, New York Central — 68
Rails to Trails — 13, 71, 338
Railway Post Office (RPO) — 64
Raines hotels — 331
Raines Act | Raines Law — 79-80, 331
Rand, A. H. — 320-321
Rappel, Joey — 68
rappings — 191-193
Ray, Dorothy and Fred — 88
Redmond, John — 136, 178
regulars — 38, 103, 144, 159, 167, 169, 176, 180, 267, 280, 289
religion(s) — Contents, 32, 36, 39-40, 191
religious — 33, 38, 44, 46-47, 52, 79, 190
Republican — 280
revival(s) | revivalism — 35, 190, 212
Richards, Fred — 329
Richards, Willard — 49
Rickard, Joseph ("Joe") — 211, 213
Rimmer, Raymond — 363, 374
road(s) | crossroads — 3, 6-7, 14, 16-17, 42, 178, 200, 213, 237, 290, 324, 333. *See: railroad(s)* and *individual roads*.
Rochester, New York — 1, 11, 19, 21, 33-34, 58, 81-82, 87, 96, 107, 121, 123, 125, 128, 132-133, 145, 167, 179-180, 215, 231, 261, 288, 309, 320, 330, 344, 347, 349-350, 360
Rochester Anti-Slavery Society — 34
Rochester Democrat & Chronicle — 50, 64, 67, 82, 89, 96, 144, 150, 202, 211, 218, 259, 310, 313, 322, 325, 333-334, 338, 343
Rochester Gas & Electric — 28, 337
Rochester Historical Society — 43, 350
Rochester Express — 8
Rochester Historical Society — 43, 339
Rochester Junction — 58, 70, 327
Rochester, University of — 167, 288, 373
Rockwell, Kent — 279
Rolling Stones — 256
Rome, New York — 20
Rome Daily Sentinel — 59, 62
Ross, John Urquhart ("Burdock") — Dedication, In Memoriam, Contents, 114, 133, 135-139, 209, 303, 306, 310-311, 338-340, 342, 350-351, 359. *See: Burdock*.
Rose, Jennie — 362
roundheads — 20

rubble—20-21
rumrunner—78, 81
Rush-Mendon Road—317, 329

S
St. Catherine of Sienna Catholic Church |
  St. Catherine's—239, 296, 331
St. Mark's Lutheran Church—332
Saints' Herald, The—47-48
Saints, Latter-day—40-42, 191, 324. *See: Church of Jesus Christ of Latter-day Saints.*
saloon(s)—Contents, 14, 79, 81, 101, 130
Sandman—187
Sartain, Alan—278, 300
sawmill—38, 320, 322-323, 329. *See: mill | milling.*
Schenectady, New York—75
Schlaefer, Jacob and Mary—65, 315, 323, 329, 332
Schlaefer, Lillian, 65, 329
schnapps | peppermint schnapps—133, 167, 241, 258
Schwarz, Jim—168
scriptures—39, 43, 346
scrying—44-46, 344
Seager, Fred—125-126, 262-263, 357
seances—193
Sears, Roebuck & Co.—95
seer stones—45, 47. *See: peepstones.*
Selden, George—330
Selke, Phil—263
Seneca | Seneca Indian—38-39, 47, 92, 318-320
Sesquicentennial, Town of Mendon—120, 350
sex—Contents, 163, 172-173, 202-203
Shady Rest—238
Shakers—36, 191
Shackleton, Ernest—326, 329
Shaffer, Chris—250
Shelby, John—273
Sheldon, Dr. Milton—41-42, 323-324
Sheldon, Ezra—14, 75, 315, 321
shenanigans—Contents, 202, 354
Sheret, John G.—25, 30, 43, 97, 346, 348
Sherlock Holmes—193
Sherry, Hugh—324
shrooms—205
Sibleyville, New York—327
Silos, Peter—165
Simmons, Bud—187, 198
Sindel, Shoey—363, 373
Slaght, Robert—65
Slipton Fell—133, 139, 179, 235-244, 255, 342, 359
Smith, Deb and Tim—148, 163-164, 283-286, 349, 357-358
Smith, Emma Hale—48
Smith, Hyrum—42, 49, 324, 326, 328-329
Smith, Jackson—62-63, 66
Smith, John and Mary—305, 308
Smith, Joseph—39, 41-42, 44-52, 323-326, 342-343
Smith, Loren—253
Smith, Mark—227
Smith, Samuel H.—324
Smule Ocarina—98
Sno-Cone—154, 313, 340
Society of Friends | Friends Society (Quakers)— 33, 36, 324-325
South Park—51, 342
spaghetti suppers—102, 132, 150
speakeasies—101
spiritual(ly)—Contents, 33, 39, 48, 350

Spiritualism—52, 191-194, 348
Spiritualist(s)—36, 191, 193
Splitgerber, Jeff—362
Springwater Inn—38, 262, 316-317, 335, 337
Stackman, Ron | Ronnie—168-169
stagecoach(s)—Title Page, Contents, Preface, 85, 1, 3-18, 26, 38, 64, 75, 78-79, 107-108, 134, 303-304, 307, 320-322, 330, 345, 348-350
Stanley, Hazel—270
Stanley, Howard ("Ike")—29, 270, 339
Stanley, Howie—68
Stark, Sandra ("Sandy")—211, 213
station-keepers—4
steam whistles—Contents
steam-powered—38, 329
steamboats—1
steamships—13
Stimson, Elder Hiram K.—75-78, 347
Stimson, Samuel—75
Stone, George S. and Jeremy—16-18, 20, 24, 303-304, 307-308, 322, 327
Stone, Nathan—324
Stone, Susan—304, 307, 327
Stott, Amanda—153, 281-282, 285, 292, 312, 358
Stott, David ("Dave")—9, 27, 106, 114, 117, 142-143, 151-156, 159, 172, 188, 201, 219, 274, 277, 279, 282, 303, 306, 309, 311, 313-314, 340-341, 352
Stott, Hilary—9, 27, 106, 114-115, 117, 142-143, 148, 151-156, 159, 162, 165, 170, 172, 188, 195, 201, 203, 219, 229-230, 243, 244, 274-275, 277-282, 295, 303, 306, 309, 311, 313-314, 340-341, 352
Stouten, Margaret ("Molly")—212-213
Streb, Paul—305, 309, 312, 335
Strong, Edward—80, 315, 331
Strowe, Paul—102, 136, 224-226, 229, 360
Stuckless, Randy—227
Suffrage—84. *See 19th Amendment.*
Suffragette—33
Sunday Afternoon Free Band, 224
supernatural—199-201
Swamp Root Singers | String Band—132, 166, 210, 212-213, 360
Swedenborg, Emanuel—37

T
t-shirt(s)—101, 183-189, 201, 356-357
tariff(s)—94-95, 345
tavern(s)—Contents, 7, 17-18, 26, 38, 40, 72, 75, 83, 108, 125, 128, 170, 201, 263, 265, 279, 303-304, 307-308, 315-317, 321-322, 335, 337, 341, 350, 357
tavern keepers—4, 8, 17, 308, 315, 321
tequila—Contents, 205, 258
Teschner, Frederica—88
Teschner, Rudolph—Contents, 85-99, 328, 345, 355
Theosophists | Theosophy—36-37, 191
Thermo Scientific—109, 110, 112
This Song—232-234
Thomas, Albert ("Alby")—88
Thompson, Erick—165, 311
Thompson, Tommy—259
Thornbush—129
thorough-braces—6
Todd Hobin Band—224
Tom Petty & the Heartbreakers—236

Tomlinson, John E. — 18, 315, 323, 330
Tomlinson's Corners | Cemetery — 40, 325
Torpy, Don — 235
Totiakton, Village of — 318
track(s), music — 14-15, 246
track(s) | trackside — 55, 62-65, 67-71, 117, 331, 338, 349
trail(s) — Contents, Preface, 13, 53, 71-72, 107, 320, 338, 344, 350
train(s) — Contents, Preface, 14, 53-73, 88, 237, 330-331, 337
Trickey, Ari — 278
Trickey, Kyle — 269-270, 358
Trickey, Madison ("Maddie") (Babigian) — 171, 278-279, 358
Trickey, River — 278
Trickey, Zane — 278
Trickey, Zoey — 278
Trout Creek — 42, 48
Tubbs, Steve — 159, 172, 341
Turner, Darwin W. — 330
Tuttle, Chauncy D. and Matilda — 304, 308, 327-328
Twain, Mark — 193
typhoid — 123

U
Uncle Dale's Readings in Early Mormon History — 47, 350
underage — 240, 355
Utopianism — 36

V
Valby, John — 218
Valentino, Rudy — 168
Valentown Museum — 92
Valium — 206
Van Castiles — 121-122, 305, 309-310, 336
Van Zandt, Carol — 363
Van Zandt, Tad — 252, 358
Venton, Brian — 223, 226-228, 342, 360
Venton Clark Band — 227
Vermont — 40, 44
Victor, New York — 132, 163, 296, 310, 316, 331, 337, 346
Victor Historical Society — 346
Victor-Mendon Road — 7, 25, 310, 321, 332
video(s) — 272, 342
video(s), game(s) — 98, 152, 264, 283
video(s), music — 15, 233, 236, 342
village(s) — 4, 8, 10, 238
Village, East Mendon — 75
Village, Honeoye Falls — 38, 327, 348
Village, Mendon — 43, 81, 238, 320-321, 344

Village, Rochesterville — 322
visionary — 32, 38, 46, 78
Volstead Act — Contents, 78-79, 81, 332-333

W
wagon(s) — 4, 13, 21, 28, 320, 326, 350
Wahlers, Ricky — 219
Wallman, John — 164
Wangman, Charles — 315, 332
Washington, George — 319
waybill — 4
Waylon Jennings — 256
Wee Willy — 210
Weiland, Debbie — 258
Welch, Philip J. — 358
West, Joe — 235
Weyl, John — 254
whisky | whiskey — 75, 77, 239
Whitney, Hannah — Dedication page, 358
Whittier, John Greenleaf — 33
Williams, Craig ("Craiger") — 187, 198, 237, 274
Williams, Jeff — 132, 139, 223, 250-254, 342, 347, 360
Williams, Julie — 347
Williams, Marina Leigh Mendez, 364
Wilson Junior High School — 96
Willie Nelson — 256
Wilson-Gorman Tariff Act — 94
Wizard of Oz — 96, 193
Woodard, Dell and Earl — 121-122, 310, 336
Woodward, Lewis D. — 261, 310, 336
Worboys, Paul S. — 55-56, 65, 95, 347, 350, 353. *See P. J. Erbley.*
Works, Miriam (Young) — 42, 324-325
Wurlitzer Company, Rudolph — 94, 96

Y
Yankee Tom — *See: Finucane, Thomas ("Yankee Tom").*
Yates, Anah B. — 349
Yates, Gus — 165, 311
Ye Olde Mendon Tavern — 38, 72, 201, 316-317, 335, 337
You'll Never Feel Alone | At the Cottage Hotel — 236-237
Young, Brigham — 40-49, 324-326, 346
Young, Elizabeth — 42
Young, John and Abigail ("Nabby") Howe — 42
Young, Miriam Angeline Works — 42, 314, 328
YouTube — 51, 57, 139, 233, 236, 342

Z
Zeigfield Follies of 1919 — 74
Zero Blues Band — 254

About the Author

Karen Mireau
(Photo by Shoey Sindel.)

As a young girl in western Upstate New York, Karen Mireau spent countless delicious hours exploring the lakes, rivers, and woodlands where she grew up—but her true creative adventures began when she discovered her passion for poetry.

In her early twenties, Karen studied English Literature and Philosophy at the University of Rochester, living the life of a full-time writer, and homesteading a fifty-acre farm on Canadice Lake in the Finger Lakes region.

This didn't put much bread on the table, but it did lead to a career in writing for television and film in Los Angeles—including creating original animated concepts such as *Troubles the Cat*, part of a Jim Henson series that aired for two seasons on Cartoon Network.

In her early thirties, Karen had the honor and wonder of birthing a beautiful, talented daughter, Marina Leigh Mendez Williams, and helping raise an extended family of marvelous and wildly creative sons and daughters, all of whom she adores dearly to this day.

During that time, she also developed *Satori*, a permaculture farm and healing center in Kentucky, where she continued her life-long commitment as a self-avowed "Agricultural Anarchist."

In 2008, Karen officially became a "Literary Midwife," helping people write their life stories, and founded Azalea Art Press, a boutique publishing company specializing in creating beautiful, meaningful, and imaginative books.

It's been her bliss ever since—but she has never abandoned her love for the natural world. She continues to plant gardens of nurturing food, flowers, and medicinal plants wherever she lives.

Karen now calls Sonoma, California, home. Alongside her husband, photographer Raymond Rimmer, she continues to write, garden, paint, publish, and shower her friends, family, and grandchildren with unending affection and love.

Closing Time

Whoe'er has travell'd life's dull round,
Where'er his stages may have been,
May sigh to think he still has found
The warmest welcome – at an inn.[1]

All good things, as they say, must come to an end, yet there are still many more fascinating tales yet to be told about the *Cottage Hotel*.

With any luck, the stories I have shared with you have brought you on an entertaining, enlightening, and perhaps even memorable journey.

When all is said and done, it is our memories that define us. It is my hope that this book will inspire you to explore your own personal and local history more deeply.

May we all live this wonderful life fully and create stories that are worth telling long after we're gone.

Happy remembering,

Karen Mireau

---

[1] William Shenstone, *Written at an Inn at Henley*, 1735.

To Contact the Author
please email:
Karen Mireau
Azalea.Art.Press@gmail.com

For Direct Online Book Orders
please visit:
lulu.com, amazon.com
and other online venues

For more information
or to share your own stories
please visit:
cottagehotelstories.blogspot.com

www.ingramcontent.com/pod-product-compliance
Lightning Source LLC
Chambersburg PA
CBHW030133170426
43199CB00008B/51